# WATER
## IN THE
# GARDEN

# WATER
## IN THE
# GARDEN

### JAMES ALLISON

No. 16051

# A SALAMANDER BOOK

A Salamander Book

© 1991 Salamander Books Limited,
Published in the USA by
Tetra Press,
3001 Commerce Street,
Blacksburg,
VA 24060.

ISBN 1-56465-181-9

## CREDITS

Editor: Anne McDowall
Designer: Jill Coote
Color reproductions: Magnum
Graphics Ltd.
Filmset: SX Composing Ltd.
Indexer: Stuart Craik
Color artwork: Jane Winton
Printed in China

## ACKNOWLEDGEMENTS

The author and publishers would like
to thank the many individuals and
organizations who gave help in the
preparation of this book, in particular:

The Aquatic Habitat, Chris Ball,
Blagdon Water Garden Products,
Bennetts Water Lily Farm, The
Garden Picture Library, Hozelock
Limited, D. Jones Landscapes, Kent
Koi Ko., Bill Le Fever (illustrations on
pages 114–115), A. J. Mann, Perry's
Water Gardens N.C. (USA), The
Royal Horticultural Society, Stapeley
Water Gardens, Charles Thomas and
Rolf Nelson of Lilypons Water
Gardens (USA), World of Koi.

# CONTENTS

# INTRODUCTION

Water is a valuable asset in any garden, an inspiring element in the overall design, guaranteed to attract interest. Subtle reflections, soothing splashes, gentle, cool streams and cascading falls all play their part. The level plane of a body of water acts as a natural foil for surrounding plants and breaks up the monotony of areas of paving or grass. Its adaptability allows it to be used in any garden, formal or informal; and on any scale from a tiny tub to an expansive lake.

Any garden project requires a little prior thought, and a water feature, in particular, benefits from some planning. This book aims to guide you through every stage, whether you are an experienced gardener already or a total newcomer. Each step is considered, from choosing the style, size and position of your pond, fountain, stream or waterfall, through to preparing the site and making allowance for additional features. The various construction methods are outlined in turn, with practical advice on obtaining the very best results, and the most effective use of any pumps and fountains. Finishing touches such as bridges, stepping stones, ornaments, edging effects and lighting add yet another dimension.

They also help to integrate the water feature into the overall garden plan. All these additional elements are illustrated to give you more ideas, with plenty of practical hints on their installation. Exotic water plants and pond fish are a source of extra life and colour, especially if they are well chosen to suit your specific design. A chapter on water plants covers all the major varieties, including eye-catching water lilies, decorative poolside aquatics, and luxuriant foliage plants for bog areas. Pond fish are dealt with in another chapter, from the humble goldfish to the imposing koi. In all cases advice is given on individual requirements and the appropriate choice of species for different sites. Essential information is provided to help you obtain balanced conditions in your pond, with clear water and healthy plants and fish, through following simple guidelines on stocking and seasonal maintenance, and by monitoring water quality and making use of filtration where necessary.

Increasing awareness of the importance of wildlife in the garden has highlighted the role of ponds – magnets for amphibians, birds and a profusion of water life. The design of these oases in the garden is considered with emphasis on attracting wildlife at the same time as creating a decorative feature.

*Left: Interesting edging effects highlight a water feature while poolside plants revel in the moist conditions provided.*

*Above: A stream cuts into the landscape; a blend of sound and movement to complement the peacefulness of a leafy glade.*

*Below: Colourful waterside plants surround this soothing, gentle stream, making an ideal place to stop and relax.*

*Left: Water lilies have pride of place in the pond with their giant floating pads and immense cup-shaped blooms in glorious shades.*

*Below: Frogs, dragonflies and other wildlife will soon take up residence in a pond, bringing a new dimension to the garden.*

# CHAPTER ONE

# WATER GARDEN DESIGN

At the planning stage for any water feature it is important to consider which components of the overall design are to be the most important. For example, if a reflective water surface is your key aim, then it should be visible from the main viewpoints in the garden and should not be obscured by dense plant growth. For a moving water feature to draw the eye it must be significant enough to be visible at a distance, with a pond that is large enough to catch the splashes from tall cascades and bold fountain sprays.

Water plants and fish add an exciting dimension to a garden and are common reasons for choosing to include water in the landscape. Water plants can spread quite rapidly and need plenty of room to grow and a fair amount of sunlight if they are to bloom well. You may also need to create different depths in the pond to suit different plants, and perhaps a buffer zone at the edge filled with moisture-loving plants to help the pond merge effectively with surrounding planted areas.

For many people, fish, with their bright colours and graceful movements, are a prime reason for having water in the garden and, given a little extra thought, they can be kept in most ponds. Hardy varieties, such as the common goldfish, are very adaptable and not too fussy about their environment. Fancy goldfish may require winter protection and exotic koi need deeper ponds. Both prefer good-quality water so it makes sense, if you want to keep such fish, to allow room for a water filter.

# STYLE, PROPORTION AND POSITION

Wherever water is used in the garden it should complement the surrounding features, not detract from them. It is therefore important that any water feature fits the style and proportion of its settings, some of which, unless you are planning a garden from scratch, will have already been decided for you.

## FORMAL AND INFORMAL GARDENS

Formal gardens have the hallmarks of regularity with straight paths, sharply defined paved areas and walling. Small town gardens are frequently boxed in on all sides by walling or fencing, and these outlines force a level of formality on the garden. More classical formal gardens will often have been designed to complement the houses they surround, with matching stonework and ornaments. If this formal atmosphere is to be maintained, then it is the natural choice to include a water feature with suitably formal design elements.

Ponds may have geometric outlines – squares, oblongs, staggered oblongs, L-shapes or hexagons – or be perfectly round or oval. If there are walls or steps in the garden, why not build a raised pond to butt up against them to create an eye-catching variety of levels. Alternatively, sink a pond into a paved area if this is practical. If space precludes the incorporation of a pond in your garden, you may decide to include a self-contained fountain ornament, which will be ideally suited to a formal situation. These recirculate water, usually using the lower section of the ornament as a reservoir.

You can choose an ornament in a style that will blend with the surrounding garden and house – a large classical ornament could act as a focal point in a period garden; more abstract ornaments might be more fitting in the garden of a modern house. However, don't be bound by the existing pattern of the garden; a contrast in styles can often provide great interest. Just take care to ensure that different styles complement rather than clash with each other.

Informal garden designs are very popular; many people want their garden to reflect the soft irregularity of nature and so create a haven in which they can relax. Here a pond with a simple curved shape will best suit the sweeping edges of lawns, bushes, hedges and borders of flowers. A reflective pool of water can stretch between lush plant growth and winding paths and such a setting is ideal for the inclusion of streams and waterfalls, which can follow the variations of contour that are often found in informal garden settings.

To describe gardens as formal or informal is an oversimplification, however; in many cases, the garden design will be a compromise between the two. Many gardeners are torn between, on the one hand, the desire to create a natural and informal garden and, on the other, the restrictions of

*Right: This well-proportioned pond fits in neatly between the hedge, path and patio, forming a good foreground feature that blends in with the garden design.*

**Mixing styles**

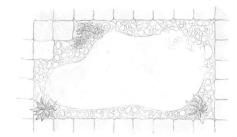

*Above: An informal pool can be cleverly sited within formal paving by filling the remaining area with softer materials, such as pebbles and plants.*

*Right: Use a pool as a cool and restful focal feature which can be easily viewed from a relaxing seat. Here the water is sited at the centre of the garden axes.*

the site itself, which may be symmetrical, flat and decidedly formal. A happy compromise can be reached by incorporating aspects of both styles.

A pool situated in such a garden might have one or two sides bounded by the straight edges of a path or patio, while plants border the remaining edges. One very effective way of mixing styles is to place a pool of informal outline within the bounds of a paved area. The space between the pool and the paving can be filled with a mixture of cobbles and plants.

## THINKING ABOUT PROPORTION

You will already have given some thought, hopefully, to your priorities in creating a water garden. It is worth noting here, however, that when introducing any new features into a garden, you should try to keep a balance between them so that no one feature overpowers the others. The aim may be to create a new focal point, but a garden will be all the more interesting if there are a variety of attractions that compete equally for attention.

Large lakes suit large perspectives with expansive plantings of trees to provide a backdrop that will be reflected by the water; trying to imitate such large-scale landscaping in too small a space is a recipe for disaster. On the other hand, small features can often be totally overlooked in large spaces. This is a common problem with water features; by the time plants

have grown up around, and in, the water, the visible surface area is considerably reduced and this can result in a small pond being completely hidden from view. The same can apply to intricate bays and inlets set into the sides of larger ponds, and also to narrow trickling streams. Ponds with wide, open expanses of water and simple unfussy edges are both more sensible and easier to construct.

Similar guidelines apply to fountain statuary and waterfalls; they should ideally be in proportion, not only to the rest of the garden, but also to the body of water from which they arise.

## SITING THE POND

There are both practical and aesthetic issues to consider when siting a pond. Having decided upon the style and approximate proportions of the water feature, consider from which perspectives it is most likely to be viewed. A pond can act as a centrepoint in the middle of a patio, the main feature in a paved area, or can complement other features in the garden, such as seating

areas or a pergola. A raised or sunken pool set up against a wall could be enhanced by siting a spouting ornament into the wall.

Don't forget about reflections. From which side will the pond be most frequently viewed? Are the reflections of interest? Bold groupings of plants can act as a backdrop and will cast shimmering reflections onto the water surface. So, too, will a backdrop of distant trees, a rockery (with or without waterfall), or an ornament or grouping of pots. However, you might want to avoid the reflections of certain buildings and fences.

A pool could be situated at the end of a path, just visible between plants or hedging on each side of the path. If the water surface is masked from view, a bold fountain or fountain ornament will help to bring water up and into the picture. Such a vista draws the attention and encourages the viewer to wander down the path for a closer look. This technique is suited to larger gardens where there are greater possibilities to create separate areas within the garden.

The 'gardens within a garden' approach is popular wherever space allows and can be used even in small gardens. The idea is usually that not all areas of the garden should be visible at once; the inquisitive looker will thus want to stay longer in the garden to ensure that he or she has explored all sections. Another advantage of creating separate 'pockets' within the garden is that you can mix different styles while reducing the risk that they will clash. A more formal section might provide a suitable site for a raised pool with a fountain ornament, while at the other end of the garden the surrounds may give the impression of being virtually unmanaged — an ideal setting for a wildlife pond.

Make use of the local environment of each specific area. Close to the house, the soil may be of poor quality, and the space available limited to rectangular areas bounded by house extensions and dividing walls. Such an area suits paving, gravel, raised planting beds and potted plants and is also an ideal site for a formal pond, either raised or sunken. Self-contained fountain ornaments also suit these areas, sheltered from strong winds and close enough to the house to be appreciated all year round.

Further away from the house, the soil quality may improve, and you can make full use of this by growing appropriate plants. A moist shady area could suit a bog garden; a dry, sunny slope could be adapted to create a rockery, perhaps enlivened with a cascading stream. If your garden lacks the extra contours you desire, remember that a pool excavation can provide the necessary spoil to build up areas.

A pond could be sited virtually anywhere in the garden. However, if it is to be a success in the longer term, you must consider the practicalities of maintenance.

Avoid overhanging trees whenever possible; they may look fitting beside a large lake, but they are a major source of problems for smaller pools. Falling leaves and blossoms can rapidly pollute ponds and are a common cause of fish deaths. Trees also shade out sunlight and too little sunlight will result in a cold, gloomy pond where plants and fish fail to flourish. Large tree roots can also make pond excavation troublesome. If nearby

trees are unavoidable, then consider a partially raised pond, which will be less likely to collect leaves. In any case it is worth covering ponds with a net in the autumn to reduce leaf pollution.

Choose a situation that obtains a reasonable amount of sunlight; water lilies in particular require direct sunlight if they are to flower at their best. The pond need not receive sunlight for the whole day, but some afternoon light will be beneficial. If possible, the pond should have some protection from cold winds. A sheltered position will warm up more quickly in sunlight, and any fountain or waterfall feature will be less disturbed by wind.

The natural place for a pond in the environment is in a hollow. However, for practical reasons, this is not usually the best place for an artificial pond. Muddy water tends to drain into such hollows along with blown leaves and it is generally better to reserve such spots for a bog area, where moisture-loving plants can flourish. The pond itself can be built close by, but on a slightly higher elevation.

If your soil is very sandy, it will be more difficult to dig steep slopes into the side of the pond. The pond may therefore have to be enlarged to allow the sides to slope more gently. In rocky soils the excavation will be hard work and if you want to build a fairly deep pond, it may make sense to partially raise the pond above the ground to avoid deep excavation. (See pages 48-49 for more on raised ponds.)

*Above: Good use of stone links the fountain, paving and seat, resulting in an effective central feature of this garden.*

*Below: Siting a garden pond close to the house allows it to be appreciated in all seasons and from many viewpoints.*

If there is a high water table in your area, you may come across water during the excavation. This is not an insurmountable problem; excavation work is best carried out during a dry season and you can use a sump pump to keep the hollow reasonably free from water until the pond is installed. However, if you were planning a particularly deep pool, the sides of the excavation may be prone to collapse and you may need to construct extra foundations and supports for the wall.

The closer any water feature is to existing water and electric supplies, the better. A pond close to the house has other advantages too; it can be viewed from the house, whatever the weather and will attract wildlife, such as bathing birds, while unwanted wildlife, such as herons, will be less likely to approach. Take care if you are planning to build a pond directly beside the house walls; it should not interfere with the house foundations or bridge any damp courses.

Where the garden is fortunate enough to have a natural supply of water you can make use of this. Although existing ditches and streams

**A silt trap**

Water flow

may not always be the most manageable of features, it may be possible to insert a silt trap to prevent a small stream from silting up, and a small trickling stream can be dammed to create pools with more stable water levels that are beneficial for water plants. It is not always a good idea to create pools within larger streams; storms can wash in considerable amounts of debris, and wash out any valuable fish. The constant flow of cool water also tends to stunt the growth of plants and ornamental fish.

A better alternative is to create a small dam in the stream and feed a small flow of water into a newly created pond. This new pond need not have any flow through it, but can be topped up by the stream water. If such a pond is fed by a pipe, the outlet can

*Above: A silt trap placed in the upper reaches of a natural stream will help prevent an excessive build-up of solids in ponds downstream.*

be protected with mesh to prevent fish escapes. The level of the pond will obviously be decided by the level of the stream, but beyond that the pond could be sited where you like in the garden and need not be restricted to the stream area alone. Bear in mind, if you plan to keep fish, that the purity of the water should not be in doubt. The redirection of larger streams may be subject to the approval of local water authorities and the introduction of ornamental fish into bodies of water that drain into rivers is also covered by legislation.

Having decided upon the site, style and proportion of any proposed water feature, you will want to gain a more accurate idea of its eventual size and shape before you start excavation. A well-tried method is to lay out a hosepipe or rope in the shape of the feature, which you can view from various perspectives and adjust as necessary. When you have decided on the final shape mark it out with pegs and measure up. This will enable you to make an estimate of the materials that will be required for the necessary construction work.

When you are considering the size of the feature, bear in mind all the elements that will be situated around it; leave plenty of room for planting areas, paved sections, waterfalls, poolside ornaments, filters and whatever else you plan to include. If you are intending to create a balanced, planted pool (rather than just a fountain feature), then make the pond as large as possible. Smaller ponds are often quite difficult to keep clear without some form of filtration. Few people complain of building too large a pond, but many, wishing that they had built something bigger in the first place, have to go to the trouble of enlarging their ponds.

# DESIGN IDEAS

## INFORMAL PONDS

Informal ponds should look natural and blend in with associated planting schemes and the overall outline of the garden. Very popular designs include simple bean and figure-of-eight shapes; both are uncomplicated designs and are relatively easy to construct with pond-lining materials.

Many gardeners choose to situate such a feature (often edged with crazy paving) in the middle of a lawn, but while this may involve less work in moving existing plants, the design tends to have a somewhat clichéd appearance. Isolating a pond from any other garden features is only really appropriate in a formal setting; an informal pool will rarely look natural in such a situation. The key to blending a pond into its surrounds is the design of the buffer zone around the water's edge. Careful choice of the landscaping materials used to edge the pond and thoughtful positioning of the pond in relation to other features in the garden are essential. Hide the pool construction material or any natural semblance will be lost.

Concrete paving can look too harsh around an informal pool, though you may decide to use some slabs, especially where wear and tear might damage other materials. For informal ponds, natural and reconstituted-stone paving are definitely preferable to concrete types. Other suitable forms of edging include natural stone, boulders, rocks and pebbles. If you have used stone elsewhere in the garden, such as a rockery, it will help if the two match. From a practical viewpoint it is best to avoid stones that tend to break up in water. Gravel beach edges look very effective when new, but tend to wash into the pond, and certain types of gravel can also make the water too alkaline. It is better to stick to larger cobbles for beach-like edges.

Lush growths of plants can very effectively mask the sharp edges of the water; a careful juxtaposition of true aquatic plants in the pond and moisture-loving plants around its edges can blur the ground between. If the pond leads into a bog or moisture area situated to the side or rear of the pond, there will also be the advantage of the reflections of these plants in the water. Choose plants that will not become too large for their situation.

The spoil removed from the pond excavation can very easily be used to create or add to a rockery or raised area within the garden. If situated behind the pool, the mound will be reflected in the water. Waterfalls can also be built into the slope.

Rockeries should blend into the contours of the garden, and this might involve creating a lower mound that spreads over a greater area. One or two steep slopes could be built into the rockery for effect, but if the garden is relatively flat, it is much better to stick to gentler slopes. Steep slopes can erode, washing soil into the pond if it is close by, and large walls of rocks by a pool edge will require some form of foundation to prevent slippage. The rocks in the mound should be of varying sizes, with some large and bold pieces, and positioned so that any strata line up. Partly bury the rocks to give the impression that they

*Below: A backing of foliage plants and decking provides soft edging and interesting reflections for informal ponds.*

have always been there, and not simply placed on top of the soil.

Raised areas will give you the opportunity to include pools at higher levels. By terracing pools within the contours of a rockery, you can create a series of natural-looking waterfall pools. Some landscapers specialize in constructing such features, often using large amounts of weather-worn rock or slate. These rocks are often carried well below the waterline to give the impression that it is the rocks themselves that are retaining the water. If you are planning on building a large-scale rockery, it may be worthwhile contacting a reputable landscaper for help and advice; very large rocks will often need specialist equipment to move them.

Alternatives to natural rock include reconstituted hollow rocks and rocks made from glassfibre or a mixture of glassfibre and cement. These are considerably lighter than real rock and can look very realistic. Some manufacturers even produce lipped rocks, which can be positioned to hang over the pool edge, disguising the lining material. Unfortunately, artificial rocks are usually fairly expensive and it may be difficult to match them with real stone used elsewhere in the garden. (For more on pond edgings see pages 50-55.)

For larger ponds, an interesting feature can be created by the inclusion

*Above: A stream has been widened to create a more visible feature in this hollow. It is highlighted by the surrounding lush growths of* Hosta *and the simple bridge.*

*Below: A large pond can tolerate dense planting of taller moisture-loving plants at its edge without becoming lost in the foliage of this well-stocked garden.*

of an island within the pond (see also pages 78-79). Almost as effective, but easier to construct and maintain, is the horseshoe pond. By building up the spit of land that juts into the pond and planting it up carefully, the promontory will be disguised when viewed from certain angles, creating the impression of an island.

If the pond is in a slight hollow, a stream can be extended from one end to create a small gully. This could be planted with moisture-loving plants and perhaps bridged with a simple wooden structure. Alternatively, large flat stones on either side of the stream could act as stepping points, creating another interesting feature.

Wildlife ponds and larger lakes benefit from fairly simple edging. Turf can run down to the water's edge or, if necessary, wooden piling or battens can be used to hold back the soil, with turf or plants growing up to the boundary. Lakes benefit from large-scale planting; the small ornamental plant varieties grown in and around garden ponds can look lost in such a situation. The giant moisture plants – *Gunnera spp., Rheum palmatum, Inula magnifica* – and other large varieties, such as larger forms of *Hemerocallis, Ligularia,* and *Lythrum,* are ideal for such a setting, perhaps with a backdrop of *Rhododendrons.*

## SEMI-FORMAL PONDS

In gardens that contain a mixture of styles, a pond can act as a buffer zone between formal and informal sections of the garden. One side of the pool may border a patio, for example, while the other side butts up against an area of contrasting style, perhaps a lawn or plant border. The pool itself can be of either style, or a mixture of the two, with one or two straight sides and the others irregular. The formal edging does not always have to be paving. A section of wooden decking could jut out over the edge of an otherwise informal pool, providing a platform suspended over the water, from which to view the pond. An alternative idea, but one that includes a similar contrasting of styles, is to build an informal pool around the base of the corner of a wall, allowing the water to lap up against its base.

An attractive effect can be obtained by raising the pond partly above ground level. On a sloping site the pond could actually cut into the slope and only be raised on the lower end of the slope. Seating can be built into the wall supporting the pond, or the wall widened to take a larger coping, which can then act as a seating area or a place to display large urns of plants. Wooden coping provides a softer, warmer finish and complements any wooden decking or pergolas.

A variation in levels enhances any garden. Normally this would be achieved with steps between different levels of patio or decking, or by the use of raised flower borders; water, too, can act as another surface and another level. Ponds can be tiered or terraced with water cascading between the two if desired and the higher ponds can be held up with retaining walls. Choose appropriate materials for the garden; new brick looks well beside a modern house, second-hand brick has a softer, more aged appearance and stone or reconstituted stone has a less formal feel. Or you could use old railway sleepers or larch poles.

The higher level need not be a pool; it could be a plant border, a walkway, or a base for an ornament. The backdrop provided behind the lower pool can act as a foil for plants or ornaments situated in the pool. By curving this back wall around the sides of the pool, the pool becomes a sheltered oasis and a fountain placed in the pool will be protected from wind.

Where a semi-formal pond borders a lawn or gravel area, paviours or bricks make a neat edging. Suitable paviours can even be used on a slope to form a solid 'beach' that shelves into the water. Other forms of edging that you might want to consider include the more informal pebble beaches, logs or stones. Having a number of different edging materials around the pond will help to break up the monotony, but don't overplay this variety or the pond will have a cluttered appearance.

It may be that you have inherited a garden that already contains a formal pool and are trying to create a more informal atmosphere. Try placing lush, bushy plants (*Caltha spp,* for example) in the pool margins to camouflage the edges of the pool. You could also place clusters of densely planted terracotta urns around the outside of the pool, or remove a slab or two of paving and plant up with some bushy herbaceous plants.

*Right: A row of vertically placed wooden sleepers acts as a semi-* *formal wall supporting a cascade pool on a higher level.*

**Wooden terraces**

*Left: Here, two levels of water mirror the ornament and brick arch and the waterfall provides extra movement and reflections.*

*Right: Despite the formal constraints of the surrounding wall and patio doors, the bold use of plants provides a soft, attractive border to this informal pond.*

*Below: The harsh edges of this formal pond are overwhelmed by the clusters and spires of water plants, which transform this secluded area into an informal oasis of tranquility, enhanced by a simple fountain.*

## FORMAL PONDS

Formal ponds should be seen as part of an overall plan for a garden. The outline of a formal pond should ideally be as accurate as possible; round ponds should be truly round. (The eye is irritatingly good at picking up any inconsistencies.) You should also ensure that the straight edges of a formally designed pond are parallel with those of any nearby features, including any buildings. If you decide to use paving to edge the pond, choose a size of pond that will minimize the number of slabs that need to be cut (remember in your calculations that it is wise to let the slabs overhang the water by 5cm/2in) and try to keep to the type of paving used elsewhere in the garden. Although contrasting styles of paving can be very effective (a ring of different textured paving or paviours could be set around the pond, for example), mixing styles can prove disastrous if the finishes clash. You would be wise to obtain samples of a few types before deciding on a particular style; they may look very different 'in the flesh' from those shown in the manufacturer's catalogue, and there are often subtle differences between batches.

In larger paved areas a sunken pond can look more impressive than one on the level. Framing the pond with an area of paving 10-12cm(4-5in) below the surrounds will draw the eye down into the pond and give a different perspective to any fish and water lilies. Sunken ponds require drainage to be set in below the paving to allow water to overflow and are not recommended in sites prone to flooding.

Paving stones are now available in various geometric shapes, which makes it easy to complement hexagonal or octagonal ponds. These styles of pond look most effective when the geometric pattern is extended into other parts of the garden, for example with geometrically shaped flower beds. However, unless you particularly want a recurring geometric pattern throughout the garden, you would be better to stick to the simpler designs; mixing too many different patterns can break up the important coherency of the formal garden.

Choosing appropriate edging for a round pond requires rather more thought. A ring of bricks or paviours would be an obvious choice, or you could think about radius-style paving slabs (if you can find some with the right dimensions). A few companies manufacture reconstituted stone sections, often imitating carved Italian features, to place around circular pools. If you have rectangular paving nearby, blending this with paving used around the pool may be a problem. You could use crazy paving as an infill, but coarse gravel may achieve a more pleasing finish, providing the pool edge is high enough to keep out loose chippings. Similar guidelines apply to semicircular and wedge-shaped ponds. These are often set up against a wall, which acts as a backdrop to show off any pool ornaments.

Canal ponds have been popular for many centuries, particularly in larger formal gardens where they may form a vista looking out from the house. They may be bounded on each side by symmetrical flower borders or paths, but to complete the framework, hedges or walls are often used to enclose and shelter the rectangular area. Such canals can be quite wide – a style popular in seventeenth-century Holland. Smaller canals may lose some of the benefits of the reflections offered by wide expanses of water, but they have their charms; a narrow canal can be easily bridged, or can have a few regular stepping stones set across it. A similar effect can be achieved by linking a number of wider formal pools with narrow canals. However they are used, the result is a ribbon of reflective water, stretching into the distance and adding a very grand touch to the landscape.

Also on the grand scale are Italian-style ponds with ornate edging in carved stone. In Britain, the majority of these were built during the eighteenth and nineteenth centuries but, though the originals are naturally scarce, some companies specialize in supplying such architectural antiques and reconstituted replicas are sometimes available, usually from companies in Italy and Spain. It may also be possible to copy these designs using brick, paviour or concrete edging, and such modern materials will complement new buildings.

Simple, formal-shaped ponds – squares, oblongs, staggered oblongs and L-shapes – fit neatly into paved areas. Overlapping and interlinking

elements such as differing water levels, stepping stones and edging materials can, with restraint, create an eye-catching feature.

Formal pools are, in essence, frames for water constructed from various hard landscaping materials. This frame is a vital element of the design and it is therefore important that plants are chosen to complement rather than cover the framework. For this reason, formal pools tend to have fewer plants, especially of the emergent varieties, and the main planting is of water lilies and the various underwater plants. Choose suitably vigorous varieties of lilies for the pool size, but remember that stronger lilies may cover the water surface too quickly and cut down on the important reflective areas. Emergent plants should have fairly upright foliage rather than informal bushy growth; irises, rushes (*Scirpus*) and reedmaces (*Typha*) are all suitable choices. For architecturally interesting foliage try *Cyperus alternifolius*, arrowheads (*Sagittaria*), and the arum lily (*Zantedeschia*). Such plants are normally positioned strategically in some or all of the corners of the formal pool.

As there is a limit to how much can be squeezed into these small areas, the formal pond may be something of a disappointment for the plant enthusiast. There are, however, several ways of increasing the number of plants without masking the important outline of the pool. One way is to build plant pockets into the side of the pool, beyond the basic framework. Another would be to replace some of the slabs around the pool with soil to grow other garden plants in. Alternatively, position tubs of plants strategically around the pool. These design hints can, of course, be combined with more informal elements to suit the semi-formal garden.

*Above: There are strong Moorish influences in this formal Spanish design, but the pattern of a* square intersected with semi-circles is also widely used in classical Italian water gardens.

*Left: A sunken canal makes full use of this long garden, leading the eye to the group of plants at the far end. The open water surface clearly mirrors the distant trees and the small bridge, and the lack of water plants is offset by the rows of planted terracotta pots.*

*Right: The formal outline of a pond can be maintained while at the same time making more room for plants. You can grow some in small alcoves in the pool side, or lift the slabs at the pool edge.*

various simply shaped pools will allow water to extend into other areas of the garden, and the pools can link otherwise distinct areas.

Interlinking pools are ideal in a garden built on a range of levels. The ponds can be quite separate, or can flow from one to another, either by formal cascades or through spouting overflow pipes set into the walls of the higher ponds, which can be built into a terrace and restrained with a retaining wall. You could even build one raised pond within another, in complementing or contrasting styles.

A single pool situated below the retaining wall of a terrace is much more interesting to the eye than merely seeing two levels of paving. Steps could bank one or both sides of the pond, or even be used over the pond.

In today's small gardens it is important to make the most of available space; clever mixing and matching of

### Planting in and around the formal pool

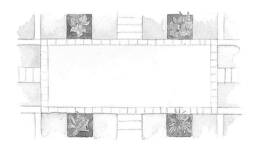

## SMALL WATER FEATURES

Dull corners or unexciting patios can be easily transformed with the addition of a small water feature. An old stone trough, painted inside with sealant or lined with butyl, makes an attractive container for water. You may be fortunate enough to find a genuine stone cattle trough, which may have a groove cut in the rim to act as an overflow, but if you cannot find the real thing, reconstituted stone troughs are widely available. Make sure that these are suitable for holding water, however; many are designed as planting tubs for alpines and are not strong enough to contain water in frosty weather.

Tubs made from halved wooden barrels can be found at most garden centres and, again, can be sealed or lined to hold water and the outside painted or varnished for durability. Both troughs and tubs can be raised on a few bricks if necessary or look very effective set slightly into a bed of gravel chippings. Cast iron well heads are still available, and can be used either purely decoratively, or functionally, situated beside a stone trough or a small formal pool.

Other tiny pond features can be built into patios and need only be deep enough for a small fountain pump if one is required. Many such tiny pools are based around small fountains and are too small for plants or fish. Troughs and tubs can be planted up with the smallest waterplants; pygmy water lilies are ideal. Other plants will probably need regular trimming back to prevent them swamping the container. Very small pools might require

*Above: A Japanese deer-scaring device (shishi-odoshi) nestles between foliage and stones. Sound is provided by the steady trickle of water and the motion of the pivoted bamboo as it hits the rock.*

*Right: The intriguing snail decoration adds interest to the waterspout above a simple stone trough sited at the base of a garden wall. Pipework is concealed behind the wall.*

*Left: This terracotta urn, surrounded by arum lilies, takes up very little space but still incorporates both the sight and sound of running water. A small pump is sited below the rocks.*

bell – or even a drilled boulder. The water provides splashing movement and gleaming reflections as it trickles down over the pebbles and into the reservoir area below. Pebble fountains are ideal if the safety of young children is an issue and the pebbles can always be removed to reveal a small pond at a later date. Pebble fountains can be set into paving or built into a raised border.

Ornaments are often used in conjunction with water features. Self-contained types, where water is re-circulated within the ornament, can be positioned on paving, in gravel, or among plants, and designs vary from classical to modern abstract.

Other ornaments can be situated in the pool or on the poolside. A large number can be fitted with a fountain jet; alternatively choose a standard ornament and direct a separate jet (or jets) up onto, or over, it. The size of ornament and the spray dimensions must be coordinated with the pool outline; fountain sprays will blow in the wind and some loss of water is likely to occur, but providing the pool is large enough this should not be a major problem.

Whichever style of ornament you choose, it is worth thinking carefully about where to position it. Take into account the angles the pool is most likely to be viewed from; in a formal garden this will often be down one of the axes of the design and it makes sense to situate any centrepiece ornament accurately on this axis. For more informal designs the precise positioning is less crucial, but, just as when you are hanging a picture on a wall, take time to experiment with different placings and angles before deciding on the most favourable.

Ornaments often benefit from some form of background to act as a foil; a light-coloured ornament will show up better if it has a lush backing of plant growth, or a contrasting building or wall in the distance. If the ornament is seen down a vista, this can often be enhanced by framing the view with hedging on each side, or a trellis arch. In larger gardens it is common to line up a number of ornaments along the same axis. Take care to choose ornaments of similar proportions whose styles are unlikely to clash.

The classical designs of nymphs and cherubs probably suit formal gardens

better than others. Other common designs include various aquatic creatures, such as fish and dolphins. Many ornaments include single or tiered bowls, either intricately moulded or plain and simple. These can be very effective, but bear in mind that a large volume of pumped water will be needed if water is to cascade over the entire circumference of such bowls. It is of enormous benefit to see fountain ornaments in operation before you make your choice; even a photograph of one in operation is useful. Remember, too, to choose an ornament that will be in proportion to the rest of the pond. Small spouting ornaments can look very fitting beside a semi-formal pond, competing for attention with plants and fish. The same ornament beside a large formal pool might look insignificant, or even out of place.

Millstones are a popular choice for fountain features; if you cannot afford the real ones there are a wide range of reconstituted and glassfibre ones to choose from. Abstract fountain features are popular in continental Europe and are often seen in public places. These often consist of individually sculpted granite pieces, or mounds constructed from various colours of cobble setts with large geyser jets fitted in the centre.

The colour of an ornament should also be considered. Some finishes will weather more than others and take on an aged look; white ornaments will often become stained with green or brown algae if they have water running over them. This will not always look unsightly, but it is worth bearing in mind. Terracotta-type ornaments usually keep their colour, but the intense hues may not blend with all surrounds; bronze ornaments will take on a green patina unless coated with a protective surface.

Smaller ponds that are built around a fountain feature will in many cases be devoid of plants; few plants like the strong water currents associated with larger fountains, and if algicides are used to keep the water clean, they will inevitably stunt plant growth. In larger ponds there should be enough room for both fountains and plants. Water-lilies provide an ideal foil for many of the more classical fountain ornaments, providing they are out of direct water spray.

draining in winter, especially if in exposed areas. The plants can be kept temporarily in a larger pool or in a large bowl in a greenhouse.

Pebble fountains – where water gushes up in the middle of a group of well-rounded pebbles – have become very popular. The jet can be of any type, but is usually a geyser, a water-

## REGIONAL STYLES

There are various different themes around which you may design your garden. The more classical, formal pools, described previously, are heavily influenced by the styles of the seventeenth and eighteenth century landscapers, who designed many of the water features in the gardens of British stately homes. In turn, these landscapers were influenced by Italian designers, who made great use of ornate Romanesque statuary, carved stone pillars and coping. The classical style has incorporated Victorian elements during its time in Britain, and today there are a number of companies specializing in the production of reconstituted stone ornaments, using designs taken from original carved pieces. Although some houses are built to neo-Georgian designs, the formal classical style does not mix well with the majority of modern housing. If your garden is big enough, then you might create a formal area – perhaps in a classical Italianate style – that is not overshadowed by the style of your house.

Oriental gardens are famed for their use of water. When the influences of oriental culture first reached the West they created a great surge of interest, with Europeans eager to purchase Chinese and Japanese porcelain, ornaments and paintings, and to build oriental gardens, with pagodas and lakes.

In recent years, there has been a resurgence of interest in oriental culture, including gardens, especially in bonsai, and the ornamental Japanese carp – koi.

It is difficult for westerners, with a different sense of design, to recreate oriental styles and some of the plants grown in China and Japan will not flourish in our climate. Nevertheless, there are features that you can incorporate into a garden to give it an oriental atmosphere.

For an instant oriental flavour, include a few suitable ornaments. Japanese lanterns (ishidoro) are available in a number of different styles and sizes, in stone or concrete. For a more Chinese feel, choose the characteristic ceramic ornaments, such as large bowls glazed in dark brown.

A pagoda or summerhouse will help to establish an oriental feel to the garden, and a bridge can also act as a striking focal point. Monet had a gracefully arched bridge included in his water garden which provided the backdrop for many of his famous paintings. Its simple form was enhanced by an oriental *Wisteria* growing along the handrail, whose hanging blooms reflected in the water.

In Japan, smaller bridges are sometimes created by laying huge, monolithic hunks of stone, or hewn granite, across the water surface. A simpler and more practical option is to use stepping stones.

Keep the design of a summerhouse or bridge fairly simple. The most ornate part of the summerhouse should be the roof, with deeply concave tiles when available. Ideally, you should build such structures from heavyweight pieces of timber, preferably unpainted, but stained if necessary. If you want to paint your summerhouse, use colours such as jet black, oriental red or antiquated jade.

Japanese garden design is very much tied in with elements of the

*Right: Rocks, moss and foliage are central elements in Japanese water garden design. The* kotoji doro *lantern helps to emphasize the oriental style.*

*Left: Various features have been effectively used to reinforce the Japanese style of this garden. The slate stepping stones abut each side of the stream, the base of which is strewn with stones and cobbles. Plants are restricted to those with bold foliage and the stone lantern and bamboo unify the oriental feel of the design.*

Shinto and Buddhist religions, with emphasis on the importance of stones, rocks, paths and waterfalls. Around the water's edge, make good use of large stones, with rounded rather than angular edges. Pebble beaches can be blended in with these larger stones, and beyond the pool edge the watery theme can be extended with 'waves' of gravel chippings, reaching out into the rest of the garden and lending some unity to the overall design. Water features tend to be based on informal designs and the pool outlines are usually irregular, any sweeping curves being interrupted by clusters of stones or, as an alternative to stone edging, upended rustic logs.

Japanese gardens are often built in a very limited space, which means that all the design features must be crammed in, often sloping up to an enclosing wall or bamboo fence. Ponds are frequently built right up to the edge of the house, and in some cases may even run under part of the house. This is of benefit to koi-keepers, who can then feed their tame koi within the comfort of their homes, through openings in the floor. Underfloor ponds are impractical in Western-style housing but the indoor/outdoor features can be adapted to suit conservatories, often to great effect.

Japanese gardens rarely have large areas of grass, the green background being provided by lush growths of moss, which flourish in Japan's humid summers. You can encourage moss to grow on more porous rocks, providing they have some shade, by spong-

## PLANTS FOR ORIENTAL WATER GARDENS

Despite the wide range of plants native to China and Japan, their minimalist gardens usually include only a small variety. Unlike Western gardens, where plants are often used to fill every corner, areas of rock and gravel are often left bare. The Japanese are, however, very fond of planting clumps of grasses, which may emerge from gravel, or between stones (these may include most European varieties or the bright green-and-gold *Hakonechloa*, the tall *Miscanthus* or, in shaded spots, smaller ferns, such as *Athyrium*). Plants are used sparingly, and the

emphasis is on their foliage, shape and leaf colour rather than flowers.

■ **Shrubs and trees**
Dwarf maples (*Acers*)
Pines (*Pinus*)
Box (*Buxus*)
*Mahonias*
Japanese laurel (*Aucuba*)
Heavenly bamboo (*Nandina*)
Barberries (*Berberis*)
■ **Flowering shrubs**
Rhododendrons, including Azaleas
Flowering cherries (*Prunus*)
*Spiraeas*
Japanese *Camellia*

■ **Pond plants**
Water lilies (*Nymphaea*)
Lotus (*Nelumbo*)
*Iris laevigata*
Japanese clematis iris (*Iris ensata/ kampferi*)
Arrowheads (*Sagittaria*)
Lizard's tail (*Saururus*)
■ **Other moisture-loving plants**
*Rodgersia*
*Ligularia*
*Hosta*
*Astilbe*
*Hemerocallis*
*Hydrangea*
*Lysichitum camtschatcense*

ing milk or yoghurt onto new rocks, and rubbing in the sporeheads from existing clumps of moss.

There are various other finishing touches which can help to add that oriental feel to the water garden. Bonsai can be placed on stones beside the water's edge, although this is not a tradition in Japan, where bonsai are normally kept in separate viewing areas. However, the Japanese do practice a form of 'giant bonsai' on the trees in the garden, which involves trimming the leaves once or twice a year, usually on pine trees, so that the majority of needles on the lower sides of the branches are removed.

Living bamboos are often avoided, due to their size and vigour, but you could use bamboo canes in oriental style fences, and larger pieces of bamboo in the water powered deer-scaring devices (*shishi-odoshi*). You could also try piping water through drilled bamboo, to pour into the pond, or into a basin beside the pond.

Koi may provide the central feature in a Japanese garden. These exotic carp can reach large sizes, and their bright colours are a dramatic contrast to the green foliage and stonework elsewhere in the garden. If they are to be an important element in your garden, you should ensure that the pool is of adequate size and depth, and that allowance has been made for water filtration (see pages 124-129).

Spanish and Moorish designs have their roots in the Middle East, where water features were a show of affluence, included in all the great palaces. Their key elements include narrow flowing canals, wider shallow canals, and splashing formal cascades. Fountain ornaments, usually in marble, consist mainly of tiered bowls, sometimes with spouts around their circumference. These fountains often play a dual role, providing soothing sounds of running water, and acting as places for drinking and washing. Designs on the ornaments often show Islamic influence, which is also reflected in the patterned screens separating the courtyards, where the fountains are often situated.

*Above: Canals and courtyards form the basis for Moorish designs. Here such a canal is enlivened by the regular rows of single jet fountains playing into the water.*

In Spain, these basic designs have been adapted. Ornaments in the Spanish style often include medieval representations of animals and plants. Fountain jets are widely used, as in one dramatic design, which incorporates a long canal, with a row of single spout jets along one side.

Moving water is a key element in such gardens, with plants and fish taking a subsidiary role. The ornaments are important in setting the style, with the careful use of paved and gravel areas, decorative setts and terrazzos. Plants around the water are often confined to large pots.

Spanish style gardens need a sunny, preferably south-facing site, to encourage sparkling reflections and sharp shadows. You can complement them with Mediterranean-type planting schemes in the garden.

## WATERCOURSES AND WATERFALLS

Moving water has always had an appeal to the gardener. The sight and sound of water trickling, running or splashing over rocks and cascades appeals to everyone; gleaming pebbles and rippling reflections add to this lively scene. It is not surprising then that many people are inspired to introduce water features into their own garden. Some will choose to have a fountain or spouting ornament, others aim to imitate nature and build their own falls and watercourses. If you are one of the latter, you should consider how these features will fit into the overall garden design and how they will blend with any other water feature – planned or existing.

Few people will be fortunate enough to have a natural stream running through their garden that can be dammed and redirected to obtain the desired effects. In most cases gardeners are faced with the difficult task of trying to recreate nature. Although recirculating pumps can provide the necessary water movement, it is quite an achievement to give the impression that a finished waterfall or stream has always been a part of the landscape. To achieve the most natural appearance, it is worthwhile taking a few lessons from nature.

## IMITATING NATURE

- *Watercourses follow the lowest points in the landscape.*
  The natural path of water is flowing downhill, cutting a niche in the landscape. Unfortunately, rainwater and fallen leaves collect in the lowest points in the garden, and can soon pollute any water feature in such a spot. It is therefore better to compromise, as when siting a pond, and position any stream low enough to appear realistic, but not in the lowest point, which is best reserved for bog plants.

- *Streams tend to cut into hillsides.*
  Water does not run over the top of the soil. Any watercourse should be set into a channel carved into the landscape.

- *The size of waterfall cascades matches the slope of surrounding land.*
  If your garden slopes only a few feet from one end to the other, a miniature Niagara will look very unnatural. Such an effect may suit a formal, or semi-formal, situation, but it will not look natural. A series of small falls would be more fitting – even an 8-10cm (3-4in) fall can provide enough noise and movement to become a focal point.

- *It is possible to see where water is coming from and where it is going.*
  This is where the gardener must use ingenuity, in order to give the impression that water is entering the garden at one side, running through, and leaving at another side. Water might emerge, spring-like, from a cluster of boulders; alternatively it may flow out from under a large slab, or walkway, as if it were a buried stream emerging, and appear to run out of the garden in the same way.

*Left: This natural stream cuts into the landscape and provides a constant source of moisture for the lush and varied selection of plants along its banks. Bear in mind, when designing a long stream, that you will need a large pump, hose bores and reservoir.*

A watercourse can take a number of forms as it flows through the garden. For a stream effect, a series of long narrow pools can be linked by small or large falls. Pools of varying width give the best effect, but, if you want to keep plants, remember that wider pools are essential – narrow streams have too strong a current for most plant growth. Avoid long stretches of sloping watercourse, because these will run dry as soon as the recirculating pump is turned off, and look most unattractive. The falls themselves can be single, clean cascades pouring from one level to another, or a film of water splashing over and between a jumble of rocks and pebbles. It will look more realistic if the water appears to run over an outcrop of rock which continues into the garden on each side of the fall. The lowest part of the watercourse should be a fairly large pool, because it provides the reservoir from which the water will be pumped.

Practical problems increase where the stream runs over a long distance.

*Left: Old railway sleepers create a series of terraces in this hillside, and also direct a winding channel of water into the pebble-lined pond.*

*Above: This informal stream tumbles between limestone rocks and groups of plants and acts as a buffer between the formal path and grassed area.*

Pumps and hose bores need to be larger, and the reservoir big enough to cope with evaporation and water loss from the stream. There is also more chance that dirt and any fish being kept in the upper reaches will be washed into the lower reservoir pond. For this reason some landscapers separate the watercourses into two or more chains. Although these appear to be linked, they actually consist of separate reservoir ponds, each with their own pumping system. For example, a stream or pond can appear to run under a path or low bridge, emerging at the other side, often as a cascade. In fact, the two bodies of water are separate, the adjoining edges being hidden under the path.

Streams can be bounded by stones set into the ground. Giant multiple cascades of slate or limestone can look very impressive, but make sure you use similar stone to that used in the rest of the garden. For the most natural effect, use rocks of different sizes, including a few really large boulders to add variety. You may also wish to use pebble beaches and bog plants among the stone edging.

For many gardeners, streams and waterfalls are accessory features, complementing one or more larger ponds; the cascades are often built into the mound of spoil that results from the excavation of a pond. The pond is usually the major feature, intended to highlight water plants and fish. For this reason the cascades are designed to be in proportion to the main pool; not detracting from it in any way. An oversized waterfall might upset the overall design, and its turbulent water could disturb the growth of water plants. To avoid disruption of the water surface, set large waterfalls back from the pool edge, perhaps cascading into a small catchment pool which then empties more sedately into the main pond. If the cascade is set into a mound, the stones on each side can direct splashes back into the catchment pool, and help to cut down on water loss. Remember that larger cascades can be noisy, which is pleasant on a hot summer's day, but can be irritating to you, and your neighbours, at night.

The limitations of many gardens prevent the creation of waterfalls and streams that appear entirely natural. Often gardens are flat and noticeably restricted by a rectangular boundary, which immediately imposes a degree of formality on the garden. You may, nevertheless, wish to maintain a level of informality in the garden, while compromising and including some obviously man-made features.

For inspiration in creating a semi-formal situation, consider some artificial water features that are found in the landscape, for example, mill-streams and canals, which, whilst being man-made, are still relatively informal. Their edges can be bounded by wooden piling or larger pieces of wood, such as railway sleepers. Mill-stream channels are often built up, above ground level, to provide sufficient height for a neatly shaped water chute, or cascade. The watercourses are often straight, and cascades can take the form of wiers. Timber decking and piers can jut out over the water surface. You could adapt these

features to suit the design of your garden, bordering the edges of the pools and streams with reconstituted stone blocks or bricks, paving or turfing right up to the water's edge, and running the watercourses and cascades parallel with paths and walls.

You may, however, prefer a more formal approach to moving water. As with formal ponds, it is important to ensure that the straight edges of formal water features really are straight, and the curves perfect. There is no need to follow land levels; many formal ponds are built in raised positions, or on different levels of terrace.

Formal streams can take the form of regular channels, lined with bricks or even tiles and edged with decorative bricks, paviours or overhanging paving slabs. Such designs complement formal bridges, stepping stones and decking. A cascade can fall from a brick raised pond into a lower pool,

*Above: A leafy glade echoes the sound of a high cascade as it trickles down into a series of formal cascade pools, which maintain the symmetry.*

and the waterfall lip can be neatly squared off, or semi-circular. Use polished concrete slabs, glassfibre, perspex or stainless steel to give the waterfall lip a smooth level finish, and ensure that the water falls in an even sheet, or create rivulets of water by using grooved slabs or bricks with deeply cut mortar joints.

As a variant on the waterfall, you may prefer to use one or more spouting tubes to direct overflowing water from a higher to a lower pond, or to introduce reconstituted stone cascade dishes, built in the tradition of the great Italian water features, with ornate scalloped shells; but beware — they are extremely expensive.

# PLANNING AHEAD

When designing your pond, remember to consider all of your aims. If you want to keep fish and plants, then you will have to plan for their requirements as well as your own – and you will need to think about the design of the pond below the waterline as well as above it.

## PLANNING FOR FISH

The basic requirements for fish are a relatively clean and stable environment, which must not overheat or dry out in the summer, or freeze solid in the winter. If the pond is of a reasonable volume and depth, then this should not be a problem. In temperate regions, ponds of around 200 litres (45 gallons) capacity and 40cm (16in) deep are about the bare minimum for hardy pond fish, such as the common goldfish. In general, the bigger the pond the better, especially if it is to be situated in an exposed windy site. The depth to aim for in the average goldfish pond is around 45-60cm (18-24in); in larger ponds (over 20m²/210ft² area) try to include a deeper section, around 90-120cm (36-48in) deep, in the centre, the rest of the base being about 60cm (24in) deep. The base itself should be fairly flat, although it may help if there is a slight slope towards the deepest point. (This will make it much easier to pump the pond dry if it should need emptying at a later date.)

A variation in depths is of benefit. A fairly shallow area will warm up rapidly in the sun and the fish will bask there in the summer. Such a shallow area can easily be created if a shelf is included for marginal plants. Another, slightly deeper, area close to the pool edge can act as a viewing and feeding point. The deepest parts of the pool are a refuge for the fish. The depth is not the only factor to consider. If you want to keep many fish then you must leave plenty of room. Larger fish, such as orfe and koi, will not flourish in small ponds.

When siting the pond, remember that ornamental pond fish benefit from sunlight, which will warm the pond and encourage fish growth. Some shelter from prevailing winds will also help to protect the pond from the excesses of the weather. A good growth of water lilies, marginal plants and oxygenators (submerged plants) are beneficial for most fish. These provide shade from the brightest sun, and shelter from bird and cat predators. Fish can nibble at the plants and the various tiny animals which live in among their leaves. During the summer months the fish may even spawn on the growths of submerged plants.

Clean, well-oxygenated water is essential if fish are to remain in good health, so it is important to minimize all forms of pollution. Fallen leaves are one of the most common forms of pollution, but you can intercept these by fixing a net over the water in the autumn. Nearby roads might be a source of dust, fumes and oily runoff; try to protect the pond from these,

*Above: Pools specifically for koi need thoughtful planning. Allowance has been made for a filter system under the decking beside this deep pond, and the Japanese theme is continued in the pool surrounds.*

## KOI

Koi, the Japanese ornamental carp, are an increasingly popular choice of fish for garden pools. Although smaller koi can be kept in similar conditions to goldfish, they are not as tolerant of poor water quality, and they can grow to almost three times the length of goldfish. For this reason, if you intend to keep any number of koi, you should design the pool accordingly. The basic design requirements for a koi pool are:

- Plenty of room for larger fish to swim freely. This means a minimum length of 3-4 metres (10-13ft), longer if possible.
- Adequate depth. The deeper sections of the pool should ideally be at least 1.2 metres (4ft) deep. Avoid large areas that are less than 60cm (2ft) deep.
- No sharp projections. Large koi can easily injure themselves on overhanging or submerged angular rocks.
- Good water quality. This is usually achieved by either stocking at a very low level, or by installing some form of water filtration to keep the water healthy, well aerated and reasonably clear. A filter for a large pond could take up a fair amount of space – and money.
- Some shade. Bear in mind that large koi will disrupt most plants in the pond, so these cannot be relied upon to provide shelter.

The requirements of koi are discussed further on pages 112-113.

perhaps with a stout hedge.

Densely stocked ponds can suffer from oxygen depletion in hot sultry weather, fish such as orfe being especially at risk. The solution is either to stock your pool sparingly with fish, or to aerate the pool artificially with a fountain or waterfall. If you install a pump to run such a feature, you can use it to run a pond filter. Biological pond filters have become increasingly popular in recent years; they not only keep the water healthy for fish, but also keep green water at bay so that you can see fish clearly, all year round. These filters can be quite bulky, so do make sure that you leave enough room for one at the design stage.

Do not rely on waterfalls to keep fish apart, fish are very adept at working their way over them. If you want to keep separate groups of fish you should build separate pools from the outset. You should also separate koi and water plants, as the two do not mix very successfully. Like any other pet, fish do require some maintenance. If you keep very few fish, they will usually find enough natural food in the pond, but most pond fish benefit from some additional food and will become more tame if they are fed regularly during the summer.

## PLANNING FOR PLANTS

The only basic requirements common to all plants are light and water. In the pond, lack of water is unlikely to be a problem, but a lack of sunlight will result in poor growth of most plants. The pond should ideally receive at least half a day's sunlight; full sunlight will encourage the best plant growth. Plants are similar to other natural organisms, in that conditions which are ideal for one may be lethal to another. If you wish to keep a wide variety of plants in the pond, then you must provide a variety of different environments. Some water plants should have just the tips of their roots in the water, others needs to have water lapping up their stems, and others to be totally submerged. The easiest way to provide for these different requirements is to design the pond with a series of different levels. This is commonly achieved by constructing a shelf, or shelves, around the inner edge of the pond, varying the depth of the shelf if necessary.

Water plants are usually planted in basket-type containers, which have a number of advantages, not least the ability to move plants around with ease and raise or lower them as required. (Details of planting are given on pages 84-87.) Various sizes of container are available to suit different plants and various sizes of pool. The depth and width of the shelves should be planned to accommodate the sizes

of basket you want to use. A good width will allow planting baskets to sit firmly on the shelf and not overhang. The sides of the pond should slope fairly steeply down to the shelf so that plants can be grown close to the edge. Many of the preformed pools incorporate shelves around 20cm (8in) deep and 20-25cm (8-10in) wide. This is a good guide for most medium-sized pools, but, if in doubt, it is wise to make the shelves a little deeper and wider. It is easy to raise containers, but inconvenient to cut them down in size. If you wish to have bold clumps of plants, using more than a single row of containers, the shelf will need to be wider.

These shelves are suitable for most of the marginal plants grown in the pond. A few plants prefer slightly deeper water (as described in the plant descriptions on pages 96-101) and if you want these to flourish, you should include a shelf about 30cm (12in) below the pond surface, or a little deeper if you are using large containers. In sunny situations, put some shelving on the south side of the pool, so that plants situated here will provide some shade to the water, reducing summer growth of green algae.

Water lilies and lily-like aquatics can vary greatly in vigour, miniature water lilies requiring only 15cm (6in) water cover, while the giant varieties can tolerate up to 200cm (72in) of water. However, many common water lily varieties grow best with 25-40cm water cover (10-16in). If you grow these in planting baskets of around 20cm (8in) depth, an ideal depth for the lily shelf would be 45-60cm (18-24in); in most cases this is as deep as the pool needs to be.

*Below: Provide shelves at different depths to cater for the needs of the* *various types of plants. Make sure that they are broad enough for the containers.*

**Planting shelves**

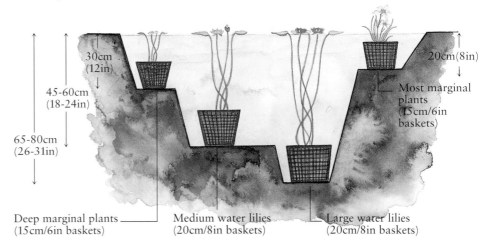

30cm (12in)

45-60cm (18-24in)

65-80cm (26-31in)

20cm(8in)

Most marginal plants (15cm/6in baskets)

Deep marginal plants (15cm/6in baskets)

Medium water lilies (20cm/8in baskets)

Large water lilies (20cm/8in baskets)

Larger, more vigorous lilies will grow better with around 45-60cm (18-24in) water cover over their crowns, so, using containers, the pool depth could be 65-80cm (26-32in). When established, the most vigorous lilies will tolerate much deeper water, but as this is generally cooler in summer, it will restrict the growth and flowering of some of the lily varieties. In general, you should raise these plants up if necessary, so that they have no more than 75cm (30in) of water over their crowns.

If you are planning to have a fountain or waterfall, remember that many water plants, including all water lilies, grow less well in moving water. It is therefore wise to keep such features in a separate area of the pool from the plants.

If the prime reason for your pond is the ability to grow water plants, allow plenty of room. Some varieties can spread rapidly and take up a fair amount of space, particularly in the bog garden where growth is unrestricted by containers. Informal and wildlife ponds often require an edging of moisture-loving plants. The various methods of constructing such bog areas are described on page 55.

When you are planning ahead, bear the timing in mind. Although container-grown plants can theoretically be planted all year round, 'bare-root' water plants are best moved during their growing season. Most temperate water plants are only available commercially during this growing season – spring to early autumn. This is in contrast to many bare-root perennial garden plants (including some bog plants), which are usually available in late autumn and early spring.

*Below: A planting pocket for marginal plants has been built into this pond; separate baskets would facilitate maintenance.*

## PLANNING FOR FOUNTAINS AND WATERFALLS

Space is, once again, an important consideration when planning water features. There must be enough room for all the fountain sprays and waterfall splashes to fall back into the water, and enough water volume to eliminate frequent topping up.

The variety and choice of fountains is dealt with on pages 58-61, but it is wise to decide on the size of any fountain before you finalize the shape and size of the pond. If the pond is only intended to house a fountain, the depth can be reduced to around 30cm(12in), sufficient to cover any submersible pump and deep enough to avoid rapid evaporation.

When planning waterfalls, you should decide on the method of construction, and consider how this will blend in with the materials used to construct the reservoir pond at the base of the cascade. Do not be over ambitious in the scope of your design. Tall falls require steep slopes, and these can be difficult to construct without supports or retaining walls. The waterfall must be accessible for construction and maintenance, without any danger of landslips.

You must remember to leave space for the pumps and plumbing for both fountains and waterfalls. Submersible pumps are the most popular, but they must be accessible for occasional maintenance. The pump inlet strainers can clog, and might need to be cleaned weekly if the pond contains much debris. Where ponds are built in public areas, care must be taken to protect pumps and valves from tampering. This may involve siting external ('surface') pumps away from the pond in a lockable dry chamber.

Remember that fish benefit from moving water as this helps to increase the level of oxygen. However, water lily blooms can become submerged by fountain sprays, so you should design the pond with still water regions if a variety of plants are to be grown.

Electricity is required for waterfall, fountain and filter pumps. It will also be necessary if lighting or heating is required for the pond. If you intend to add extra pumps and lights at a later date, it is wise to use a supply cable of sufficient size for present and future

## ELECTRIC SUPPLIES

Water and electricity do not mix. Although water is not an excellent conductor of electricity, it is quite good enough to transfer a powerful current from an unprotected electric supply to someone dabbling in the water nearby. Despite this, mains supply is safe to use providing sensible precautions are taken. The basic precautions to note are:

- Only use apparatus designed for use in and around water.
- Use a suitable residual current circuit breaker (RCCB) on the supply; (30mA, 30millisecond rating).
- Protect the cable from damage. The cable between the pond and the house supply should either be of an armoured type, or laid in a protective conduit.
- Any cable connections must use suitably rated waterproof or weatherproof junctions. Such connecting devices are only as good as their weakest point and must be fitted in accordance with the manufacturer's instructions. Even if waterproof junctions are used, it is better to situate these above the water level where possible.
- Double check all connections and earth leads, and ensure that a suitably rated fuse is fitted.
- Disconnect any apparatus before handling.

### Electrical wiring from the pond

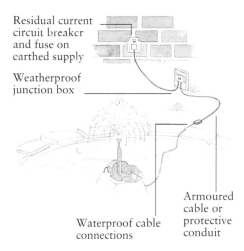

Residual current circuit breaker and fuse on earthed supply

Weatherproof junction box

Armoured cable or protective conduit

Waterproof cable connections

*Above: The pump cable should be connected to an extension by a waterproof junction near the pool, through a switch box, to an RCCB in the house.*

There are two main alternatives — mains-voltage or low-voltage supply. Mains-voltage equipment tends to be more powerful than low-voltage types, and as no transformer is required, it is often a little cheaper, but low-voltage appliances are useful where cables might be prone to tampering, and in some countries legislation allows only low-voltage appliances to be used in and around water. These usually require a 12- or 24-volt supply, which must come from a transformer intended for use with the appliance. Low-voltage supplies can still give a nasty shock if handled incorrectly, so take care when making connections.

Treat the mains supply to the transformer with the same respect as any other mains supply. It is very important that the transformer is protected from moisture. If there is a long length of low-voltage cable between the transformer and the appliance, some loss of power may result. Use the largest gauge cable possible to minimize this problem. Again, if you are in doubt call in a professional.

You should also plan water supplies carefully. Tap water is usually the best source for filling and topping up water features, although in some cases it may require extra treatment to make it suitable for fish. (This is explained in *Water Garden Care* on page 120.) Extend a hose from the nearest supply point when necessary, if possible using an automatic metering device, which will turn the supply off after a period of time, so preventing the floods which can occur if a running hose is overlooked.

Water features that require regular topping up, can, if necessary, be plumbed into the water supply through a permanent link. To do this you should set a small reservoir tank in the ground beside the pool, and link them together with a buried pipe. The water supply is fed to the reservoir tank, where it is controlled by a ballcock valve. Any drop in the pool level will automatically trigger the refilling operation. There may be legal restrictions on the connection of outdoor pools to the mains supply; contact your local water supply company first.

If a tapped supply is too distant, it is possible to use natural supplies, such as a nearby stream, or collected rainwater, but both of these are prone to contamination. You should check such water chemically for purity, before use. Do not collect rainwater from metal roofs, and feed it through a filter of floss and carbon to remove other impurities. Storage containers and pipework should all be of non-toxic materials.

needs. Remember also to leave a gap or duct under any pond edging, so that cables can be easily threaded in.

There is a wide range of electrical fittings now available to allow simple DIY installation of pumps and lights. Weatherproofed switched junction boxes also allow safe control of such appliances while in the garden. If you are in any doubt about electrical wiring, ask a qualified electrician to help. It is also important to check on any local regulations applying to electricity in the garden.

### An automatic topping-up system for large ponds

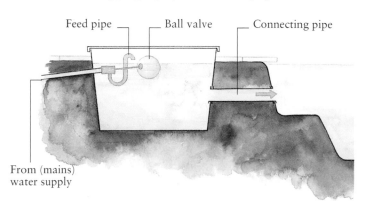

Feed pipe    Ball valve    Connecting pipe

From (mains) water supply

*Left: To allow large ponds to be topped up automatically, the pond can be filled from a protective tank housing a ballcock, which regulates the flow of water into the pond. Ensure that water cannot siphon back into the supply system.*

# LIGHTING THE WATER GARDEN

Lighting can bring the garden to life at night, and is particularly effective with water features. In the home, thoughtful use of light can transform an ordinary room into something much more inviting, and much the same principles apply to the garden.

If buildings are floodlit, they will stand out in the garden and reflected light will brighten the garden around them. As an alternative, more selective lighting of features in the garden will draw the attention to particular areas. Fountains and cascades take on a whole new aspect if lit at night, becoming vibrant displays of moving, glowing water. Ornaments, figures and sculptures can be spotlit, and will stand out in the landscape even more than in daylight. The glow of submerged lights can create eerily attractive pools of incandescent colour within the main pool.

By lighting up patios, poolsides, paths, decks, steps, bridges and barbecues, you can safely make full use of such areas at night. The safety aspect of lighting must be emphasized, as poor lighting can turn a charming daytime landscape into a potentially hazardous one at night. Lighting also improves security – well-lit gardens tend to deter possible intruders. You can further enhance security by linking some lights to passive infrared detectors, which will turn on lights only as people pass by.

## LIGHTING DESIGN

There are two methods of highlighting water in the garden, either from above the water surface or below. Above the water, floodlights can be hidden in trees, among plants, or even fixed to buildings. If you direct these down onto the water surface, they will lift the pool out from the darkness, but you should avoid any possible reflections of the light source into the viewer's eyes, as these can dazzle, and will spoil the desired effect of diffuse lighting. Shine light at waterfalls to obtain glittering, moving reflections of the cascade. Try using a hidden spotlight to pick out the detail on a fountain ornament, or sculpture, and reflect it in the water surface.

For reasons of safety, as well as aesthetics, illuminate bridges and paths around the pool. Use either a few bright floodlamps or a number of smaller lights. Remember that, as in a room, uniform bright lighting removes interesting shadows and fails to distinguish between areas of interest. If instead the landscape is lit by discrete pools of light, the more interesting sections can be emphasized and the eye will dwell on each area in turn. One method of achieving this is to use a series of low-power downlighters that stand around 45-60cm (18-24in) high and can be used to cast pools of light along paths. Ideally you should place lamps of similar intensity at regular intervals, directing the light to avoid glare. Downlighters can also be hidden under bridges, illuminating the water, nearby plants and fish.

Shine uplighters into trees around the pool to obtain a green glow, which will illuminate the surrounding area. The moving leaves will create a constantly changing pattern, and this will be stunningly reflected in the water.

Below the water, inpool lighting can be used in a variety of ways. You could direct floodlighting across a body of water, causing a diffuse glow to emanate from the pool, or in ponds with clear water and pale coloured bases, light can be directed at, and reflected from, the base. This is generally only suited to shallower formal ponds and swimming pools.

Geyser-type jets are among the most effective types to use with lighting as the foaming water scatters light well. Very fine jets tend not to show up well, unless massed together, and it may be better to swap a fine jet head for a bolder spray if the fountain is to be lit. When lighting fountains, take care to avoid directing spotlights at viewers. Tall fountain ornaments with multiple bowls are often difficult to illuminate successfully from within the pond, but it is possible to place lights in the bowls to effectively illuminate the sections of ornament above them.

Lights positioned below cascades will transform them into ribbons of shimmering water, glowing in the darkness. If you direct submerged spot or floodlights onto fountains, the result will be bright jet streams contrasting against their background, which need not only be darkness, it could be lights of contrasting colours, for example the fountains could be lit in an icy white to stand out against an amber highlighted building behind.

Tastes differ as to the use of different colours of lighting in the garden. A string of multicoloured lights may look very cheerful when strung over a barbecue area, or hung as Christmas decorations, but this style of lighting is difficult to blend with many garden designs, and some colours can clash. You could use just a few colours in order to contrast different areas, rather than mixing them at random, but a single tint throughout the garden is often just as effective. Amber is the most popular tint, with red and green following. Colour filters are usually fitted over the light source to obtain the desired effect. Remember that filters can noticeably reduce the output of lamps. Blue filters, in particular, need to be used with bright, white output bulbs to obtain reasonable levels of illumination.

## TYPES OF LIGHTING

There are a number of units on the market for use as outdoor lighting including some intended for use under water. For general garden floodlighting, the cheapest units tend to use standard household tungsten bulbs, often in a rainproof bulkhead. This type of lighting is non-directional and can normally only use lower wattage bulbs. These are ideal for the illumination of patios and areas around the house, where the units can be fixed directly to the outside wall. You can

*Right: Copious use of light allows this decking to be used safely at night and at the same time casts reflections of the pergola onto the mirror-like pond.*

# CHAPTER TWO

# PONDS

Having decided upon a design for your pond, you are faced with the further choice of method of construction. The most popular are flexible liner, preformed pools and concrete. None of these options can be considered as the outright first choice for every situation; each has different attributes, and you will have to make your own judgements based on the relative importance to you of such factors as cost, durability, ease of installation and flexibility to match your chosen design and edging materials.

You may be faced with a choice of different coloured materials; light colours enhance the details of the wildlife within the pond but show up any dirt on the surfaces; darker colours give an illusion of more depth, and increase the reflections from the surface – black and brown are two of the most popular colours for pool liners.

It is vital to plan ahead, especially if you want a deep or raised pond. The excavation can involve major effort (especially in unseasonable weather) and you will need to make arrangements to deal with the resulting voluminous amounts of soil and rubble. Take care to avoid buried pipes and cables, and make sure that you don't disturb nearby foundations. Steep-sided pools and soft soils require extra attention to ensure that finished surfaces are firm and sound, and the more unusual edging effects can add significantly to the costs. Preparation and advance planning are the keys to success and will help you to obtain perfect results. This chapter aims to guide you through these important stages.

# LINER PONDS

Pond liners are a very popular method of pool construction. Liner materials are available in virtually any size, and many of the small and medium sizes are available off the shelf, ready to be taken home in the boot of a car. For square, round or other regularly shaped pools you can obtain custom-made liners, welded so as to fit snugly in the excavation. Even large lakes can be lined, as smaller sheets can be joined together on site; ask a specialist supplier for details.

The liner's flexibility allows corresponding flexibility in the design of the pond, as the materials will conform to the intricacies of your excavation, and the better qualities have a long lifespan. They are probably the easiest of the pond materials to install, and the

method of anchoring around the top edge can be adapted to suit a wide variety of edging styles. Any minor variations in the level of the pool edge can be overcome at a late stage in the installation by simply packing earth under some edges and removing it from others. It is even possible to lift some liners and relay them if necessary, although extending liners successfully is difficult without the use of factory welding equipment.

Liners are usually the most economic method of pond construction, too, though the wide choice of lining materials varies considerably in price and performance.

To their disadvantage, liners can be punctured by sharp implements, sharp-edged stones and the roots of

certain invasive plants, such as bamboo, but repairs are possible in most cases. If stony soil is a problem, use a protective underlay material, and where particularly sharp-tipped plant roots are prevalent, lay a barrier of persistent herbicide under the liner. Unfortunately, malicious damage is difficult to protect against, and liners are therefore sometimes unsuitable for ponds in public places.

In excavations with complex shapes there may be a number of folds left in the liner, which can look unsightly when the pond is new and bare, and can be difficult to clean if the pond is drained.

The liner's main advantage of taking up the shape of the excavation can become a disadvantage if the soil should slip. Shelves may tend to lose their shape with time, and although quality liners should last a lifetime, many of the cheaper grades can start to break up after only a few years.

*Below: Use a liner for a pond in a tight corner as access may be too limited for a preformed pool.*

## CHOOSING A POND LINER

Flexible pond liners have been in use since the 1940s, when polythene was the only material widely available. Polythene is still used, because it is fairly cheap, but it is easily punctured, can stretch very thin, and is rapidly degraded by sunlight into a brittle material. It is also difficult to join, and once it has become brittle, it is virtually impossible to repair. If you are using polythene, choose a thick grade (1000 or 1500 gauge) and ensure that all surfaces are protected from sunlight. Polythene is an economical choice for larger wildlife ponds, where the liner can be buried under a layer of soil to prevent physical damage and ultra-violet degradation.

PVC (Polyvinylchloride) liners are more expensive than standard polythene, but they are much stronger. They have some elasticity and they are more resistant to ultra-violet damage, but although PVC is longer lasting than polythene, it still becomes brittle with age and is difficult to repair once

*Left: Paviours create an unusual sloping beach effect. A liner laid in first provides the necessary waterproofing while the paviours protect the liner from malicious damage. Leave a level base for the plants and a duct for a pump cable.*

it has lost its flexibility. It is available in many different sizes, as sheets can be heat welded together. There are a number of different grades of PVC; the thicker grades (0.5-0.75mm/0.02-0.03in) usually last longer, carrying guarantees of up to 10 or 12 years. PVC is available in a range of different colours, including twin-laminate PVC, which is a different colour on each side, giving you the choice of which to place uppermost. Twin-laminate PVC reinforced with mesh is

tougher than ordinary PVC but has a similar lifespan. Be sure to choose PVC intended for pond use as some types contain chemicals that may prove toxic to pondlife.

Butyl is generally considered to be the best-quality lining material available for ponds. Butyl liners are made from a synthetic rubber (isobutylene with isoprene), which has excellent flexibility and elasticity and a very long lifespan. The material has been used to line canals and reservoirs since

| CHOOSING YOUR POND MATERIAL | | | | | | |
|---|---|---|---|---|---|---|
| Type | Costs | Durability | Ease of installation | Flexibility in design | Ease of repair | Comments |
| **Liners** | | | | | | |
| ■ Standard polythene | Cheap | Poor | Fairly easy | Good | Difficult | Frail |
| ■ PVC types | Fairly cheap | Fair to good | Easy | Very good | Possible if still supple | Can be punctured and |
| ■ Butyl | Moderate | Very good | Easy | Excellent | Possible at all ages | finding holes is tricky |
| **Preformed pools** | Moderate to expensive | Fair to very good depending on materials and installation | Average | Limited | Possible with most materials | Smooth finish |
| **Concrete pools** | | | | | | |
| ■ Standard type | Moderate to very expensive | Poor to excellent dependent on workmanship | Difficult | Good to very good | Difficult | Very solid. Need to seal lime |
| ■ Butyl-topped concrete | Expensive | Very good | Fairly difficult | Good to very good | Possible | Solid. No need to seal lime |
| ■ Butyl sandwiched in concrete | Very expensive | Very good-excellent | Difficult | Good to very good | Very difficult, but damage unlikely | Ideal for public sites. Need to seal lime |

the 1940s, and in normal use it should last well in excess of 20 years. The grade normally supplied for ponds is 0.75mm (0.03in) thick (although thicker grades are available) and contains a small amount of EPDM rubber, as this blend has the best longlife properties. Sheets of butyl are heat-sealed (vulcanized) together to give

*Below: Overhang decking to mask the edges of the pond liner and provide some shade for fish. Plants soften the deck border.*

the size of liner required.

Butyl is normally only available in black (an ideal colour for natural ponds) but it is sometimes possible to obtain liners with a coloured surface layer. Butyl has the advantage over PVC in that it remains flexible in cold weather even when it is old. Its stretchy nature allows it to be installed with fewer creases than PVC or polythene, and accidental punctures in the material can be repaired with patches of butyl mastic.

Butyl is also used for roofing, tyre

tubes and cable insulation, but not all grades are suitable for ponds. It is therefore very important to ensure that you obtain vulcanized butyl intended for pond use from a reputable source, and with a valid guarantee of longevity. Other rubber blends may prove toxic to fish, and may have unreliable glued joints.

The 1990s have seen the arrival of a number of new types of pond liner based on modified plastics and varieties of polythene. These liners are generally black in colour and are often

## CALCULATING YOUR LINER SIZE

To calculate the size of liner required, take the dimensions for the maximum length and width of your pool and add twice the maximum depth to each measurement. For example, a pond 3m×2m and 60cm deep would require a liner [3+0.6+0.6] × [2+0.6+0.6] = 4.2m×3.2m. However many shelves there are, if the pond has some slope to the sides, there will be enough overlap for most forms of edging. If the sides are sheer, or if there are to be extra edging effects or islands, then you may require a larger liner.

very extensible. Some will stretch until they are alarmingly thin, but are difficult to puncture. As yet they do not have the longterm proven record of butyl, but if they achieve the manufacturers' claims, they may well overtake butyl as the first choice.

## INSTALLATION

Dig out the pond to the shape required, remembering that if you dig down to the shelf level first, you can firm the soil before continuing. This will give you a solid shelf that is resistant to crumbling. Remove any large stones or roots, and, if the soil is excessively weedy, consider laying down a layer of persistent herbicide granules. Finally, compact the base, sides and shelves firmly. For most ponds the sides should slope inwards fairly steeply, with a drop of about 3cm for every 1cm. If the soil is very crumbly it may be necessary to slope the sides more gradually and make the shelves slightly wider. In such soft soil it is worthwhile working a layer of cement into the surface for extra support (see page 47).

Check that the pond edges are level; this is easiest with a spirit level placed on a stout plank. For very large ponds you may have to use a series of levelling pegs around the pond edge.

Protective underlay materials are available for pond liners. These tough, rotproof materials (usually polyester) cushion the liner from sharp stones and, should the soil shrink and crack,

leaving small sections of liner unsupported, these underlays will protect it from damage. The better-quality underlays are not cheap but they are very worthwhile. As alternatives, you could use a layer of soft sand (2-3cm/ 0.75-1.25in) deep), or old carpet, or generous layers of dampened newspapers. Take particular care to protect the edges of the pond and the shelves.

Place the folded liner in the middle of the excavation and carefully unfold it, moving it into position as you proceed. For PVC liners, you should choose a warm sunny day when the material will be more supple. For informal ponds, stretch the liner slightly and hold its edges in place with stones or other weights, making sure that none of the weights can fall into the pond and damage the liner. A few extra hands can be helpful at this stage. The middle of the liner should sag onto the base of the pond. Overstretching the liner will reduce the strength of the material, so be careful to avoid this, and remember that some of the cheaper polythene materials should not be stretched at all.

Start to fill the pond with water. As it fills, and the liner stretches, ease off the weights around the edge. Make use of the elasticity in the liner to even out as many creases as possible.

Try to avoid folding the liner edges back down, especially in corners, where there are more folds, which can draw water out by capillary action. Slow seepage may make it difficult to keep the pond brim full, and can sometimes give the false impression that the liner is punctured. Disguise the liner with some form of edging.

Fitting liners into formal ponds with tight corners requires a different technique. Once the liner has been loosely laid into the excavation, smooth out the base to minimize creases. Fill the pond with 2-3cm (0.75-1.25in) of water to hold the base down, then fold or pleat the corners of the liner. Carry on filling until the pond is full; then check that the edges are level and add or remove soil as necessary. Trim back any excess liner with sharp scissors – an overlap of 15-20cm (6-8in) is usually adequate for simple edging, such as paving, though other forms of edging may require more overlap (see pages 50-55). Keep any large pieces of spare liner, they may be useful in future.

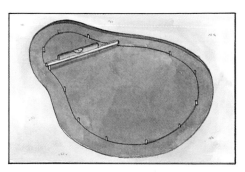

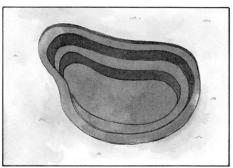

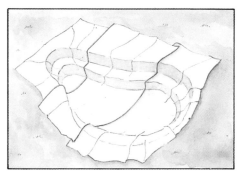

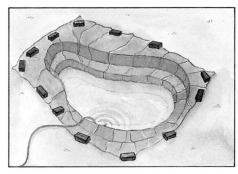

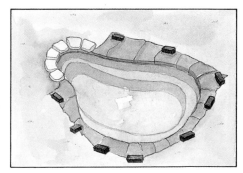

*Above: Liners provide an easy way to build a pond to the shape you want. Check levels, remove all stones and firm all the surfaces, using protective matting or sand under the liner. Leave enough overlap for your chosen edging.*

# PREFORMED PONDS

Preformed or moulded units are another popular means of installing a water feature in the garden. They are available in a range of sizes and in many different designs. Most of the newer designs have a reasonable depth and are an improvement on the early models, which tended to be too shallow. One of the main advantages of preformed pools is that all the design work has been done for you; the shelves are all included, hopefully at the correct depths, and the smooth finish on the units is wrinkle free and fairly easy to clean.

Preformed ponds are much easier to install than concrete pools, especially the medium-sized and smaller designs, which are fairly light and can be handled by one or two people – they will normally fit onto a roof rack for transporting home. Their tough finish is resistant to minor knocks and sharp instruments, and if a small area becomes damaged you can repair it without too much difficulty.

Preformed pools do have some disadvantages, however. They may look deceptively large when displayed out of the ground, but will seem much smaller when they are installed and edged; indeed a number of the smaller designs are just not large enough to accommodate fish. Larger preformed ponds tend to be expensive in comparison to liners and they are not easy to transport.

Although there are a wide range of designs available, you may still be unable to find one that you like, and the number of deeper ponds (over 60cm/24in) is very limited. As with liners, you generally get what you pay for, so the longer life materials will cost more. Despite manufacturers' claims, preformed ponds do require a fair amount of care in installation, and generally take longer to fit than similar-sized liner ponds. It is very important that the top edge of the pool is set level, and the unit must be carefully backfilled so that all shelves are well supported.

The edges of preformed pools can be a little tricky to disguise; you could try using overhanging paving or rocks, but remember that if heavy rocks rest on the pool edge they will need extra support or the pond material may warp or buckle. If the supporting soil slips or shifts, the pressure can deform the pond and may even split the material. You can prevent this problem by laying a concrete foundation before the pond is set in.

## CHOOSING A PREFORMED POND

Over the years various containers have been used for ponds – old metal baths, earthenware sinks and lead cisterns. In the 1950s the first mass-produced preformed ponds came onto the market, and soon became accepted as an easy method of building a pond in the garden.

These ponds were made from glass-fibre- (or fibreglass-) reinforced plastic (GRP or FRP), which is used widely in manufacturing boat hulls, kit cars and watertanks, for example. The finished products are light but very strong.

Glassfibre ponds are produced by spraying layers of polyester resin and glassfibre strands onto an upturned mould. The inside surface of the pond is very smooth, and there are many different shapes available, some of them similar to designs first produced in the 1960s. More recent designs include giant models up to 120cm (48in) deep. GRP is tough and resistant to ageing, but it is a little brittle and can be damaged by sharp knocks (though it is easy to repair). The lifespan of a glass-fibre pond depends very much on the quality of construction, and upon how well it is installed. Water can penetrate from underneath the pond and frost can slowly weaken the structure. The better ponds have a coating of polyester resin on the underside as well as the inside, and this reduces such damage. Ponds with a thicker shell are less prone to damage and buckling than thin models but obviously cost more. Even the best pools will eventually start to leak as the polyester resins will gradually break down. In ideal conditions a good-quality pool could last over 50 years; 10 to 30 years is a more realistic estimate for the average pool.

Glassfibre is not the only material for preformed pools. A number of companies produce vacuum-moulded ponds in various plastics, such as ABS (Acrylonitrile Butadiene Styrene), polypropylene, HDP (high-density polythene) and other forms of polythene. These tend to be cheaper than glassfibre, but as most are moulded from a single sheet of material, there is a limit to the size and depth attainable. When new, they are less easily damaged than glassfibre, but they tend to become more brittle with age and not all types are easy to repair. Their lifespan depends upon how well they are installed and upon the stability of the plastic in sunlight. Many are black, as the black pigment helps to protect the plastic from ultra-violet damage. The best materials should last over 10 years, but some of the poorer qualities may break up after only three or four years.

*Right: Preformed ponds are available in many different shapes and materials, some manageable enough to take home on a roof-rack. Be warned; they will always look much smaller after you have installed and edged them.*

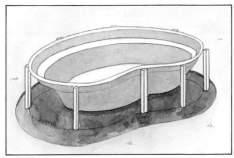

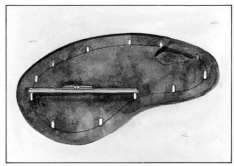

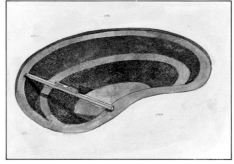

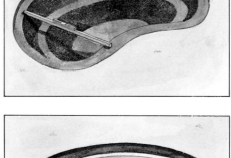

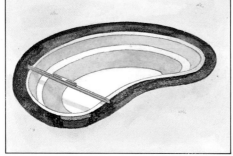

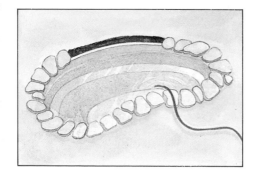

*Above: Regular-shaped preformed ponds provide a perfect template for formal edging, such as brick. A simple fountain adds the finishing touch to this pond.*

Whichever pool you choose, remember that it will look much smaller once it is in the ground. Make sure that it is undamaged, and that the top edge is level and unwarped, before you buy.

## INSTALLATION

Moulded ponds are often described as ridged or semi-ridged, and their flexibility is much more limited than that of liners. A pond full of water can weigh over a tonne; if the moulded pond is poorly supported by the soil around it, or rests on a bump or stone, there is a high risk that the material may become buckled or damaged. Careful installation of the unit is therefore essential if the pond is to last its theoretical lifespan.

For sunken ponds, dig a hole somewhat larger than the mould itself. Compact the base thoroughly and remove all large stones from the base and sides. Place a layer of sifted soil on the base and compact it firmly. Lower the pond into position and check the level carefully using a spirit level on a firm plank across the pond – it will be difficult to rectify any inaccuracies in level at a later stage.

Run some water into the pool to hold it firmly in place and then start to backfill behind the pond sides. Firm the backfill as you proceed, making sure that the shelves are well supported. You can gradually fill the pond with water as you are backfilling. Sifted soil is a better material to use than sand, as it is less likely to wash away, but even soil can shift with time. Some landscapers use different materials to provide a more stable backfill; small, rounded gravel is one option; another is to use concrete for the base and backfill, but remember that glassfibre ponds without a resin laminate on the underside can be damaged by the lime in cement. Paint a protective layer of resin gelcoat onto the underside of such ponds before installation.

Moulded ponds can also be used in raised situations; some are strong enough to be used freestanding, providing the base is well supported; others will require support on all sides, so you should build a wall around them to hold up the top rim.

*Above: A preformed pond has a smooth wrinkle-free surface and all the design work has been done for you. Make sure it is set level and is supported by a firm backfill. Avoid stressing the lip with heavy edging materials.*

# CONCRETE PONDS

For many years, concrete was the only method of making an artificial pool, but with the advent of modern materials its popularity has waned and now few ponds are constructed from concrete. Having said that, it still has a number of advantages: a well-made concrete pond is very sturdy and resistant to damage, can be built to suit virtually any de-sign, and any size, and can incorporate a range of different edging effects, such as rock edges and pebble beaches. Concrete is particularly well suited to deeper ponds; blockwork or shuttered concrete can be used to create sheer walls with firm edges. A strong concrete shell is more resistant to shifting soil than are liners or pre-formed pond units.

The price of a concrete pond depends heavily on the construction method used and on labour costs. A well-made concrete pond can last many years; a poorly built one may fail at the first heavy frost.

Concrete does have disadvantages. The materials are bulky and heavy to handle and transport, with the potential to create a fair amount of mess if cement and gravel are not stored and handled carefully. The construction itself will require a certain amount of skill, and it will take longer than that

*Below: The thick concrete shell of this pond has been raised above ground to create a bold edging, hidden by plants in places.*

of liners or preformed pools. For these reasons most concrete pools are installed by professional builders, who know the pitfalls, and who should be able to install a pond in much less time than the most ardent DIY fanatic.

As concrete does not flex like liners and, to a lesser extent, preformed pools, it is prone to frost damage. (Contrary to popular belief, sloping the walls outwards will do little to prevent this.) To overcome such problems the concrete shell needs to be thick and may require extra reinforcement. Once the pond has cracked it is very difficult to repair successfully, as the crack will tend to open up again after being repaired. Often the only solution is to place a pond liner inside the concrete shell.

Concrete is a fairly permanent material; it is difficult to alter or remove at a later date. The levels must therefore be correct at the first attempt and this is not always easy, especially with very large ponds, which tend to be more difficult to construct in concrete.

Concrete has two other major disadvantages. It is porous and it contains lime. To overcome porosity, it is necessary to include waterproofing compounds in the cement render, or apply a waterproof paint. Lime, which is toxic to fish, can be sealed in with waterproof paint, or neutralized with special acid chemicals applied to the finished concrete. These treatments add to the overall cost.

## INSTALLATION

A concrete pool is basically a tough concrete shell, reinforced and topped with a smooth waterproof rendering. if the pond has gently sloping sides, it is possible to lay stiff concrete directly onto the prepared soil surface, but for steep- or sheer-sided ponds you will need to use blockwork or shuttering. Blockwork is also useful in constructing raised ponds (see pages 48-49). Shuttering involves the use of a frame-work to create a mould into which concrete can be poured and is a time-consuming and expensive process.

For maximum strength the concrete should all be laid on the same day, because joins between one day's work and the next will always be a source of weakness. For larger pools this will involve extra labour to ensure everything is completed quickly; unless you are a confident DIY expert you would be better to call in a professional to do the work for you.

The excavation should be large enough to allow for the thickness of the walls and base; 10-15cm (4-6in) thick is the minimum for small pools, 15-20cm (6-8in) for medium-sized pools, and 20-25cm (8-10in) for large pools. The base and sides of the excavation should be firmly tamped, and in soft soils a layer of hardcore should be worked into the soil. Drains were traditionally set into the pond base, but this, leading to a sump below, weakens the pond and can wash the supporting soil away. Drains are not necessary for most ponds, but if you do install one, it should lead to a sump remote from the pond.

Do not lay the concrete in frosty or hot weather. Frost can damage the finish, and in hot weather the concrete will dry too quickly and lose its strength. For large areas it is often wise to order ready-mixed concrete from a local firm and have this poured directly into the required area. Usually some form of reinforcement is placed in the concrete as it is laid. Steel rods, thick galvanized mesh or chain-link fencing are all possibilities. Where these overlap they should be firmly tied together with wire. The reinforcement should be buried in the concrete, at least 25mm (1in) away from the surfaces. Pegs can be used to mark off the top edge, which should be level. Decide on any edging effects before the pool is finished, as it is virtually impossible to alter the concrete once it is set.

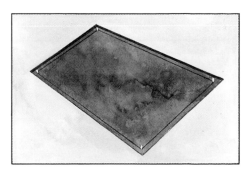

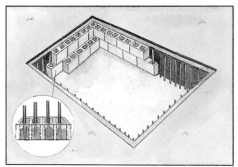

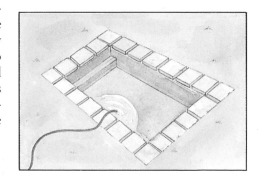

## TYPICAL CONCRETE MIXES

- Foundations: 1 part cement/2 parts sharp sand/4 parts aggregate
- Pond walls/bases: 1 part cement/2 parts sharp concreting sand/3 parts (5-20mm/(0.25-1in) aggregate.
- Waterproof render: 1 part cement/3 parts builders' sand/+ waterproofing agent

*Above: For greatest strength, lay a thick base in one operation and incorporate steel mesh and re-inforcing rods.*

*Blockwork is easier to use than shuttered concrete for the walls and shelves. Finish with waterproof render.*

The pond is finished off with a smoother render coat about 12-25mm (0.5-1in) thick, which normally incorporates a waterproofing agent – either a powder or a liquid additive. Use the correct proportions, as too much additive can sometimes weaken the concrete. It is possible to include reinforcing plastic fibres in the final render, which will make it a little stiffer to spread and will result in a much stronger finish, even if the render coat is only 6-10mm (0.25-0.4in) thick. Any fibres protruding from the dried surface can be sanded off or melted with a blow-torch.

If the finished pond is left unpainted, it will need to have the lime in the cement neutralized. Alternatively, a coat of paint will seal in the lime and waterproof the surface at the same time. Draining and refilling the pond a number of times will neutralize the lime, which is toxic to fish and plant life, but this is laborious and not always effective. Another method is to use commercial lime neutralizers. These normally consist of a powder dissolved in water, which is brushed onto the dry surface. Silica-based acids in the mixture react with the lime and neutralize it, at the same time forming insoluble silicates, which reduce lime seepage from deeper in the concrete. The pond is then rinsed, drained and filled.

Alternative methods include filling the pond with dilute solutions of acetic acid. After a few weeks the pond can be drained, rinsed and refilled. An old method depended upon soaking with potassium permanganate, but this is not very effective.

Check the pH of the water some days after refilling to ensure that lime has been removed before introducing plants and fish. Values in excess of pH 8.5 indicate that lime is a problem.

Paints for concrete pools include plastic and polyurethane types, synthetic rubber paints, epoxy resins and

*Below: Concrete provides the necessary strength for the steep walls of this deep koi pond. A glass-fibre-reinforced plastic coating gives a smooth waterproof finish.*

bitumenastic paints. Some require primers, others cannot be applied in cold weather; most require the concrete to be fully dried before use. For repairs and patches, bear in mind that many paints are incompatible with other paint finishes. Choose a paint that has a long waterproof life, is non-toxic, and bonds well to concrete.

## CONCRETE AND LINERS

Concrete can be used together with flexible liners in a compromise that incorporates the best of both materials; the liner provides a waterproof membrane, unaffected by frost, and the concrete acts as a solid support for the liner. Much less concrete is required than would be necessary for a concrete-only pond, as the concrete structure does not have to be watertight and minor frost damage will not result in leaks. This type of construction is well suited to raised ponds, where the waterproof liner is supported by a wall of concrete or brickwork.

A foundation of concrete also ensures firmer shelves and edges for the pond, less affected by soil movement than ordinary liner ponds. Such a foundation is especially valuable where heavy stones are to be placed around the pond edge, where sheer walls are required, or where the soil is particularly crumbly.

If the pond is in a situation where the liner might be prone to accidental or malicious damage, a layer of concrete or brickwork can be laid over the liner. This may require extra treatment to neutralize lime, but it does protect the liner. Some specialist pond-building companies use the 'concrete and liner' approach, but in-

### Concrete reinforcement

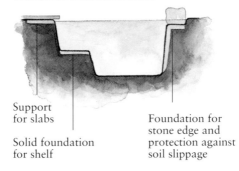

Support for slabs

Solid foundation for shelf

Foundation for stone edge and protection against soil slippage

*Above: Before fitting a liner, work a layer of concrete into the soil in areas to reduce slippage and provide a firm edge.*

stead of fitting a flexible liner, coat the inside of the concrete shell with glass-fibre-reinforced plastic. The tough layers of glassfibre and resin give a smooth wrinkle-free finish, but this does cost more than liners.

The simplest form of reinforcement mix a fairly stiff concrete containing fine aggregate. This is worked into the soil in the excavation to give a layer 25-50mm (1-2in) thick. The reinforcing layer is most useful around the top edge, on the shelves, and on any steep sides. It is not necessary to use concrete all over the excavation. The rough finish should be covered with a thick layer of liner underlay before the liner itself is installed.

For deep ponds, such as koi pools, ponds with sheer sides and ponds in soft soils, it is worthwhile incorporating a concrete collar. This needs to be built before construction takes place by digging a trench around the outside of the proposed pond. Pack the base of the trench with hardcore and tamp firm before pouring in a foundation mixture of concrete. Depending upon the size of the pond, the softness of the soil, and the weight of any pond edging stones, the collar should be 15-30cm (6-12in) deep, and 45-90cm (18-36in) wide. The collar should be level, and at the right depth for your chosen edging. When the concrete has set, excavate the soil in the centre. You may also want to lay another collar to support a shelf. Remember to leave gaps in the collar if you intend to fit any pipework into the side of the pond.

Liners in exposed public areas can be protected by laying concrete or setts over the top. Setts normally have to be laid on a gentle slope, and any cement containing finish will need treatment with a lime neutralizer. An alternative is to sandwich the liner between two brick walls (see page 48).

## OTHER POND CONSTRUCTION METHODS

Clay has traditionally been used to provide a fairly impermeable lining for ponds. If necessary, clay-rich soil can be brought in from another site and worked into the base of the pond, pounded down to give a dense watertight layer. This process is known as puddling. Because such a clay lining can crack and leak if it dries out, pud-

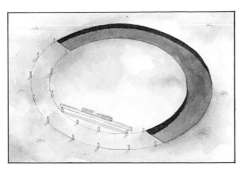

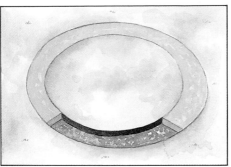

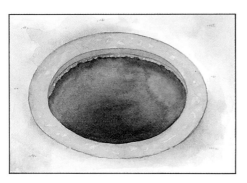

*Above: Use a thick concrete collar to give a firm safe edge to steep-sided and deep ponds. Install this some days before you excavate the pond, double-checking levels and making allowances for any pipework. Protect liners with underlay.*

dled clay ponds are usually built in sites with naturally high water tables.

A more modern variation on this method uses fibrous matting impregnated with a bentonite clay, which is buried under soil or gravel on the base of the pond. When the pond is filled with water, the clay swells to form an impermeable layer.

The advantage of these methods is that any minor punctures to the clay layer tend to repair themselves, as surrounding clay moves in to fill the gap. However, as using puddling clay is labour intensive and not always successful, you would be wise to take advice from someone experienced in building such ponds. Bentonite matting is often expensive, and is not always available.

# RAISED PONDS

There are a number of advantages in raising water levels closer to the eye; new perspectives are created with different reflections, fish and lily blooms will be closer to view, and fragrant plants appreciated more readily. Where the pond is retained by a wall, easy access can be obtained to the marginal plants without kneeling, which will help the elderly or infirm. Raising the water level also reduces the risk of inquisitive young children falling in. An elevated pond requires much less in the way of excavation, and it is easy to drain waste from the pond with a siphon.

Build the pond walls from bricks or use a mound of excavated soil. Soil walls need to be fairly wide and will result in a slope up to the pool edge – a feature that may be difficult to blend into the overall garden design. Walling is more popular as it takes up less space, is easy to maintain, and – with carefully chosen materials – will complement other elements.

For fully raised ponds, the only excavation required is for the wall foundations. Higher walls obviously need to be more sturdy as they are holding back a considerable weight of water. In exposed sites you should include some form of insulation within the wall, otherwise the pond will be prone to rapid temperature fluctuations.

Partially raised pools will require some excavation and you may need to remove some soil from the site. The original soil level could be used as the marginal planting shelf.

## USING A LINER

Pond liners are well suited to raised pond construction. Tamp the base and shelves of the pond firm and line them with sand or underlay. Incorporate a concrete collar if necessary to act as the wall foundations, and fit the liner in much the same way as for a sunken pond. For low walls (up to 30cm/12in) a single width of house bricks is adequate; run the liner up the

### A partly raised pond

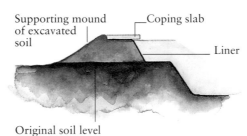

Supporting mound of excavated soil — Coping slab — Liner — Original soil level

*Above: Firm a wide mound of excavated soil to support the edge of a partly raised pond, and don't forget that the soil will settle. Use the old soil level as a shelf.*

inside wall and trap it under the coping. Build higher walls, and those with wider coping, with a double row of house bricks, or a single row of wider, decorative bricks. Enlist professional help if you are in any doubt.

If you choose a twin wall, the inner wall can be of second-quality bricks or concrete blocks. Tie the two walls together with the occasional brick laid across the gap, or insert butterfly ties between the mortar layers to increase the overall strength, placing insulation (polystyrene chips) between the walls if necessary. If you include a damp course at the base of the wall, it will prevent unsightly white crystals (efflorescence) forming on the brick surfaces. Hide the liner between the walls around water level. Wherever

*Right: A wall requires a firm concrete foundation at least 10cm (4in) deep and 10cm (4in) wider than the wall. At water level hide the liner between the twin wall. For ease, build shelves under, rather than over, the liner.*

bricks are constantly in contact with the water, use those of engineering quality, which will minimize the risk of frost damage.

You could extend the wall at lower levels, on the inside or the outside, to provide marginal shelves or seating, using wider forms of coping as seating, but remember to leave a duct under the coping if you wish to fit electric pump cables at a later date.

## USING A PREFORMED UNIT

The toughest glassfibre moulded ponds may be strong enough to use freestanding, with only a decorative brick or wooden support built around the edge. In most cases, however, you will need to provide a greater level of support. For a partly raised pond, sink the mould to shelf level, and build the wall from ground level to the edge, backfilling the space between at each

### A raised preformed pond

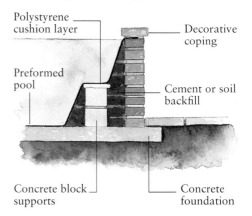

Polystyrene cushion layer — Decorative coping — Preformed pool — Cement or soil backfill — Concrete block supports — Concrete foundation

*Above: A raised preformed pond must be very well supported. Use bricks and blocks and fill gaps with tamped soil or cement as you lay each course of bricks.*

### A raised brick-walled pond

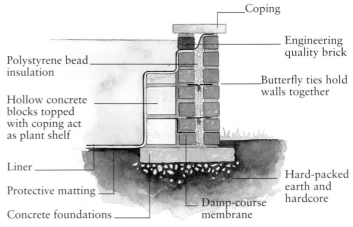

Coping — Engineering quality brick — Butterfly ties hold walls together — Polystyrene bead insulation — Hollow concrete blocks topped with coping act as plant shelf — Liner — Protective matting — Concrete foundations — Damp-course membrane — Hard-packed earth and hardcore

stage. Fully raised preformed ponds need a firm level base, usually a concrete foundation. Build a wall to support the shelf, filling any minor gaps with a cushioning layer of polystyrene, then build another wall to support the edge and backfill any gaps. As when installing a sunken preformed pond, check the levels at every stage and ensure that the mould is well supported and free of avoidable stress.

## USING CONCRETE

The concrete base of the pond can act as the foundation for the walls, which must be thick enough to withstand the pressure of any ice in the pond. You will need to run a layer of waterproof render over all the inside surfaces, preferably all on the same day, to increase the strength of the finish, which can be painted if necessary. The joins between the floor and walls are a weak point, and in deeper ponds you should link these together with reinforcing bars set into the concrete base. Remember that wherever you have used mortar, fresh concrete slabs, coping or reconstituted stone, you will need to treat all surfaces adjacent to the water with a lime neutralizer.

*Below: The coping and formal brick retaining wall around this raised pond complement both the adjacent back wall and the gravel area in the foreground.*

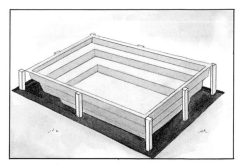

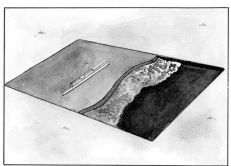

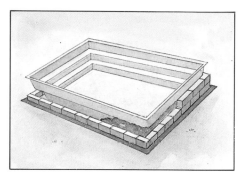

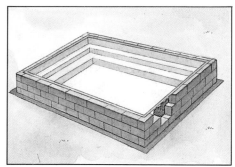

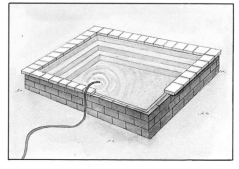

*Above: You will need a concrete foundation to support a raised preformed pond. Make it level and wide enough for the supporting wall. Fill the pond gradually, as you backfill, and disguise the top flange with coping.*

# POND EDGING

The way in which the pond is edged will have a major influence on how well it blends in with its surrounds. You should also consider the different levels of effort involved in the various design options, especially if you intend to build the pond by yourself. For example, where large amounts of brickwork are involved, it might be better to enlist the help of an experienced builder or landscaper.

Before you start constructing any edging make sure that the levels are correct. Whichever form of edging you decide upon, try to forecast how much wear and tear it will have to cope with: areas that are frequently walked upon, or where children have regular access, need to be sturdily constructed. This involves fixing edging materials in place rather than just positioning them. You should also incorporate some form of reinforcement to avoid soil subsidence at the pool edge. For average-depth garden ponds in stable soils, a skim of cement mortar 3-5cm (1-2in) deep worked into the soil around the top edge, will be sufficient to support light stonework and paving. Concrete collars (see page 47) are recommended for steep-sided ponds and heavy forms of edging. Remember to leave gaps or ducts in the edging to take any electric cables or hoses that may be needed.

## PAVING

Prepare the ground around the pool before excavations commence by tamping down the soil firmly, then putting down a layer of hardcore if the paving is to be wider than one or two slabs from the pond edge. The edge itself may need extra reinforcement. Take into account the final level of the paving, which is best set below the level of any surrounding turf.

For liner pond edges, trim the overlap back to around 15cm (6in) from the pool before laying the paving slabs, then bed the slabs in on a cement mortar to hold them firmly in place. If you use slabs of variable size, lay the larger ones at the points where people are most likely to stand to reduce the risk of paving tipping into the water. The slabs should slope away from the pool slightly, to prevent rain washing dirt into the water, and should overhang the pond by about 5cm (2in) to help mask the liner from view and protect it from damage by strong sunlight.

When laying slabs around a preformed pool, ensure that the weight of the slabs rests mainly on the surrounding area and not on the pool itself; excessive weight on the edge of a preformed pool can buckle or even crack the material.

There is a great temptation to simply cement slabs directly onto the top of the walls of a concrete pond; this may look very neat but has long-term disadvantages. In frosty weather the water in the pond expands at a different rate to the soil around the pond.

## Paved edging

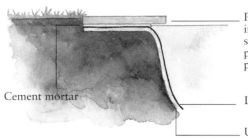

Cement mortar

Paving recessed into lawn slopes slightly away from pool and overhangs pool edge

Liner

Underlay or sand

This puts a great stress on the join between the wall and any edging slabs. To avoid damage to the pond walls it is wise to leave a small gap between the wall and the slabs. A few sheets of polythene can be placed over the top of the wall before mortaring the paving slabs on top. Make sure that the main weight of the slabs rests on the surrounding area wherever possible.

Remember that wherever cement has been used – in the edging, in mortar, in slabs, or in reconstituted materials – there is a danger from lime, which can damage plant growth and kill fish. Remove all loose cement, treat all surfaces with a commercial lime neutralizer, and, if mortar has fallen into the pond, change the water, before introducing fish.

*Above: Recess paved edging into surrounding turf, bedding it on cement mortar. Remember to leave room for cables and hose.*

*Right: This pond is nestled between the raised terrace and the steps. Harsh edges are softened by plants and mellow red bricks.*

*Left: A statuette is the focal feature of this formal pond, surrounded with mellow, aged crazy paving encrusted with lichen and creeping thyme.*

*Above: The Japanese theme of this pond is enhanced by the decorative brick edging, some pebbles and boulders, and minimalist use of foliage plants.*

## BRICKWORK

The simplest brick edging is a single row positioned around the pool edge in a radial pattern. Make sure that the surrounds are level and firm enough to support the bricks. With a liner pond, if the intended water level is to be no higher than the base of the bricks, then trim the liner back to leave a flap of about 8 to 10cm (3 to 4in), then mortar the bricks onto the surrounds, trapping the liner in place. If you want the water to lap up the sides of the bricks, leave a larger flap of liner. Mortar the bricks on top of the liner and bring the liner up behind the bricks before trimming the excess. If the foundations are not solid the bricks may work loose, as mortar will not stick firmly to lining materials.

With a preformed pond, follow a similar method to that for paving, ensuring that the main weight of the bricks rests on the pool surrounds and not on the preformed pool itself. It is virtually impossible to create a waterproof bond between brickwork and the pool material, so water should rest no higher than the pool edge.

On concrete ponds, cement the bricks directly onto the pool edge, but leave a small gap between these bricks and any solid structure (i.e. paving, concrete path) surrounding the pool to allow for expansion.

## WALLING

If you are building a wall around the pool edge, you must install suitable foundations in the form of a concrete collar around 10cm (4in) deep. To construct this pour the concrete onto a prepared base of hard-packed earth/ hardcore around 10-15cm (4-6in) deep before beginning to excavate the pond. Ideally the collar should extend at least 10cm (4in) beyond the width of any proposed wall.

A single width of brick will suffice for decorative walls of up to about 60cm (24in) high, though many walls are made of a double thickness for extra strength — a wise precaution if the wall is to hold back any weight of soil or water. Walls over 60cm (24in) high may require more substantial foundations and it is better to enlist the help of a builder in such cases. Walls around a preformed pool must not rest on the pool edge itself unless the edge is set on a substantial concrete foundation.

## STONE

Stone is an excellent edging material for more informal ponds. In nature, edging stones rarely rest at water level; the water is bounded by the stones, which rest below water level and protrude above the surface to varying extents. Follow this lead and position stones on a shelf set below water level. Heavy stones will require good foundations to reduce the risk of the pool walls slipping. Choose good solid rocks and avoid soft and crumbly types of stone, which can break up in frosts. Certain soft stones also release minerals into the water, which can upset the chemistry of the pond water.

Protect a liner pond from damage by sandwiching it between layers of polyester, or similar matting, before resting the stones in place. If protective matting on top of the liner reaches above water level and over the edge, there is a danger that it will act as a wick, drawing water out of the pond, so trim it back if necessary. Always take help when moving heavy stones, so that you avoid damaging the liner – or your back! Use cement to hold loose rocks in place, and bring the liner close up behind the stones or, alternatively, leave small pockets for water plants. Back-fill the area behind the liner with soil or concrete, and top it off with gravel or pebbles if you wish. Make sure that you construct the edge in a way that will prevent rainwater draining into the pool.

It is unwise to place large stones around the edge of a preformed pool, or on its shelves, unless the pool mould has been bedded onto concrete. Without this extra support there is a real danger that the mould will become distorted or damaged. To disguise the pool edge, the rocks should overhang by a few inches, which will, unfortunately, cut down on the visible water surface of the pond. It is difficult to overcome the appearance that the rocks have simply been laid around the edge of a pre-formed pool. Reconstituted hollow rocks are available with a lip that hangs over the edge of the pool, disguising the pool material and giving the effect that the water is bounded by rock. They are much lighter than real rock, and require less support. Or,

### Edging with boulders

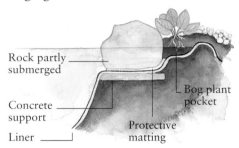

Rock partly submerged

Concrete support

Liner

Bog plant pocket

Protective matting

*Above: For the most natural effect, partly submerge boulders. Flap the liner up behind to form a pocket for bog plants.*

*Below: Stone is the unifying element in this water garden, with boulders and gravel complementing the dyke.*

*Above: Sweeping curves of log edging provide a striking backdrop to the pond and blend naturally with the bold clumps of plants.*

you may be able to obtain glassfibre rocks, which are lighter still.

Rocks can be placed on the edge of a concrete pool providing the support is sufficient. As with a liner pool, it is often more effective to place the rocks on a shallow shelf inside the pool boundaries. Avoid cementing edging rocks to other rocks beyond the pool edge, as this will increase stress on the pool walls in icy weather.

Whichever form of rock you use it will often look very 'new' at first. To encourage aging, mix up a paint of moss or lichens in a milk or yogurt base and dab it onto the rocks. This should speed up the growth of cover, and give a more aged appearance, though it is a rather messy task and it has a mixed success rate. Moss will grow most readily on absorbent rocks in partially shaded positions.

### Pebble beaches

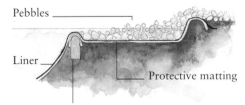

Pebbles

Liner

Protective matting

Piece of kerb set in soil prevents pebbles slipping into the water

*Above: A pebble beach is best sited on a wide shallow shelf.*

*Ideally, use matting both on top of and under the liner.*

## PEBBLE BEACHES

To create a pebble beach you should build a wide shallow shelf around the inside edge of the pool, which is normally only possible with liner and concrete ponds. The shelf should be level and have a rim on the inside edge. Pile pebbles and cobbles onto the shelf to form a gradual slope up onto the dry ground around the pool. Where pebbles are likely to slip or be moved, cement them into place.

Gravel beaches can be constructed in a similar manner. You will need to maintain them carefully to keep the correct slope, and to remove algae and dirt, which might become trapped in the gravel. Ensure that the slope is very gradual and make a large rim to prevent slippage of gravel into the deeper areas of the pond. Wash the gravel before positioning it and avoid crumbly soft gravels. In liner pools lay a protective layer of polyester matting between the gravel and the liner, and avoid sharp angular gravel.

Whether using pebbles or gravel, remember that children delight in throwing stones into water. The only solutions are to cement all pebbles into place, to avoid using such materials, or to (attempt to) ban children from the pool area.

## WOOD

The use of wood around the pond edge, whether it be upright logs or railway sleepers, is very effective visually, but tricky in practice. The major problem is that wherever wood is frequently exposed to water it will tend to warp and rot. Wood preservatives are not recommended because although the less toxic types may be safe with plants, in the confines of a garden pond the residues can build up and poison fish. There are a number of ways around the problem, which are dealt with on page 73.

Make sure that all wood is held firmly in place, whether it is set in a groove around the pond edge, nailed to a glassfibre support plate, or fixed to a wall or concrete support with steel straps.

### Edging with logs

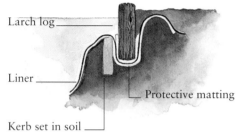

Larch log

Liner

Protective matting

Kerb set in soil

*Above: Logs can be set into the very edge of the pond excavation,*

*like teeth in their sockets. Take care to protect the liner.*

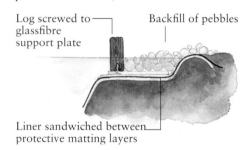

Log screwed to glassfibre support plate

Backfill of pebbles

Liner sandwiched between protective matting layers

*Above: On a shallow shelf, logs can be fixed to a strip of*

*plastic board held in place with a backfill of pebbles or soil.*

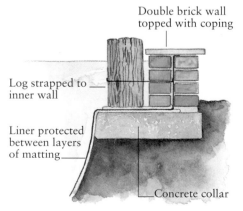

Double brick wall topped with coping

Log strapped to inner wall

Liner protected between layers of matting

Concrete collar

*Above: Strap large logs to a supporting wall with steel wire or*

*bolts. The wall can be merely decorative, or functional.*

## *TURF*

Turf is a good edging for informal and wildlife ponds, and fish like to browse in among the roots that hang into the water. However, it does require more maintenance than other forms of edging; the turf must not be treated with any lawn preparations, and you will have to cut the grass at the water's edge by hand. Drainage can also be a problem; before laying turf over the pool edge, create a drainage channel behind the edge and fill this with rounded gravel. Water draining into this channel should be directed away from the pool to reduce the risk of soil washing into the water. Occasional slabs set into the grass will help to prevent bare and boggy patches.

**Edging with turf**

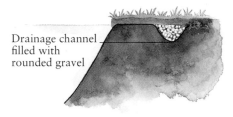

Drainage channel filled with rounded gravel

*Above: Turf is a very natural form of edging. A drainage channel will reduce muddying.*

*Below: By using turf and a profusion of plants, the edges of the pond in this hollow are made indistinct, maintaining a very informal design.*

*Right: An unusual wattle edging, utilizing traditional craftsmanship, has been used very effectively to border this natural-looking stream.*

## PLANTS

Plants provide a useful and decorative way of disguising the water's edge. The best method is to grow plants in the plastic baskets designed for the purpose, and place these on a marginal shelf. If the pond wall slopes steeply to the marginal shelf, you should be able to move the plants right up to the pool edge.

A marginal planting area filled with soil is a good alternative for koi pools, where large boisterous fish might otherwise upset planting containers. A brick wall can be built along a shelf edge to hold back an area of soil. Leave some open joints in the wall to allow water movement. Line the shelf side of the openings with filter wool to reduce soil seepage into the pool. Lay a protective layer of thick polythene,

### Planting pockets

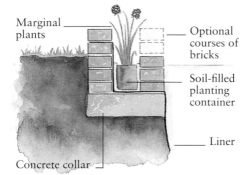

Marginal plants — Optional courses of bricks — Soil-filled planting container — Liner — Concrete collar

*Above: Koi can disrupt planting baskets so consider a planting pocket lined with matting to protect the liner and prevent soil erosion.*

or an offcut of liner, on top of the pool liner before adding the soil, to prevent damage to a pond liner.

Any pockets of water behind stone edgings can be lined with filter wool and filled with soil and will be ideal for planting shallow-rooting marginal and bog plants.

## BOG AREAS

Soil-filled marginal plant areas can be extended to create bog areas providing constantly moist conditions for plants. Unfortunately, soil nutrients

are constantly leached into the pond, and in small ponds, in particular, this will result in murky green water. The bog area remains so wet that it is very difficult to dig it over, and digging may, in any case, damage any lining material and so drain the pond.

A much better method is to construct a separate bog area outside the pond itself. Dig out an area around 40-45cm (15-18in) deep beside the pond, taking care not to weaken the pond walls. Line the excavation with old pond liner, thin polythene, or old plastic sacks. If you use a single sheet, perforate it a short distance up from the base to prevent large quantities of stagnant water collecting. With a liner pond, flap the overlap into this excavation so that water can overflow from the pond into the bog area, and refill the hollow with the excavated soil, enriching it with compost, chopped bark or peat. Providing the pond overflows into this area, and is topped up in dry weather, the bog area will be kept moist. An alternative is to sink a perforated tube into the bog area as it is being filled. One end is sealed, the other extends to the soil surface and has a removable plug. In dry weather, pipe water into this tube to nourish the bog plants' root system without disturbing the soil surface.

### In-pool bog areas

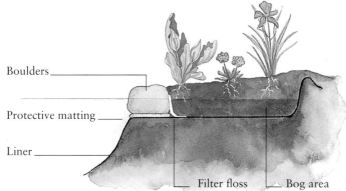

Boulders — Protective matting — Liner — Filter floss — Bog area

*Left: Bog areas can be built on boulder-edged wide shelves; a layer of filter floss will reduce soil seepage into the pond. Although they do provide constantly boggy conditions they have a number of drawbacks.*

### Bog areas beside the pool

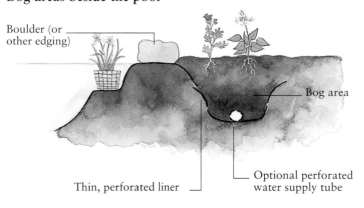

Boulder (or other edging) — Bog area — Thin, perforated liner — Optional perforated water supply tube

*Left: Poolside bog areas are more easily maintained than in-pool ones and can also be added to existing pools or even built away from the pool. Ensure that the pond walls are not weakened by excavation.*

# CHAPTER THREE

# MOVING WATER

The fascination of moving water
begins for many of us in childhood and it is therefore not
surprising that after plants and fish a moving water feature is the
most popular addition to a garden pond.

It is very relaxing to sit back on a summer's day and watch a
fountain play; there are the captivating sights and sounds of jets of
water leaping into the air, glittering in the sunlight, and splashing
back down. And there is a wide selection of jets to choose from;
even if you don't have enough room for a pond, you can probably
fit in a self-contained fountain ornament. Small submersible pumps
make it very easy to fit and plumb these types of feature, and range
in size to match most situations. They provide beneficial aeration
for fish and can also be used to feed a water filter.

A simple cascade pool can be positioned in a raised area beside the
pond with a minimum of effort. Alternatively you may want to
install a more ambitious series of large falls, or a long stream.
There is plenty of scope for your imagination and the end results
can be really spectacular.

Whatever type of feature you choose to include, think through the
practical issues before you begin; effective fountains, leak-proof
waterfalls, frustration-free plumbing and suitably specified pumps
all have a part to play in obtaining the results you desire. Impulse
purchases of equipment may not always accomplish all you
intended, so it helps if you have a clear idea of the effect you hope
to create before you decide what to buy.

# FOUNTAINS

Simple fountains are very easy to install and submersible pond pumps are readily available; many come as a complete kit with a fountain jet included. Provided that you installed a suitable power supply when building the pool, you should be able to wire in the fountain and have it running in under an hour. Simply place the pump in the water, usually on a plinth near the centre of the pond, with the outlet of the pump facing upwards, and attach the jet to this outlet, either directly, or via a tee piece. Usually there is some form of flow adjuster so that the height of the fountain can be varied. The maximum size of the fountain will depend upon the size of the pump and the type of jet used. One limitation of such kits is the quality of the jet supplied, but it is usually easy to fit a different jet onto the pump.

## FOUNTAIN ORNAMENTS

There are many different ornaments available for use in and around the pond, from simple spouting frogs and gushing lions' heads at the poolside, to complex multi-tiered bowls, situated in the middle of the pool. In between fall an array of cherub-type ornaments, millstones and abstract sculptures. The range is vast, not only in design, but also in quality and price. You should be able to find something in a size and style to suit the proportions of your pool, and at the same time to match your taste and pocket.

Most ornaments are made from concrete or reconstituted stone, sometimes with a coloured coating. Larger bowls often contain reinforcing rings of steel, buried in the material. Ornaments are also made of lead, terracotta, carved stone, bronze and glassfibre (GRP). Lead ornaments often have very fine detailing, and look ideal in more classical situations. However, they are usually very heavy and very expensive. Terracotta is used mainly for smaller ornaments, and is popular throughout Europe. It has a clean smooth finish and keeps its colour.

Few new ornaments are carved from stone due to the expense, but antique stone ornaments are sometimes available from specialist dealers. It may be worth seeking one out for a particular focal point. Old millstones make popular fountain ornaments, but are exceptionally heavy. Most of those available are simulations constructed from concrete or GRP with a suitable coating, and look surprisingly realistic. Bronze ornaments are less widely available, but they do help to create a very individual character for a pond. Some are cold cast from a resin containing bronze particles; make sure that the resin is suitable for use in water.

Whichever type of ornament you choose, it is wise to find out how frost-resistant the material is. This can be a problem with ornaments containing bowls, as ice may fracture certain materials. The ornaments will usually

*Left: An imposing feature for a large garden. The jet is purposefully restrained so that it does not overshadow this grand centrepiece fountain with its bold colonnade supporting the main bowl.*

*Right: The component parts of these ornaments are fitted together on site, and incorporate a small pump in the main, reservoir, bowl. The overflow standpipe acts as a duct for the electric cable and can be unthreaded to drain the bowl.*

*Left: A millstone fountain blends most effectively into the brick, stone and gravel theme of this informal garden. The reservoir is safely hidden under the cobbles.*

**A self-contained fountain**

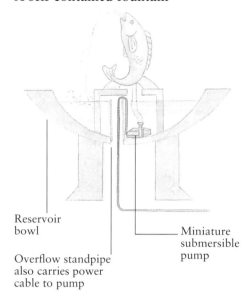

Reservoir bowl

Overflow standpipe also carries power cable to pump

Miniature submersible pump

fall onto surfaces that might be damaged by moisture. If necessary, you can use quite potent algicides in the water, as damage to plants or fish is not a problem.

The electric cable for the pump usually runs down an overflow tube hidden in the lower bowl of the fountain, and out through a duct in the base of the ornament, but in some cases the cable may lead out from the back of the ornament above ground level, and you may need to disguise it.

*Below: The small reservoir pond below this eye-catching modern fountain restricts its positioning to a wind-free site.*

have a pipe running up through them to carry water from the pumped supply to the outlet. Some may only have a narrow-bore pipe, and this will restrict the size of fountain obtainable. The end of the pipe may simply spout water, or it might be fitted with a thread to allow a suitable jet to be attached. If the ornament has a painted finish, you may need to touch it up at a later date, so make sure that the paint is available. The darker finishes can show up water scale, and might require periodic cleaning with a limescale remover. Light finishes will become stained with algae, which will lend an aged appearance to the ornament, but can be cleaned off.

## SELF-CONTAINED ORNAMENTS

These ornaments require no pool to stand in, as the lower bowl of the ornament acts as the reservoir from which water is pumped. With the advent of miniature submersible pumps, self-contained fountain ornaments have become increasingly popular. Previously such ornaments had to be powered by cumbersome external pumps plumbed in below the ornament or in some remote position.

Self-contained ornaments are particularly suited to sheltered positions, such as an enclosed patio, sunken garden or covered terrace; in exposed areas, wind can blow the spray out, and you will need to top up the bowl more frequently. Conservatories are ideal for these ornaments, but make sure that any splashes of water do not

**A fountain ornament**

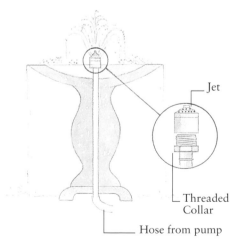

Jet

Threaded Collar

Hose from pump

*Above: Many fountains are supplied fitted with a central pipe. The top often has a standard thread, allowing you to fit a jet. The supply hose is attached at the base.*

## PLUMBING AND FITTING FOUNTAINS

Fitting a jet on top of a submersible pump often involves no more than a push-fit connection onto a tapered pipe, or simple screw fitting (for non-standard jets use an adaptor). The jet itself should protrude out of the water, but not excessively. Raise the pump off the base of the pond to obtain the correct jet level, or fit an extension between the pump and the jet.

Problems can arise when the pump strainer needs cleaning, or if the jet height needs adjusting. In small pools it is easy to reach in and carry out these tasks without moving the pump, but in larger pools you might need to wade in. A neat way around this problem is to situate the pump and flow adjuster at the edge of the pool on a readily accessible shelf, and run a pipe to the jet in the centre. The jet can be supported either on a plinth – the base disguised with stones or an imitation glassfibre rock – or on one of the various stands and tripods available commercially. Whichever way the jet is supported, it must be at the correct angle, or the fountain spray will fall irregularly.

Fine-nozzle jets are prone to clogging with debris, so it is a good idea to fit a fine filter in, or over, the pump inlet strainer to avoid having to clean the fountain jet frequently. In-line filters are also available to fit in the jet supply hose. You may need to clean them every few weeks, but they are generally more accessible than the jet.

Use adequate-bore hose between the pump and fountain, otherwise much of the pump's output will be wasted in friction losses; 12mm (0.5in) hose is ideal for most smaller jets and ornaments, but will prove inadequate for larger displays. For multiple-jet features use dividing tees or crosses with control valves.

Fountain ornaments need to be well supported. They are usually fairly heavy, which helps to prevent them from blowing over in strong winds, but they are often tricky to handle and larger pieces may need two or more people to lift them. You may need to cement multiple bowl ornaments together, or at least to put some mastic between pieces, to fill any irregularities in the surfaces and reduce rocking. It is very important that the bowls

**A fountain jet with separate pump**

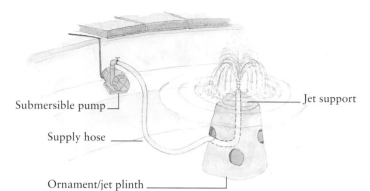

Submersible pump

Supply hose

Ornament/jet plinth

Jet support

*Left: Position the pump near the pool edge so that you can easily reach the flow-adjuster and inlet strainer. The jet can be mounted on one of the hollow rock-like stands that come complete with convenient ducts for hose feeds.*

are level, especially if water is to cascade evenly over the edges.

Poolside ornaments have hose fittings either in the base or in the back of the ornament; you may wish to disguise the hose feed by leading it through a hole in the supporting slab. Test the ornament before fixing it permanently to check that all the water is directed back into the pond.

Pool-centre ornaments normally have hose connections in the base. If they are supported on one of the hollow stands often sold for the purpose, holes will have been cut in the stand to allow for hose access. Spread the weight of heavy ornaments by laying a large flat slab on the base of the pool, putting a cushioning layer of polyester matting, or expanded polystyrene, between this and any pond liner underneath where necessary. For very heavy ornaments, build a specially reinforced section in the pool base. If the pool is less deep in this area, it will avoid the need for excessive supports within the pool.

Self-contained ornaments need a firm level base. Make allowances for the cable to be hidden before positioning the ornament. You will need to fit any loose overflow pipes and plugs in place using PTFE plumbing tape. Build the ornament up piece by piece, fitting in the pump and hoses as you work. It is usually a good idea to use a reinforced hose rather than the cheap hose often supplied with fountains because it is less prone to kinking, although it may be too coarse to fit into any small hose ducts in the ornament. Remember that you may need to dismantle or drain the unit for winter storage or pump maintenance, so avoid permanently cementing any cables or parts that you may have to move later.

## CHOOSING A FOUNTAIN JET

There are a vast number of different jets to choose from, at a wide range of prices. If you cannot obtain the jet you want locally, you may have to order it from one of the specialist suppliers, but most general suppliers should be able to order jets for you.

The simplest jets are of moulded plastic and push on to the cone outlet provided with most small and medium-sized pumps. A number of different patterns are available, and some jets even have interchangeable heads. This type of jet is often included in pump kits and is reasonably cheap. Many have very fine nozzles, which give a high jet, even on small pumps. Disadvantages are that fine jets of water tend to be overlooked at a distance, and the small nozzles are very prone to clogging with debris. The cheapest jets do not dismantle for cleaning, which makes it more difficult to clear any blockage.

Better-quality plastic jets have more precise mouldings, may include built-in flow-regulators, and pull apart, or unscrew, for cleaning. They often come complete with adaptors to allow fitting onto threaded or push-fit connectors. Drilled brass jets are widely available, with fine or coarse holes, and some of the more compact designs are ideal for fitting to the tops of fountain ornaments.

All of the simpler jets are designed to give variations on the traditional tiered fountain spray. For very large

*Right: The fine-jet spray in this pool does not disrupt the Nymphoides*     *growing in it, but the fountain is less visible from the seat at the end of the vista.*

pumps, substantial drilled brass fountainheads are available to give the same effect, but on a larger and more impressive scale.

In recent years there has been a proliferation of new fountain designs, many of which are plastic mouldings of older metal-type jets, which were generally very expensive. Some of the more popular new styles include bell, tulip and geyser jets. Bell and tulip jets depend upon water being forced out evenly around the circumference of a disc or cone. The smallest types do not require large pumps and can even be fitted to the top of fountain ornaments. Larger bell jets (over 30cm/12in high in the centre) need more powerful pumps if the bell is to remain intact. They are not suited to windy sites, as the thin films of water are easily disrupted.

Geyser jets have been popular in mainland Europe for some time and are now gaining wider popularity elsewhere. By introducing air bubbles into a single jet of water, the overall bulk of the jet is increased, giving a constantly changing column of foaming water. Geysers are ideal for exposed sites as the bold column of water does not look unsightly when disrupted by wind. The wide-bore nozzle is unlikely to clog and therefore needs less maintenance. Geysers – also known as foaming nozzles and Schaumsprudlers – do require quite powerful pumps, especially if a higher jet (over 40cm/15in) is required. There are two main types of jet; one requires the nozzle to be set at a precise water depth to work correctly. These are generally being superceded by those that draw in air from near the top of the jet, and can operate in a range of water depths.

### A three-tier jet

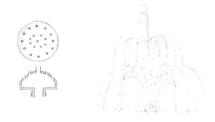

### A water-bell jet

### A water-tulip jet

*Above: A plethora of jet designs are available from larger suppliers at a wide range of prices. Many have standard fittings that are easy to connect to pumps and some allow adjustment of jet shape or height.*

There are also a number of unusual jets available for special effects, including multi-nozzle pirouette designs and combinations of tiered and bell jets. If you have a central ornament, why not fit a spray-ring? These look particularly good on classical ornaments, either fitted in one of the bowls, or situated in the pond around the ornament. Heavy-duty spray-rings have nozzles that can be removed for cleaning, and in some cases these can be swivelled to the desired angle. Lightweight rings lack these refinements but are much cheaper.

Electronic fountain controllers are available, which will switch pumps on and off in sequence and direct water through solenoid valves to different spray heads. These are often linked with underwater lighting to give a fascinating display. Such a feature may be out of place in many gardens, but it can create a stunning focal point in public areas and foyer ponds.

# WATERCOURSES AND WATERFALLS

It may have been your intention to create a waterfall feature at the design stage of your pond, or you may be wondering what to do with the large mound of spoil from the excavation. Either way, the resulting raised area gives you the opportunity to include a series of cascades and pools, powered by a recirculating pump.

Streams and cascades can be constructed in a number of ways. If you are fortunate enough to have a natural stream in your garden, this could be adapted or dammed to create a new feature. In general, the two main methods involve either using preformed cascade units or building a natural stone waterfall over a waterproof liner.

## USING PREFORMED UNITS

Preformed units of informal design are widely available and allow you to install a cascade fairly quickly. They have a number of advantages: the design work has been carried out for you, and the lips should pour water neatly into the next unit. Various pool and stream designs are available, mostly in convenient sizes that will fit comfortably into a large car. Some designs incorporate falls within the unit itself; others have small pockets for water plants. These units can cope with a range of water flow rates; the smallest units are designed to cope with flows of around 15 to 35 l/min (200-500 gph), matching the output of many smaller pond pumps, while larger units can cope with over 100 l/min (1300 gph).

The materials used to make these type of units include glassfibre, plastic, cement and reconstituted stone. Glassfibre units are probably the most popular; they are relatively light and

very strong, the surfaces are often tinted to imitate natural rocks, and they may have a coating of sand or grit to help camouflage them. It is sometimes possible to purchase 'bolt-on' waterfall lips for formally designed glassfibre ponds, which can be used to convert the pond into a cascade pool.

Plastic units are available in a number of moulded shapes, which are very light and easy to handle, but may require more careful anchoring to prevent the wind from dislodging them. Plastic units can be produced cheaply,

but the smooth finish and uniform colour can be difficult to disguise. The areas under the water will soon be covered by a natural greenish coating, but the areas above water can be glaringly obvious. If the plastic colour does not match the surrounding stone you may be able to abrade the surface and glue on a layer of suitably coloured grit or sand. This is not particularly easy, but it does have the added advantage of protecting the plastic from the damaging effects of sunlight, which shorten the lifespan of moulded plastic units.

Concrete and reconstituted stone cascades are considerably heavier than glassfibre or plastic models, but they are solid and substantial. Their size is limited by the strength of the materials. Reconstituted stone cascades have a more natural appearance, and may be available in the same

*Right: Use very large rocks, or reconstituted stone, to construct an impressive waterfall. The layout of rocks and a concealed liner help to reduce water loss.*

*Above: Preformed cascades units are available in various materials.*

*This reconstituted stone unit has a hose fitting in its underside.*

colour as your local stone. Some units even have built-in hose connections to allow easy connection of water pumps. The finish on these materials is sometimes slightly porous, and lime can often seep out into the water and cause problems. Coat the units with a lime-neutralizing compound if this is the case.

## INSTALLING PREFORMED UNITS

Preformed units must overlap sufficiently for the lower units to catch all the water falling from those above. Bear this in mind as you measure up. With larger flow rates and high waterfalls there will be a greater risk of water loss from splashing. In these cases, and whenever more than two or three units are being used, put a liner underneath the units to catch any seepage and direct it back into the pool. The liner will be hidden by the units and surrounding stones and soil, and in these conditions, a long life will

be obtained from even the cheaper grades of PVC liner.

For a series of cascade pools it is best to start at the base, beside the reservoir pond, and work up. To disguise the hose, set it in place before positioning the unit, but make sure that it is not crushed. Position the pump inlet near the base of the waterfall to prevent excessive circulation of water through the pond. Level the units carefully, filling with water if necessary to gain an impression of how they will look; set them in loosely at first and give each unit a trial run with pumped water, or using the garden hose, before fixing permanently.

Once you have checked that all the units will fit into the available space, you will find it easiest to fix each unit firmly, before you proceed to the next one up. Pack the soil foundations very firm and place the unit into position, putting a few blobs of cement under it to help support it, just as you would if laying a paving slab. Ensure that there is at least a 2cm (1in) clearance above the water level around the edges of the units when running to avoid problems of seepage. This can occur when heavier units settle, when algae growing on the lip of the waterfall causes the water level to gradually rise in the unit and when algae around the edge of the units draws water out into surrounding soil by capillary action.

You should only grow plants in cascade units when you are certain that they will not clog up the waterfall lips and cause the water to overflow around the sides. As a finishing touch, disguise the edges of waterfalls, and any liner used, by covering them with rocks and soil, and position plants around them to help them blend into the landscape.

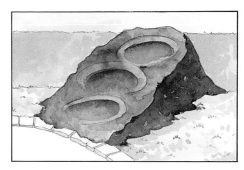

*Above: Preformed units allow you to install a series of waterfalls in the minimum of time. Ensure that the units overlap*

*sufficiently and carry out a trial run before fixing them firmly. Long runs benefit from a liner underneath to catch seepage.*

## WATERFALL WIDTHS AND FLOW RATES

Minimum flows required to give:

|  | A thin film of water over a smooth lip | A bold film of water over a waterfall lip |
|---|---|---|
| 10cm (4in) lip | 15 l/min (200 gph) | 30 l/min (400 gph) |
| 15cm (6in) lip | 22 l/min (300 gph) | 45 l/min (600 gph) |
| 25cm (10in) lip | 55 l/min (700 gph) | 90 l/min (1200 gph) |
| 40cm (16in) lip | 100 l/min (1300 gph) | 160 l/min (2100 gph) |
| 60cm (24in) lip | 225 l/min (3000 gph) | >300 l/min (4000 gph) |

This is a guide; results are very dependent on the shape and texture of the waterfall lip.

## LINER-CONSTRUCTED WATERFALLS

Although preformed cascades are fairly easy to handle and install, they are only available in a limited range of sizes and designs. In large gardens they will become dwarfed by their surrounds, and longer series of pools and falls will become increasingly expensive. In these cases you should consider a liner-constructed waterfall.

Liner-constructed waterfalls give complete freedom in the extent of the pools and size of the falls, being adaptable to virtually any style of pond, including formal designs. The liner acts as a waterproof layer under the main decorative materials of the waterfall – stone, large rocks, pebbles, or timbers and, for more formal designs, slabs, bricks, or even tiles.

In general, the aim is to create a series of small pools linked by cascades, which eventually empty into the lowest, reservoir, pond. Long, sloping streams are unsightly as they will run dry if the pump is turned off, but a few short sections can look effective. On a smaller scale you may choose to have a single raised pool, emptying into the main pond by a single cascade feature. If you construct the main pond with a liner, and build the raised pools at the same time, then you can buy a single sheet of liner, with an extending 'arm', which is used to line the waterfall. This gives a seamless join between the pond and waterfall, and reduces the risk of leaks, but, in practice, it is not always easy to match up the liner with the waterfall excavation.

In many cases it is preferable to use a separate piece of liner for the waterfall. If you buy an oversized liner for the main pool, you can cut a strip from it, remembering that it is often cheaper to buy one large liner, and cut it as required, than to order a number of separate smaller liners amounting to the same area. You can either construct a series of ponds and streams from a single strip of lining material of uniform width, or use a larger rectangular liner and cut it into a series of strips of different sizes to form waterfall pools and stream sections of different lengths and widths, which will help to create a more natural effect.

As most parts of the liner will be covered by other materials, degrada-

**Liner-constructed waterfalls**

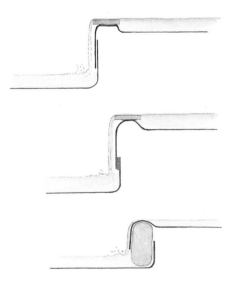

*Above: Use mastic or cement to fill gaps under the rocks at the waterfall lip.*

*Overlap liners well, using mastic if required to prevent capillary seepage of water.*

*Above: A well-proportioned waterfall provides an attractive backdrop to the interesting variety of plants in this pond with its simple edges of swept curves.*

tion by sunlight will be reduced, and you could use cheaper lining materials, but the better-quality butyl rubber types are the most flexible, and will conform best to the intricate shapes of waterfalls and streams. When you use rocks and liners together, the risk of puncturing increases, so always use protective layers, both under and over the liner, remembering to make sure that protective matting used on top of the liner cannot act as a wick, drawing water out into surrounding soil.

You should start the construction at the base and work upwards, in the same way as indicated for preformed units. If the lower pond has a large flap of liner at the edge, use it to construct a shallow basin, which will catch the water falling from the cascade above. It is very important to build up the sides of such basins, especially with larger cascades, where splashing is more likely, and remember that the basin's dimensions will shrink once stonework has been placed over the liner.

The liner from the upper pond must overlap the lower liner by a reasonable amount, as capillary action can draw water up folds and overlapping sections. The liners can overlap directly, or be separated by stones or supporting blocks. Use non-toxic mastic or mastic tape to stick them together where there is a danger of capillary leakage. You can also use mastic tape to join butyl liners in submerged sections, but longer joins are prone to failure if the liner is under tension.

It is normally best to fit the liners into place before starting to position any rocks, and fill the empty liner basins temporarily to check the water levels and possible leakage points. Construction of the various cascade pools and stream sections is much the same as that for any other liner pond (see pages 38-41). Whichever form of edging you use, take care to carefully disguise all visible areas of liner. For the most natural effect, edge streams with rocks or pebble beaches, using shallow areas at the stream sides, and pockets of soil behind the rock edges, for plants. You could also line the base of the ponds or streams with stone, but avoid gravel on the stream base, as this will simply clog with silt.

Either lay stone loose onto the liner,

*Below: A concealed liner allows great design flexibility and is the best means of waterproofing a cascade.*

or, ideally, cement it into place to give a firm finish. (Always use a lime neutralizer with cement.) If you are positioning heavy stones on top of the liner, especially at the pond edge, make sure that they are sufficiently well supported – build concrete foundations if necessary – and protect the liner with suitable matting. At the waterfall lip the liner can lap over a support in the lower pool or you can fix stones on top of the liner. Fill the gap between the stone and the liner with cement or mastic to ensure that all the water flows over the stone, and fix stones at each side of the fall to direct the flow. The width of the waterfall lip should be sufficient to cope with the intended flow of water, and at the same time give the desired effect, which can take time and patience to obtain.

For sheets of water, the top surface of the lip must be very smooth and level. It should overhang the lower pool and the piece of stone used must not encourage water to run back under the lip. Various tricks have been employed by landscapers to create more even sheets of water, for example glueing on strips of perspex, fixing glassfibre lips or sculpting cement lips can all help, but it is possible to achieve the desired effect with carefully cut stone; visit your local stone merchant or quarry to choose pieces of stone suited to this purpose.

The pool below a high cascade should ideally cut into the landscape, and the sides of this part of the pool be built up with rock and stone to direct splashes back into the pond.

Formal waterfalls are constructed in much the same manner, but with different materials, such as brick. Take good care to ensure that all water falls neatly over the lip, as any water trickling down a backing wall will soon lead to growth of algae, which can look very unsightly. If you use tiles, be sure that the grouting is non toxic and that the materials will withstand weather conditions.

Timbers can create a very effective water chute, but they are not easy to combine with liner ponds, although you could tack the liner to the wood above water level and disguise it with a thin facing of wood. Fix the liner extending into the chute with mastic, and treat the inside of the wooden chute with a waterproofing paint.

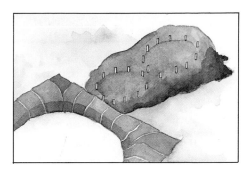

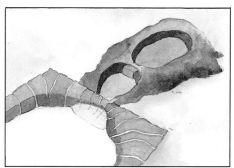

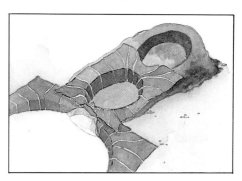

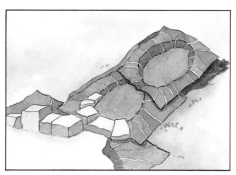

*Above: Start at the base and work up, creating a catchment basin in the main pond if possible. Make sure that the sides and lips of the cascade pools are firm and place stones on each side of the fall to direct splashes into the pond.*

# PUMPS

Water pumps are at the heart of water features, powering fountains, waterfalls and filters. Modern compact recirculating pumps make it easy to create moving water features; before the advent of this technology, fountains required elaborate piping systems connected to elevated storage reservoirs, which restricted most decorative fountains to the gardens of wealthy landowners. Now pumps are available at prices to suit most pockets, and in a range of sizes to match different applications.

There are two main types of water pump: submersible and externally mounted. Submersible pumps sit in the pool and often have fountain jets fitted directly on top of them with a strainer on the inlet to remove debris that could clog the interior. These pumps are now the most popular, as they are relatively easy both to install and to remove for maintenance and cleaning, they require no priming, and the water helps to cool the motor.

External (or surface) pumps sit outside the pool; a reinforced suction hose leads from the strainer positioned in the pond to the pump inlet, and other pipes lead the water back to the fountain or waterfall. External pumps do not have the benefit of water around them to aid cooling, and not all models have waterproof motors, so, depending on the design of the pump, a dry, ventilated housing chamber may be required. The pump and inlet hose are best situated near the pond at a point below the pool surface level; you will need to fix the inlet hose through the side of the pond. Alternatively, the pump and inlet hose can be sited above pond water level, in which case you will need to prime the pump and fit a non-return valve. More powerful external pumps can be placed some distance above and away from the pond, but this will reduce their output.

External pumps can be noisy, and extra plumbing can increase their expense considerably, but they do have some advantages: there is no pump or electric cable to be seen in the pond, which is especially valuable in public situations vulnerable to damage; they can use larger motors than submersible pumps, allowing the high-pressure, high-volume outputs to suit very large features; as the motor is often a separate unit from the pumping chamber, it is more easily accessible for repair and maintenance, and often, in the case of larger motors, more reliable in external than submersed situations.

In most cases you will find a submersible pump to suit your requirements, but consider surface pumps for very large features. Some of the newer designs of submersible pumps can be adapted to run externally, which gives you extra choice in siting the pump.

## CHOOSING A PUMP

Choosing a pump can seem a little daunting as major stockists may have 20 or more pump models on offer, but fortunately these outlets usually have specialist staff to advise on pumps and any other equipment you might require. There are a number of factors to consider when making your choice.

Output figures will give an indication of the pump's performance. They are usually quoted in litres per minute (l/min) or gallons per hour (gph), at a particular head (i.e. the distance between the surface of the pond and the outlet height). The maximum head is the height at which pump output drops to virtually zero. It gives a relative indication of the pressure of the pump output, so that pumps with a high maximum head have high-pressure output and are well suited to high fountains, and waterfalls and tall fountain ornaments.

Typical output figures refer to the flow measured through a short length of wide-bore hose at a specific head,

## MAINS/LOW-VOLTAGE PUMPS

Mains-voltage electric pumps are generally the most widely available type. They are usually double insulated, and must be earthed if you use them out of doors. If you take sensible precautions, they should be safe. Protect the cable from damage, use suitable cable connectors and fit a residual current circuit breaker and fuse. Many modern pumps have all the electrical components in a sealed compartment, totally separate from the pumping chamber, for added protection.

In some countries, regulations specify that all submersible pumps should be low voltage. A transformer situated indoors reduces the mains voltage to the 12 or 24 volts required; make sure that it is sited according to the maker's instructions. Long lengths of low-voltage cable will reduce the current reaching the pump, and can affect the pump output. Transformer failure (often due to overheating) can be a problem with less reliable brands. Low-voltage pumps tend to have relatively small outputs, and the few larger output models available are rather expensive. If you decide against a mains submersible pump, but cannot obtain a suitably sized low-voltage submersible pump, you may have to substitute an external mains-voltage one.

**An external pump**

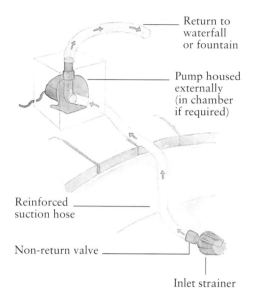

Return to waterfall or fountain

Pump housed externally (in chamber if required)

Reinforced suction hose

Non-return valve

Inlet strainer

and are much more indicative of pump performance than maximum outputs (quoted at zero head). Ideally, you should ascertain the typical output for the head at which you will be running the pump. Remember that in normal use the pump flow will be reduced by long hose runs, narrow-bore hoses, pipe fittings, dirty inlet strainers and pump ageing, so you should choose a pump a little on the large side: you can always restrict its output if necessary. Output figures are meaningless unless you known what a given output looks like; some shops have displays to demonstrate the various pumps, and as the height and size of fountains is very dependent on the type of jet chosen, they may also demonstrate a jet before you buy it.

## ESTIMATING WATERFALL FLOW RATES

You can replicate a given waterfall flow rate by filling a standard nine-litre (two-gallon) bucket, and pouring it out as evenly as possible.

Poured out in
    1 min =   9 l/min (120 gph)
  40 secs = 13 l/min (180 gph)
  30 secs = 18 l/min (240 gph)
  20 secs = 27 l/min (360 gph)
  12 secs = 45 l/min (600 gph)

These figures are within the range of many small to medium-sized pumps.

*Above: Some pumps can be mounted remote from the pond and fed via a reinforced inlet hose from a foot-valve and strainer in the pond.*

*Left: Submersible pumps are the most popular types; they are readily available, easy to install and often come complete with tee-piece, flow-adjuster and jet.*

*Right: Geysers are becoming very popular. They require quite large output pumps, but their foaming jets are easily seen from a distance, suit both formal and informal designs, and, spreading over a small area, are less affected by wind. The nozzles are also less prone to clogging with dirt, and help to aerate the water.*

Most pond pumps work on a centrifugal principle, with an impeller running in a pump chamber, which forces water outwards and through the outlet. Some pumps have enclosed impellers, which tend to be more efficient but which can become blocked with debris if you fail to use the inlet strainers supplied with the pump. Open impeller pumps can pass large solids without clogging and are well suited for pumping dirty water when draining a pond.

Check that your pump is suited to continuous running, that the bearings are repairable or replaceable, and that the pump can be dismantled sufficiently to clean the moving parts —

### A direct-drive pump

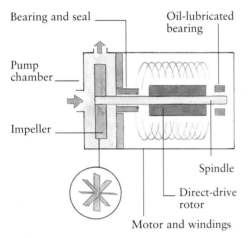

*Above: The main shaft runs through a seal and bearing directly to the motor, giving a powerful output, but wear on the seal can eventually let water into the motor.*

### An induction-drive pump

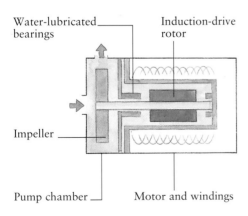

*Above: Indirect-drive and water-lubricated bearings reduce the torque of the pump, but by avoiding the need for seals reliability is often improved.*

carrying out simple maintenance yourself can significantly extend the life of the pump. Some pumps are described as needing no maintenance, being sealed for life, which unfortunately may not be as long as desired. Others may have routine 'in-factory' maintenance, but this can prove quite expensive. There are many different pump brands on the market, some of which have excellent reputations, but others are notoriously unreliable. A good dealer will advise on pump reliability, service and guarantees.

It is worthwhile noting the design of pumps. Direct-drive pumps have a shaft running from the motor section into the pump chamber with a lipped seal between the two. They have a very good output ratio and are available in a wide range of sizes, but the seals break down in time and if they are not replaced, water can seep past towards the motor (especially in submersed models) and irreparably damage the motor.

Many small to medium-sized pond pumps now have the motor windings quite separate from the impeller, which is powered by a magnetic or induction drive, requiring no connecting shaft and no troublesome seals. New designs incorporate many of the engineering advances gained in the production of central heating pumps. Better-quality materials and longlife bearings, often ceramic, mean that pumps are becoming considerably more reliable.

You should choose a sturdy-looking model, as the fittings on some of the flimsier plastic pumps can become brittle in time. A well-designed large strainer saves time by reducing the frequency with which you have to clean it. Make sure that the cable on a submersible pump is long enough to reach an external connector, and leave a gap in any paving around the pond so that the cable can be fitted, remembering not to fix the cable permanently, as you may have to remove the pump. Grommets can be fitted to feed the cable through the side of the pool, but they are fiddly to fit and make pump removal a nightmare.

Power consumption on continuously run pumps can be expensive, so consider a more expensive pump if it has lower running costs. Note the power rating on the pump — usually the higher of the two figures if two are

*Right: Limestone rocks have been used to create this impressive series of falls. A pump is submerged in the lowest pool and in this case is supplying over of a thousand gallons per hour to the top of the waterfall.*

shown. As a guide, a 100-watt pump run continuously will use 17 units of electricity per week.

Extras provided with the pump can greatly increase their value, for example, outlet tee-pieces, hose connectors and fountain jets, which would otherwise be an added expense. Some pumps come complete with float switches to prevent them from running dry. Don't forget all the accessories you will need to get your pump up and running; a submersible pump might require outlet hose and clips, an extension for the fountain and alternative jets, flow adjusters or valves, a waterproof cable connector and perhaps a foam pre-filter to fit on the pump inlet. External pumps may require a housing chamber, reinforced inlet hose, an electrical junction box, a non-return valve and a strainer.

## PUMP MAINTENANCE

A few simple precautions will keep your pump running smoothly:

- Don't run the pump dry, this overheats the motor and damages bearings.
- Avoid pumping gritty solids as this wears the bearings. Raise the pump inlet off the pond base and use a suitable inlet strainer and pre-filter.
- Don't lift the pump by its cable, and check the cable routinely for damage.
- Clean the pump and strainer as recommended by the manufacturer, and replace bearings as soon as they show signs of wear.
- In hard water areas, run the pump regularly. Before storing dry, take care to clean the pump well, and check that parts move freely before re-starting. Use a descaler to clean the pump and impeller if recommended by the manufacturer.

well to remove any loose metal particles. Plastic ballvalves are probably the most useful form of flow controller and are generally trouble free.

Most connections can be made with hose, although you can use glued ('solvent-weld') solid pipe for long feeds of water, or even pushfit waste pipe for low-pressure feeds. Ordinary garden hose is only suitable for small feeds to ornaments, and is totally unsuited to larger ornaments and waterfalls where you must use a larger bore hose to obtain the full benefits of your pump performance. The ideal hose is tough yet supple, longlife, non-toxic, of a suitable colour, but often hard to find. Algae, which can restrict flow considerably, may be a problem with the cheap clear PVC hose sold by many outlets. Clear PVC hose also ages rapidly, becoming inflexible, and is prone to kinking. If you intend to run the hose under soil or rocks, or on a suction intake, use spirally reinforced hose, which resists crushing.

Remember to leave room for your hose when building around the pond; it is very frustrating, trying (and failing) to fit a large-bore hose through an inadequately sized duct left under paving or through walls. Fit hose clips on all connections, as leaks and loose hoses can cause havoc. When feeding hose into the top of a waterfall or raised pool, try to minimize splashing. It helps to fit a short length of wide-bore hose, perforated pipe, or a wide-bore bend, over the end of the feed to reduce the pressure at the outlet. Alternatively the hose can be connected through the side of the upper pond, just below water level, using an appropriate fitting. Make sure that there is no danger of water siphoning back into the lower pond when the pump is turned off.

## PLUMBING

A certain amount of plumbing is necessary with any pump, whether it is to feed a simple fountain, or a more complex series of outlets. Use non-toxic plastic fittings, which will usually thread onto the pump, either directly or via a pushfit adapter. Many pumps include a tee-piece to feed a fountain and waterfall at the same time, but you can often change these if you require alternative fittings. When using threaded fittings, seal the gaps with plumbing tape (PTFE), which at the same time lubricates the threads. Avoid narrow fittings and sharp bends, both of which will reduce the pump output.

Keep metal fittings to a minimum, as they can corrode, and some are toxic to fish. If you are using new brass jets or gatevalves, rinse them

### RECOMMENDED PIPE SIZES
*(Hose inside diameter)*

|  | Short pipe runs | Long pipe runs |
|---|---|---|
| Small ornaments | 10mm (3/8in) | 12mm (1/2in) |
| Flows up to: |  |  |
| 7 l/min (100 gph) | 12mm (0.5in) | 19mm (0.75in) |
| 25 l/min (330 gph) | 19mm (0.75in) | 25mm (1in) |
| 40 l/min (530 gph) | 25mm (1in) | 32mm (1.25in) |
| 75 l/min (1000 gph) | 32mm (1.25in) | 38mm (1.5in) |
| 150 l/min (2000 gph) | 38mm (1.5in) | 50mm (2in) |

# CHAPTER FOUR

# BRIDGING WATER

A water garden can benefit from
additional design elements that can enhance and complement the
existing attributes of a pool, and may also serve a very useful
and practical function.

By extending decking, a bridge or stepping stones over the pool
you will achieve a link between the two elements in the garden –
an eyecatching combination of water and landscaping. A bridge
may be a practical means of access to the rest of the garden, or to
an island, or simply a feature in itself.

An uncomplicated footbridge is ideal for small spans, while a
more elaborate arched bridge could be draped with climbing
plants, which will reflect in the water surface. Stepping stones form
a less conspicuous passage across the water; rocks are ideal for
more naturalistic settings; use slabs for formal designs. (If there is
even a slight chance that you may add a bridge or stepping stones
to your water garden at a later date, make allowances at the initial
design stage, or you could be faced with a lot of extra work.)

Why not include an island in your design? A heavily planted
island will form a backdrop, casting colourful reflections in the
water, while a tiny one can act as a simple plinth for an ornament
– a stunning focal point to the water feature.

Wooden decking at the water margins is less harsh as a border
than stone or slabs; experiment with different arrays of wood to
create bold straight edges, or gentle curves, and consider extending
a deck on a uniform level to form piers and bridges.

# BRIDGES

A simple bridge can greatly enhance a water feature, but you should consider its design carefully so that it will successfully complement the other elements of the water garden. If you are planning the bridge at the same time as the rest of the water garden, take trouble to ensure that the pond and its surrounds are suitably adapted to the bridge. Adding a bridge later may involve some alteration to the pond edging, or a compromise in the size and shape of the bridge. There are a number of positioning and design points to consider.

## FUNCTION

Where does the bridge originate and where does it lead? Bridges normally serve a purpose – a means to overcome an obstacle, in this case your pond, stream or bog area. It is possible to have a bridge that leads to a dead end, or that offers no appreciable short cut over an obstacle, serving only as a suitable viewing platform, and as a feature in itself, but it should ideally lead somewhere.

## HEIGHT

The height of the bridge should be in proportion to the rest of the garden. High bridges will allow a different viewing perspective, not only of the pond, but also of the surrounding garden. They will also be visible from other parts of the garden, and for this reason it is important that they blend in well. A bridge that is too large, or too high, can become very intrusive on the overall garden design, especially if it is built in a contrasting style.

Lower bridges look very effective – the lowest can give the impression that they are floating on the water surface and are often only fully visible at close range, being disguised by plants from a distance. Enticing glimpses of the bridge will encourage viewers to draw closer to find out where it leads.

*Above: A simple wooden bridge enhances this informal garden. Its straight-forward design is within DIY capabilities.*

*Below: This elegant Japanese bridge, finished in red laquer, complements the stream and cobbled 'dry riverbed'.*

## WIDTH

The width of the bridge must strike a compromise between being wide enough to cross safely, and yet still in proportion with surrounding features. The general intention is normally to create a water feature with a bridge, not a bridge that happens to have water under it.

## STYLE

Style is another consideration: simple flat bridges suit informal settings, their uncomplicated design being less likely to detract from the surrounding plants. Arched bridges add character to a semi-formal setting, casting interesting reflections and shadows, but are a little more difficult to construct.

The style of any handrail will have a large influence on the overall style of the bridge. The width of, and distance between, uprights can be varied for effect, but for a more informal style these should be as plain as possible.

A fairly neutral colour will help the bridge to merge with its surrounds. Wooden bridges are often left unpainted, with an application of non-toxic stain if necessary. In oriental-style gardens bridges are sometimes painted black, red or jade, which looks effective in certain situations.

## USING WOOD IN AND AROUND THE POND

Wood is an extremely useful and versatile material – it is fairly easy to work with and its natural colour and texture fit well into most garden designs. Its main disadvantage is rot, but this problem can be overcome.

- Position wooden structures or edging so that rainwater will run off and not collect in pools.
- Hardwoods are more resistant to rot than are softwoods, though they are more expensive and difficult to cut. Because they are much stronger than softwoods, hardwoods are better suited to load-bearing structures, such as bridges. The most durable woods are African Iroko, Greenheart and Oak. Alternatives include Balau, African Ekki, Elm and Alder. (Avoid very oily woods, such as Teak, which can taint the water.)
- Softwoods can be sealed with clear polyurethane paints, or painted (on less visible surfaces) with low-toxicity bitumenastic paints (see below). Larch is one of the most rot-resistant softwoods.
- In Japan, imitation logs are moulded from concrete and used around pond edges; once they have obtained a covering of moss they can look quite effective.
- If possible, position logs behind the pool edge and separate them from the water with waterproofed render (in concrete pools) or with the pond liner. Here the cut surfaces of the wood can be safely painted with a low-toxicity preservative and the render or liner at the pool edge disguised with a pebble beach or plants.

### Using preservatives
- Don't use preservative on wood in contact with pond water.
- Make sure that you treat wood well away from the pond to ensure that preservative does not splash into the water.
- Always use low-toxicity preservative. Wood preservatives are often in a toxic-solvent base, usually including various persistent pesticides and fungicides, some of which are lethal to fish and other water life.
- Avoid solvent-based treatments when re-treating the wood; even the fumes may prove lethal to fish.
- Remember that timber is often pre-treated with preservative: check before you buy.

### Stains, paints and varnishes
Natural wood generally looks best, taking on an attractive rough texture as it weathers. If you do want to apply a finish, take precautions to protect the fish – all the above warnings apply here too. Microporous stains and paints allow the wood to breathe; surfaces sealed with ordinary – non-porous – outdoor paints or varnishes have a tendency to crack in time. If the surface is sealed unevenly there is a greater risk of the wood warping. It is also worth bearing in mind that preservative-free stains are becoming increasingly difficult to find.

### Fixing wood
For safety's sake, it is very important that wooden slats in decking and bridges are fixed securely (see page 75). Nails can work loose in time, so use rustproof screws instead, drilling pilot holes first to minimize the risk of splitting. Alternatively, strap the wood in place with steel wire. More important load-bearing beams should be bolted into position.

*Left: Large wooden sleepers allow easy construction of a simple and stable bridge, set close to the water surface to maintain the level of the landscape. Their colour blends with the bark surrounds.*

## MATERIALS

Wood is the most popular choice of material; its natural finish blends easily into the garden and anyone with basic DIY skills can cut and fix it.

Metal is also useful for bridge construction; a couple of structural support beams are often used as a sound support for wooden slats or stone slabs. Iron or steel gridding can be used as the walkway on a bridge, but it is not particularly easy to disguise and is noisy to walk on. Some firms specialize in producing iron and steel structures, from uprights and handrails through to complete bridges.

Stone is an attractive bridging material, but, although large hunks of rock are used in the construction of ornamental bridges in Japan, the practicalities involved make this method unrealistic in most cases. You can bridge narrow streams with smaller slabs, or place them along reinforcing beams to give a longer span, cementing them into place if necessary. Arched stone bridges may be

*Above: To help it merge with its surrounds, this gently arched stone bridge has been intriguingly clothed with a layer of turf.*

*Left: Strong wooden beams are laid over the stream, their ends supported by concrete footings. The cross-pieces are then fixed on with recessed screws.*

found in old gardens. Sadly the skills involved in their construction are hard to find today, and usually very expensive. Be sure to maintain an existing stone bridge as it will add a great deal of character to the garden.

Concrete is frequently chosen as an alternative to natural stone for bridge construction. Use reinforced concrete beams as the basis for a bridge and lay concrete in shuttering between the beams, with a decorative brick or stone wall on each side. You can also use shuttering to construct arched concrete bridges.

## POSITIONING

Existing landscape features, such as a path, may limit the site of the bridge but you will often have the freedom to choose its position. Try out your ideas by laying a few planks over the pool to simulate the possible positions. Take a look at them from different angles to gauge how the finished bridge might appear, bearing in mind the possible reflections and shadows. Will the bridge give you a better view of water-lilies and fish? Does the garden at the opposite end of the bridge encourage people to cross?

**A simple wooden bridge**

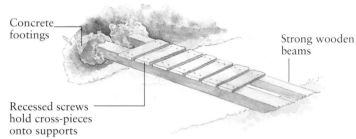

Concrete footings

Strong wooden beams

Recessed screws hold cross-pieces onto supports

*Left: This simple wooden bridge provides a place to cross a long natural stream and an opportunity to admire the view along its stretch.*

## CONSTRUCTION

Ready-made bridges are available, but can be very expensive. It may make sense to ask a local craftsman to custom build a bridge for you, but a simple wooden bridge may well be within your capabilities. Remember to relate the sturdiness of the structure to the level of its wear and tear. The bridge will be very dependent upon its foundations, and you may need to build concrete footings at each end of the bridge, and also, for bridges with a long span, a central support. A poorly built bridge is potentially very dangerous, so consider safety at each stage.

*Below: In a cross between bridge and stepping stones, the low staggered layout of these timbers leads the eye across the water into the distance, distracted only by the reflected sculpture.*

### SAFETY OF BRIDGES, DECKING AND STEPPING STONES

- Sturdy construction is essential for safety; consider the weight that the structure will have to bear and use strong, long-lasting materials.
- Non-slip surfaces will help to prevent accidents; roughen the surfaces if necessary, and make sure that water can drain away. Fix strips of steel mesh, or even chicken wire, to wooden surfaces to provide a grip.
- Solid fixing will prevent movement of the surfaces; a loose plank, slab, or stepping stone could throw someone off their balance. Sink screws into wood walkways to prevent tripping.
- Handrails are useful, especially where bridges are narrow, or particularly high above the water surface. A handrail must bear the weight of someone leaning against it and a poor handrail is worse than none, as it can give a false sense of security. Consider a stout rope as an alternative.
- Children need to be considered; handrail supports placed close together will prevent children from falling through, but in a garden where young children play unattended, you would be wise to avoid bridges altogether.
- Deep water can be dangerous, so try to keep the water near bridges, decking, and stepping stones as shallow as possible. This often makes construction easier.

# STEPPING STONES

Stepping stones, like bridges, should lead somewhere. They are often much closer to the water surface than bridges, and you can arrange them in interesting patterns – though always remember to consider safety at all stages of design and construction.

Stepping stones are useful where the water to be crossed is too wide for a bridge, or where a bridge might seem too intrusive, or out of proportion with the rest of the water feature. You can use the stones to separate the body of water they run across, giving an impression·of two linked pools, or you could even use them across the top of a waterfall, where one pool falls into another.

Adapt the style of the stepping stones to suit the design of the garden, using oblong flagstones, or paving slabs in a material similar to the pool surrounds for formal ponds. Position the stones precisely, with even spacing between them. For a less formal effect stagger the stones. Natural stone is ideal for informal stepping stones; try to use pieces around the same size – a few bold pieces are more effective than a large number of smaller rocks, and they are easier to stand on. Space the pieces evenly, so that they can be crossed safely at a steady pace. Irregular stepping stones can be either an exciting feature in the garden, or a potential hazard.

If you use more angular stones match them together to give a continuous run of stone, separated only by clefts of water. Consider running the stepping stones on into the ground beyond the pool edge, setting them into the plant border, lawn, or a bed of gravel to give continuity.

## CONSTRUCTION

Stepping stones require a good firm foundation, which the base of the pool must be able to support without subsidence. In liner and preformed pools you should tamp the base of the pool firmly before the lining is inserted. Ideally lay a concrete foundation first, and place the liner on top, protected between two layers of mat-

ting, or offcuts of liner. Obviously it is not an easy task to add stepping stones to an existing pool. Advanced planning at the design stage will minimize disruption of the lining material at a later date.

Construction will be much easier if the water around the stepping stones is relatively shallow. Either span the depth with large rocks, protruding a short way (3-15cm/1-6in) above the water level, or build up the height with layers of flat stones, or a pier of

*Right: An oriental vase and spouting bamboo lend a strong Japanese flavour to this garden with its bold arched stepping stones leading from the pond to stones set in the gravel.*

*Below: Stepping stones across the lip of a fall combine the elements of a path and moving water as well as splitting the flow into more forceful streams.*

**A stepping-stone cascade**

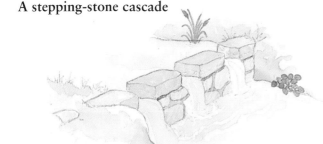

**Stepping stone supported by brick pier**

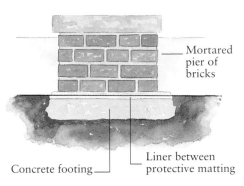

Mortared pier of bricks

Liner between protective matting

Concrete footing

*Left: These stepping stones, evenly spaced and set at the same level as the surrounding paving, act as a divider for the long expanse of this formal rectangular pond.*

*Above: When positioning large slabs or stones across a liner pond, build a foundation below the liner and wafer the liner in matting before building the support pier.*

*Above: Informality is maintained in this oriental design by laying irregularly shaped stepping stones in a curve. The stones are also set into the soil at each end.*

bricks or blocks, topped with a flagstone or slab. The supporting stones and bricks must be able to withstand constant immersion and frost. To ensure that the overall structure is stable, use cement mortar to hold stones in place and prevent rocking. Set the top of the stones at the same level, especially in formal designs, and remember to use a lime neutralizer on any cement work.

Try to choose stonework similar to that in the rest of the garden, but remember that crumbly or porous stone could prove dangerous, as it encourages growths of slippery algae and moss. Use less porous stones, preferably with a slightly rough surface. They should be set at a level that will never be submerged in normal use. Neutral-colour slabs are most likely to match the surrounds.

Construction usually demands that the pond be drained to enable the stones to be fitted. It may be possible to set stones into the base of a filled natural pond, but this is a difficult — not to say wet and messy — task.

# ISLANDS

Islands can be created in larger pools and will have a major influence on the overall appearance. Informal islands also increase the amount of pool edging and allow you to grow more waterside plants. If thoughtfully positioned, a well-planted island will cast dramatic reflections and become a stunning focal feature. Islands also provide a relatively undisturbed haven for wildlife.

Position the island in accordance with the overall pond design; informal islands should have simple outlines, and will look better when offset from the centre of the pond. In adventurous designs you might be able to link the island to the edge of the pond with bridges, or with a series of stepping stones. In a few cases the presence and position of an island may be decided by existing site conditions, for example an outcrop of rock intruding into the pond excavation. Make the most of this island enforced on your design. A rectangular island in a formal pond can enliven a dull design, forming the central section of a set of stepping stones, or serving as a plinth for an ornament.

If islands in a small pool are built in proportion they will appear ridiculously small, and if they are too large they can overwhelm the whole design. An alternative is a promontory built out into the water, which will appear like an island from many angles, and is much easier than an island both to construct and maintain.

## CONSTRUCTION

How you construct an island will depend on the lining material you have used for the pond. Most preformed pools are too small for islands; larger concrete and liner ponds are more easily adapted.

Building in a liner pond involves sandwiching the liner between protective layers of material. Consider the island as an oversized stepping stone, and follow much the same construction method. Whatever the pond material, the island can be built up with a brick, stone or concrete retaining wall. Fill the bulk of the centre of the island with non-toxic rubble, and finish with topsoil. At water level, construct the edge of the island using any of the usual pond-edging effects, including a layer of filter floss or poly-ester underlay to reduce the rate of soil erosion into the pond. Alternatively build a few narrow columns supporting a plinth just below the water surface, and construct the island on the plinth. This takes up much less room in the pond, but the finished structure has limited load-bearing capacity.

For liner ponds it is often easier to leave the island in the middle of the excavation and drape the liner over the mound of soil that is left, supporting steep sides with a wall, or a skim of cement. Trim the liner around the edge of the island and incorporate a suitable decorative edging. This avoids placing large amounts of soil and rubble in the pool and reduces the risk of the liner being punctured. However, unless a specially tailored liner is obtained, the lining material will contain numerous creases, and will need to be very large. Estimate the size by adding twice the maximum pool depth on both sides of the island

*Below: This island is built like an oversized stepping stone.*

*The layer of floss reduces soil erosion into the pond.*

**An island on a liner**

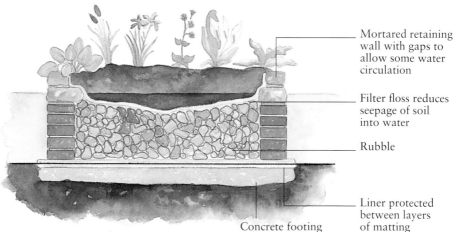

Mortared retaining wall with gaps to allow some water circulation

Filter floss reduces seepage of soil into water

Rubble

Liner protected between layers of matting

Concrete footing

**An island within a liner pond**

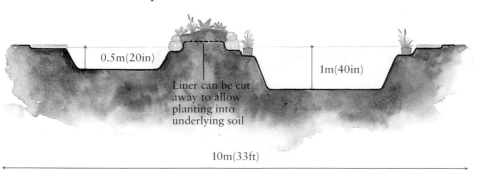

0.5m(20in)

Liner can be cut away to allow planting into underlying soil

1m(40in)

10m(33ft)

Size of liner required: 10m+(2×0.5m)+(2×1m)=13m

*Left: Here, the liner is draped over a mound left in the excavation. Strengthen any steep soil walls before laying the liner and cut away the section on the island to allow planting. You will, of course, need a*

*larger liner to cover an island; as a rough calculation, the liner will need to be the maximum length and breadth of the pond plus twice the depth of water on both sides of the island.*

to the maximum width and length of the pond. Where the pond is of an even depth, this is equivalent to adding four times the maximum depth to the pond width and length. You may need extra liner for more elaborate edging effects.

Maintaining the island can be diffi-cult. Prepare the soil well at the time of construction, and eradicate any weeds before planting up. Use fairly maintenance-free plants, strong-growing ground-cover plants, and larger foliage plants, such as *Astilbe*, *Alchemilla mollis* and *Hosta*, to help crowd out weeds.

*Above: An island in a pond can be anything from a large planted area in a grand-scale lake to a plinth for a fountain ornament in a* smaller garden pond – the method of construction is similar. Here a classical statue provides an ideal centre-piece for a formal pond.*

# DECKING, PLATFORMS AND PIERS

An increasingly popular landscaping feature, decking is less harsh than cement or stone and has a pleasant warm appearance. Where the ground conditions are rough and uneven, you can build a level deck with a minimum of earth movement. Try building out decking from the house into the garden, perhaps on varying levels, to create wooden terraces, and perhaps overhanging the water's edge to cast cool shadows. You could direct a stream or small cascade to emerge from under the decking – the hollow under the boards will enhance

*Below: Here decking provides both a convenient area from which to view koi and a removable cover to the filter system. Its texture suits the Japanese style.*

the sounds of splashing water – or use smaller areas of decking at the pool edge as viewing platforms. Do not be restricted by rectangular designs; it is not too difficult to curve decking in a wide sweep over the water.

If you extend a nearby deck from the garden at a uniform level, out and over the pond, it will draw the two elements together. A variation on this theme is a wooden jetty projected out into the water, which you can use as a viewing platform when feeding fish.

To break the monotony of large areas of decking, vary the direction of the boards. You may be able to set a pond into the decking, or a self-contained fountain ornament surrounded by a bed of cobbles. Strategically positioned urns of plants will draw the eye, you might even build a pergola

over the decking to support climbing plants and outdoor spotlights, especially if the decking is near the house when it will be used in the evenings, and will need to be well lit.

Decking has proved especially popular in the US, where wood is also used widely in house building, and its exciting potential and practical advantages are certain to encourage its more frequent use in garden designs elsewhere.

## CONSTRUCTING DECKS, PLATFORMS AND PIERS

Constructing a small area of decking is quite within the abilities of those who dabble in DIY; the methods used are not dissimilar to those involved in building simple bridges. For larger areas it is more difficult to obtain a really level surface, and the task will be made more arduous if you do not have access to a saw bench. In these cases it makes more sense to call in a local carpenter.

The supporting uprights for these types of structure must be fixed very firmly; this usually means setting

sufficient gaps between the boards to allow for water drainage and wood expansion, but not large enough to catch shoes. Reduce the risk of splintering and snagging by bevelling the top corners of the planks gently. Where possible fix the decking using countersunk screws, but if the decking has to be loose (for example for access to a filter chamber), fix small blocks on the underside of the boards to help locate them between joists.

Maintaining decking may involve periodic treatment with stains or preservatives where appropriate, but remember that even small amounts of these chemicals can be lethal to water-life (see page 73). Ensure that water is draining freely from under the deck and that no pools of water collect on the decking surface and avoid contact between decking and soil as this increases the risk of rot. If slippery algae growth is a problem, and nearby water life prevents the use of standard herbicides, try using one of the proprietary brands of pool algicide. If a small amount of these chemicals drains into the pool, it should cause little harm.

*Above: Dry decking is a pleasantly warm surface to walk on and so is ideal for leisure areas, such as this one, which extends over water and boulders.*

them into a concrete footing. Where such a support rests in the pond, the pond base must be strong enough to cope. Set a concrete footing at least 10cm (4in) deep into the ground before installing a pond liner, which should be sandwiched between protective layers of matting or liner offcuts. Place extra reinforcement in the base of concrete ponds. Use concrete blocks to form the pier, rather than wood, which will eventually rot in the water, and remember to treat the cement work to neutralize lime with a suitably coloured sealant, which will also help to disguise the pier. Where wood extends into the water, use a suitably rot-resistant hardwood and fit a damp-proof membrane between this support and the wood above it.

Fix strong crosspieces between the uprights to support the decking itself, groove and interlock the wood for extra strength and use bolts and screws for fixing. Make sure the deck material is of suitable strength and thickness for the loads it will have to bear and if the supporting joists are widely spaced use even thicker wood; in normal use the decking should not noticeably flex as it is walked upon. Use a suitable wood and, where there is no run-off into the pond, treat it with preservative. Allow freshly cut timber to weather for a while and settle into shape before fixing.

Plane and sand the deck surface if there are any splinters present, leaving

## Removable decking

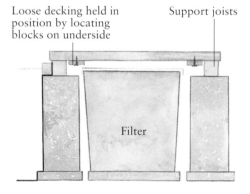

Loose decking held in position by locating blocks on underside

Support joists

Filter

*Above: Lay decking loose, held in place between joists by locating blocks, to act as a cover for a filter or pump chamber.*

## Bridge and decking supports

Recessed rustproof screws

Bridge/decking supports cut to interlock

Crosspiece strapped to uprights with damp-proof membrane between

Steel straps

Hardwood uprights

Concrete footings

*Left: Uprights are set into concrete footings and a crosspiece bolted or strapped on. Support timbers are interlocked onto this.*

# CHAPTER FIVE

# WATER GARDEN PLANTS

Water plants can make the difference between a dramatically successful pond and a dull and lifeless one. After completing the 'hard' landscaping of your pond – the shelves, waterfalls, fountains and bridges – it is time to consider the 'soft' landscaping. At this exciting stage in the project you will be able to choose from a wide range of attractive aquatic plants, and to grow them in combinations to suit your taste.

Plants have a number of very useful roles in the pond – first and foremost, they are very attractive; water lilies usually take pride of place, with their immense blooms and giant floating leaves, and for those living in warmer climates, or with conservatory ponds, there is a further range of tender species to consider, including exotic and colourful tropical lilies. But water lilies are only one type of the many eye-catching plants for the pool, which together help to obtain a natural balance in the pond; they shade the water from sunlight, provide shelter for fish and other forms of waterlife and, by absorbing nutrients from the water, help to combat the growth of unwanted algae.

A lush profusion of leafy growth will soften the harsh edges of a new pond masking the bare dividing line between the water and its surrounds and helping the pond to blend into the garden. Even in very formal ponds, where the outline remains visible as a feature in the landscape, a few bold groupings of plants will relieve monotony. A well-chosen plant will become a feature, the focal point in a picture framed by the pond edge.

# PLANTING THE WATER GARDEN

You should start planting the pond as soon as it is practicable, but if cement or building materials have fallen into the water during construction, you will need to drain and refill the pool first. Ideally, let the water age for a couple of days before you begin to introduce plants.

Unlike many herbaceous garden plants, water plants are best moved during their growing season – from late spring to the end of the summer. If you have completed your pond out of this season you may be able to obtain some ready containerized plants, which can be moved while dormant and placed into the pond, ready to spring into new growth after the winter. Underwater oxygenating plants may also be available out of season, and spring and autumn are ideal times for introducing plants into the bog garden.

A new pond may look very bare, but waterplants are surprisingly quick to settle themselves, and within a few months your pond will look mature.

## THE MAJOR GROUPS OF WATERPLANTS

Within a wild pond there are a range of different depths provided by the sloping banks, and nature has produced plants to fill all these niches. Some grow completely submerged; others mainly under the water, but sending leaves up to the surface; and others keep only their roots below the waterline; a few pond plants do not need soil and instead float on the water surface.

From this range of plants, a number of varieties have been developed and hybridized to provide more colourful blooms and more interesting foliage. These ornamental aquatics fall into the same categories as wild plants.

*Below: The fast-growing* Iris pseudacorus *is one of the many attractive and decorative marginal plants that grow well in a shallow covering of water or, as here, just beside the pond.*

■ **Water lilies and lily-like aquatics** grow on the base of the pond and send up leaves and blooms to the surface. The different varieties will grow in anything from a few centimetres of water to a couple of metres. They provide very valuable leaf cover, shading the water during the summer, and help to reduce algae growth. Fish love to bask under the large floating leaves. Try to cover at least a third to a half of the pond with floating leaves, such as those of water lilies. This will normally involve planting one lily for every one and a half to three square metres of pool surface (one for every 15-30ft$^2$).

■ **Marginal plants** grow in the shallow margins around the edge of the pond. Ideally you should have incorporated a shelf to provide a suitable area for these plants, which are very decorative, and available in many varieties. They provide shelter from winds, and a certain amount of shade. Smaller forms of pondlife take refuge around the base of their stems and in and around the roots.

As a start, you might plant around one third of the circumference of the pond with marginals, adding more if you so wish.

A few marginals – often referred to as deep marginals – can be grown on lower shelves, and some growers class them with lily-like aquatics.

■ **Oxygenating (submerged) plants** have underwater foliage, some with floating leaves and flowers as well. They may seem rather uninspiring to the new pond owner, but they have a vital role in aiding the natural balance of the pond (see page 102).

The term 'oxygenating plants' is a little misleading; during daylight hours they do produce oxygen by photosynthesis, but at night no oxygen is given out, and they even use some of the oxygen produced during the day. The main source of oxygen for pond life is the water's surface.

These submerged aquatics are most valuable for their ability to use up waste nutrients in the water, which helps to purify it, and starves the algae that cause green water and blanket-weed. They also provide cover for many microscopic forms of water life, including fish fry.

Make sure you include enough oxygenating plants in a new pond –

By shading the pond and using nutrients from the water, floating plants help to reduce levels of unwanted algae. Introduce one for every one to one and a half square metres of surface area (one per 10-15ft$^2$).

■ **Moisture-loving (bog) plants** grow in the damp soil at the edge of ponds, or in suitably constructed bog areas. Most will not tolerate water cover, preferring to have only the tips of their roots in water.

*Above: Floating plants, such as this unusual water soldier,* *provide beneficial shade for the pond depths and cover for the fish.*

about five bunches for every square metre (one bunch for every two square feet) surface area is usually adequate, though in larger ponds (over 15m$^2$/150ft$^2$) a less dense stocking rate of three to four bunches per square metre (one per three square feet) may be adequate.

■ **Floating plants** simply float on the surface, providing decoration and shade. They establish relatively quickly and can provide cover more rapidly than water lilies, but beware of varieties that grow so quickly that they can become pests and don't introduce these into very large ponds, where removal might prove difficult.

## Planting the pond

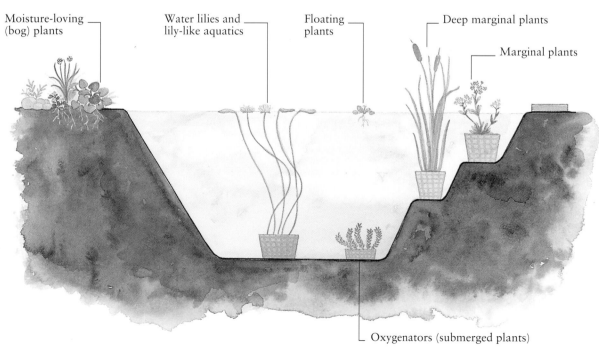

Moisture-loving (bog) plants

Water lilies and lily-like aquatics

Floating plants

Deep marginal plants

Marginal plants

Oxygenators (submerged plants)

*Above: There are a wide range of bog plants and moisture-loving shrubs that will grow in profusion in damp soil around the pond, creating a lush edging effect.*

*Left: If they are to grow well, the different categories of water plants must be set at an appropriate depth. This is made easier if planting shelves are built into the design.*

## PLANTING METHODS

You can place aquatic plants directly into pockets of soil on the pool base or shelf, but you will find it more convenient to use basket-weave containers, which allow groups of plants to be easily moved around or removed for maintenance. The risk of soil pollution is also reduced, as you will need much less soil in the pond. You can separate vigorous plants from more delicate varieties, and control their spread easily. (Don't put gravel on the base – it will just trap dirt.)

A wide range of containers are available, mostly in rot-proof plastic. Black is generally the most inconspicuous colour. The containers' sides are usually perforated, allowing the roots to grow out into the detritus on the pond base, which provides the plants with extra nutrients and allows oxygen and microscopic pond life to enter the soil, aerating it and preventing it from becoming foul. Although some plants will grow in solid-sided containers, many will become rapidly stunted and die, so only use solid containers to restrict the growth of invasive plants, or to protect large valuable koi from abrasion on the container sides.

Use the largest containers possible, with wide stable bases, and handles to make moving more easily. Small containers tend to blow over, and the limited volume of soil very quickly becomes exhausted of nutrients. Take care to pick containers that will give you the required level of water cover over the soil surface.

Basket-weave containers can seep soil, so you should line them with hessian (burlap), which swells in the water and retains the soil while the plant establishes. By the time the hessian rots, the plant roots will normally have a good hold on the soil. You can use plastic woven materials, which will not rot, but they are too impervious and can restrict plant growth.

Pile as much soil as possible into the containers, firming at all stages, and mounding it slightly, before making room for the plants. When you have transferred the plants, firm the soil around them and submerge the planting basket in a container of water or soak the container, using a watering can, to wash out any very fine particles and expel most of the air bubbles from the soil. Firm the soil again and, if the level has dropped, add more soil to the container, taking care not to smother the plant. Trim back any excess hessian and top the container with 20-25mm (0.75-1in) of lime-free gravel to keep the soil in place and prevent fish from grubbing. Lower the container gently into position; you can run cords through the perforations at the top of the basket to swing it over a large pond.

## SOILS AND FERTILIZERS

The best soil for waterplants is a heavy loam top-soil, free from herbicides, which provides a good consistency and has a reasonable nutrient content. You can use clay soil, but pure clay lacks nutrients and will restrict most plant growth; rotted turves or commercial water plant loams may also be suitable.

Avoid sandy and chalky soils, which can wash out of the planting containers and are often deficient in nutrients, and very alkaline chalk or limestone soil, which can upset some plants. Peat or peat-based composts are ideal for use in the bog garden, but below water become increasingly anaerobic. They are also very acid, lacking in nutrients, and tend to float out of underwater containers. Very few aquatic plants grow naturally in peaty soils, and most others will fair poorly or die if planted into peat. You should also avoid general garden composts and potting mixtures, which contain peat and/or high levels of soluble fertilizers.

Most fertilizers, manures and garden composts tend to leach out into the pond water, and encourage the growth of algae rather than pond plants, and poorly rotted manure can release ammonia into the water, which is dangerous to fish. A good-quality soil in a reasonable-sized container will provide plants with sufficient nutrients for three to four years. Boost plant growth with slow-release aquatic plant fertilizers in tablet form, which can be pushed into the soil by the plant roots.

*Right: Choose the largest planting containers that will fit well into your pond design and line baskets with hessian.*

*Below: Top containers with a thin layer of gravel and raise marginal plants higher until they have established.*

Fragrance adds a great deal to a garden and is particularly appreciated by those with poor eyesight. There are a limited number of aquatic plants that have strong scents, but try the following:

- *Acorus calamus* A marginal plant that releases a distinctive tangerine aroma when crushed (see page 96).
- *Aponogeton distachyus* The strong, vanilla scent of the water hawthorn can carry some distance (see page 95).
- *Filipendula spp.* The 'meadow-sweets' are moisture-loving plants, whose blooms often have a light, sweet fragrance.
- *Hemerocallis* The day lilies are moisture-loving plants, and a number have strongly scented blooms (see page 104).
- *Houttuynia spp.* Marginal plants whose foliage has an acid citrus scent when bruised (see page 97).
- *Mentha aquatica* Water mint has strongly aromatic foliage (see pages 98-99).

*Above: Water mint has a distinctive aroma but must be controlled to prevent it from spreading rampantly.*

- *Preslia cervina* The most highly aromatic marginal, which will release a sweet, minty scent as you brush past it (see page 100).
- *Primula spp.* Most primulas have a delightful fragrance and are ideal for a bog garden (see page 105).

## CHOOSING AND ARRANGING PLANTS

Choose healthy stock with signs of fresh new growth, and avoid stunted or damaged plants. Bare-root aquatic plants are available from specialist growers, and many water garden centres now supply container-grown water plants, which, though generally more expensive than bare-root stock, are often larger, and will settle more quickly. Containers vary from temporary small (1 litre/1.75 pint) pots to giant (22 litre/5 gallon) baskets.

Transfer plants from small pots to larger containers as soon as possible, and repot those in small baskets within a year or so. Larger plants that are already in full-sized baskets can be moved directly into the pond and, depending upon the quality of the soil in the containers, may not need repotting for two or three years.

*Above: In a large setting, such as this, a few bold clumps of appropriately tall-growing plants looks much more effective than numerous varieties of smaller plants.*

The layout of the plants is an integral feature of the overall design of the water garden. Bold clusters of plants usually look much more effective than a ring of plants around the edge of the pond. Consider the final height of the plants, and the combinations of foliage and flower colour. Higher marginal plants can be set as a backdrop for lower growing forms, and different types of foliage can be contrasted. Remember that the shape of the plant, whether it be a mound, a tall spire or a rambling sprawl, will be present before and after the plant flowers, and consider this when positioning the container.

# WATER LILIES
## (*Nymphaea*)

No pond should be without water lilies, even small pools have room for one or two. Their dramatic leaves and magnificent blooms instantly make them a feature.

The first leaves of hardy lilies normally hit the surface in late spring, moving out across the water before fading and sinking below the surface. They are produced in succession throughout the season until autumn, and the dying old leaves are not a sign of ill health.

Depending upon the climate and the amount of sun received, the lily blooms should start to appear in early or mid summer (at temperatures over 18°C/65°F). The first few blooms of a new plant are often a little disappointing, being smaller and paler than the blooms produced later in the season, but once established, water lilies will flower right through the summer, and often into early autumn. The flowers open during the morning and close in the late afternoon, each bloom lasting three to five days before closing finally and sinking below the surface. In hot and sunny weather, the blooms will open earlier in the morning and close earlier in the afternoon.

Water lilies prefer a warm sunny position, producing paler blooms, which will often open for a shorter time, in shady spots, or sites with cooler, moving water. Poor flowering may also be a sign that the lily is pot bound or needs fertiliser.

As they have a greedy root system, it is important to plant water lilies in the largest suitable container, with a soil depth of 15cm (6in) or more. You can transfer container-grown lilies to larger containers without disturbing the growing point. Trim off older leaves and most roots from bare root lilies and plant them as soon as possible. Plant lily rhizomes with the growing point – the crown – at soil level, exposed to the water; the shoots should be growing upright, just as they were before the lily was lifted. Take care not to smother the crown with soil or gravel or to leave it standing proud of the soil.

Lower lilies gradually to their final position. Start the containers off on an upturned basket, or other support, so that there is only 15-25cm (6-10in) of water over the crown, and, as the leaves reach the surface, lower the plant a further step. If you intend to position the plant in very deep water (1m/3ft or over), you may need to lower it over a year or two; lowering a lily too rapidly will check growth, resulting in small leaves, poor flowering, or even death.

Large and vigorous lilies are better suited to deeper water; although they may establish more quickly, they will soon swamp small ponds. Small or medium-sized varieties may look small at first, and may be more expensive than the vigorous varieties, but they will grow to a more moderate size, suitable for most ponds.

Miniature lilies are far too small to be the central lilies for a pond and are better positioned on the marginal shelf of the pond or, alternatively, or in a tub. They can be grown successfully in one-litre (quart) baskets, as they require less soil than their larger relatives. Frost can damage the crown, so ensure that the growing point is well below ice level.

## WHITE LILIES

- *alba* (vigorous)
The common white water lily, native to Europe and Asia, with cup-shaped clear white blooms, bright yellow centres and plentiful mid-green foliage. Best suited to lakes and larger wildlife ponds. When fully established, it will tolerate coldish water up to 2m (6ft) deep.

*Above:* alba

- *candida* (small)
Another native of Europe and Asia. The white flowers with golden centres are held just above the water surface.
- *caroliniana* 'Nivea' (small)
The narrow-petalled, lightly scented flowers have yellow centres and are held above the water.
- 'Gladstoniana' (large/vigorous)
Enormous, broad-petalled white blooms, with deep-yellow centres and large olive-green leaves. An excellent lily for the larger pool and lake.

*Below:* 'Gladstoniana'

*Above:* caroliniana *'Nivea'*

■ **'Gonnere'** (medium/small)
A fully double lily with globular blooms, which expand into dense clusters of pointed white petals and golden centres.

*Above:* 'Gonnere'

■ **'Hermine'** (medium)
Dainty white flowers with pointed petals are produced throughout the season. On mature plants they stand slightly above the leaves, which age from olive-bronze to mid-green in colour. A good lily for medium-sized and small ponds.

■ **x marliacea 'Albida'** (medium)
Joseph Bory Latour-Marliac introduced a large number of hardy water lily cultivars around the turn of the century, many of which are still very popular. *marliacea* 'Albida' is a reliably free-flowering, golden-centred white lily, with leaves that are a deep-olive green in colour with purply brown borders.

■ **odorata var. alba** (small/medium)
This water lily produces deep, medium-sized, cup-shaped flowers with pointed white petals and yellow centres, which contrast attractively with the round mid-green leaves. A

*Above:* × pygmaea *'Alba'*

native of North America, notable for its mild fragrance.

■ **x pygmaea 'Alba'** (miniature)
A true miniature lily producing star-shaped flowers, with relatively large golden centres. The blooms rarely exceed 4cm (1.5in) diameter, the leaves are only a little larger. It is rather delicate, but will grow in small tubs and even large bowls, setting seed freely.

■ **'Queen of the Whites'** (large)
An American variety with semi-double white blooms.

■ **tuberosa 'Richardsoni'** (medium)
An improved form of a native North American water lily, with numerous snow-white petals clustered in a globular bloom enclosed with green sepals. The strong rootstock produces round, apple-green leaves with hairy young stems.

*Below:* × marliacea *'Albida'*

## LILY SIZES

Lilies are categorized approximately according to their size, which provides a useful guide to the depth of water, in which the plants can grow when established. These sizes are meant as general guidelines; growth patterns are affected by various factors, including sunlight, soil and fertilizer. (The depths given refer to the water cover over the lily crown, not to the pool depth.)

| Lily sizes | Water cover |
| --- | --- |
| ■ Vigorous lilies | 40-90cm (16-36in) (Up to 120cm/ 48in once well established) |
| ■ Large lilies | 30-70cm (12-28in) |
| ■ Medium lilies | 25-50cm (10-20in) |
| ■ Small lilies | 20-35cm (8-14in) |
| ■ Miniature lilies | 15-25cm (6-10in) |

The spread of an established lily is usually a circle with a diameter one and a half to two times the depth of water over the crown. If a lily is grown in water that is too shallow, its leaves may be pushed up above the water level.

## YELLOW LILIES

■ **'Charlene Strawn'** (medium)
An American lily with very wide yellow blooms and pointed petals. The flowers are held slightly above the dark green leaves and have a mild fragrance.

*Above: 'Charlene Strawn'*

■ **'Colonel A J Welch'** (vigorous)
Narrow, pointed and slightly crinkly petals radiate out like a star and are held above plentiful green foliage that is flecked purply brown when young. The flowers stay open late in the afternoon, but are rather sparse in comparison to the leaves. A lily better suited to deep water and lakes.

■ ***x marliacea*** **'Chromatella'** (medium/large)
Probably the most popular yellow lily. The large, oval, olive-green leaves are streaked with purply brown and the clear yellow, wide-open blooms are cup shaped. The outermost of the broad petals are tinged pink at the base, and the centre is a golden yellow. Reliably free flowering, it can become too vigorous for small ponds.

*Below: × marliacea 'Chromatella'*

*Above: odorata 'Sulphurea'*

*Above: 'Sunrise'*

■ **'Moorei'** (medium)
Similar to 'Chromatella', but not quite as large or as free flowering. The leaves are spotted, rather than streaked, with brown.

■ ***odorata*** **'Sulphurea'** (small to medium)
Tall, pointed buds are held above the water and open into soft yellow, star-shaped blooms, with an orange-yellow centre. Given a warm, sunny position, this variety is free flowering.

■ ***x pygmaea*** **'Helvola'** (miniature)
The most popular miniature lily, with small (5cm/2in), star-shaped yellow blooms, which float between its greeny-brown speckled oval leaves. The flowers stay open into the late afternoon and are produced freely.

■ **'Sunrise'** (medium)
The bright, starry blooms stand above the water surface and the narrow pointed petals are slightly crinkled with incurved sides. The foliage is mid-green when mature, but young leaves are speckled brown and have hairy stems. 'Sunrise' needs a good summer and a warm position to be at its best, but in the right conditions will produce large blooms, and can be quite vigorous.

*Below × pygmaea 'Helvola'*

## PINK AND RED LILIES

Pink lilies range from almost white to striking rosy-carmine in colour, and red lilies between deep pink and mauve-red.

■ **'Amabilis'** (medium)
The pointed buds open to form large stellate, salmon-pink blooms, the base of the petals becoming increasingly pink on successive days. The centre of the flower is a rich golden yellow.

■ **'American Star'** (medium/large)
Spiky, narrow pointed petals with in-curving sides radiate out from the golden centres of the blooms, which are often held slightly out of the water. The petals are strong pink at the base changing to a light pink at the tips.

*Above: 'American Star'*

■ **'Atropurpurea'** (small/medium)
The very open mauvey-pink blooms darken to a deep scarlet-crimson on mature plants, contrasting with the golden-yellow-tipped red stamens and purple-tinged dark-green leaves.

■ **'Attraction'** (medium/large)
A very popular red lily, whose blooms

*Below: 'Attraction'*

are freely produced and shade from deep wine red at the base of the central petals to almost white at the tips of the outer petals. The blooms, which are complemented by golden stamens streaked fiery orange and red, may be pale for the first two or three years, but once established will flower a darker red, and tolerate much deeper water.

■ *caroliniana* **'Perfecta'** (small)
Small, light-pink, orange-centred flowers are freely produced and have a mild fragrance.

■ **'Charles de Meurville'** (large/vigorous)
Large open blooms, of a strong wine-red colour with paler outer petals and inner sepals, are freely produced. The centre is a mass of golden stamens.

■ **'Colossea'** (large/vigorous)
Large blooms have slightly pointed petals that are flesh pink at the base, fading towards the tips. A strong, free-flowering variety.

■ **'Conqueror'** (large)
Once established, the large flowers are a deep wine-crimson in colour, flecked with white. The outer petals are distinctly paler and the flowers have hairy stems.

*Above: 'Conqueror'*

■ **'Ellisiana'** (small/miniature)
The pale sepals frame the small golden-centred blooms, which are a glowing mauvey-red once established. The leaves are a purply dark green, ageing to mid-green, and often have quite long stalks.

■ **'Escarboucle'** (medium)
Few red lilies are as bright as 'Escarboucle' with its pointed blooms of intense carmine-scarlet. The outer petals are rather paler and the centre of the bloom has a ring of bright

*Above: 'Fabiola'*

golden stamens, orange on the inside and red on the outside. The blooms are freely produced and stay open till late afternoon. It needs plenty of room.

■ **'Fabiola'** (medium)
Golden-yellow stamens are surrounded by slightly pointed, purply pink, oval petals that fade to pale pink at the tips.

■ **'Firecrest'** (small/medium)
Even, pink blooms have a cluster of golden stamens in their centre, streaked with fiery orange and red.

■ **'Froebeli'** (small)
A popular red lily, with freely produced blooms, for the smaller pool. The four sepals fold back to reveal the upright blooms of deep winey red that float at, or slightly above, water level. The heart-shaped leaves are a bright apple green when mature.

■ **'Gloire du Temple sur Lot'** (medium)
Impressive double flowers have narrow petals that turn in at the tips, the inner petals clustering round the yellow centre. On first opening, the blooms are a light pink, deeper at the base, but on successive days they fade to creamy white.

*Below: 'Escarboucle'*

*Above: 'Gloriosa'*

- **'Gloriosa'** (small/medium)
Although rather pale at first, the flowers deepen to a rich, bright red with golden centres. A good red for the smaller pond.
- **'Hollandia'** (medium/large)
Almost double, pink flowers, deeper coloured at the base.

*Above: 'Hollandia'*

- **'James Brydon'** (medium/small)
Large buds open into cup-shaped, deep-pink blossoms with golden centres and a pleasant mild fragrance. On mature plants the petals

*Below: 'James Brydon'*

darken to a deep carmine pink and blooms are produced freely. Young leaves are maroon, fading to dark green with a brown edge.
- **x laydekeri 'Fulgens'** (small/medium)
The *laydekeri* group tend to be free flowering, and generally produce fewer leaves than other varieties. They are ideal for smaller ponds and large tubs, but can take a year or two to establish. The leaves are oval with a distinct 'V' cut in them, and are produced on quite long stalks. 'Fulgens' produces glowing red blooms with a magenta tint, pale inner sepals, and bright golden anthers.
- **x laydekeri 'Lilacea'** (small/miniature)
This variety has small, pale-pink blossoms with pointed petals. The colour intensifies to a deeper rose-pink as the plant matures.
- **x laydekeri 'Purpurata'** (small/miniature)
Pink blooms deepen on older plants to a wine red, streaked white. The petals are pointed and the centre of the bloom is golden orange.
- **'Lucida'** (small/medium)
The broad petals have slightly incurving sides and a distinct small point. The outer petals are a pale peachy pink, the inner ones deep vermillion pink in colour. The centre has a ring of rich golden anthers.
- **'Madame Wilfron Gonnere'** (medium)
Mid-green foliage provides a foil for the rich-pink, deep-cup-shaped double flowers. The petals fade from deep pink at the base to pale pink at the tips and are flecked white.
- **x marliacea 'Carnea'** (medium/large)
A strong-growing, reliable lily with a

*Below: 'Madame Wilfron Gonnere'*

*Above: × marliacea 'Carnea'*

mild fragrance, producing a string of blush-pink blooms throughout the season. The broad, slightly pointed petals are virtually white at first, but the plant quickly matures to produce blooms with a distinct pink shading at the base, fading to pale, flesh pink at the tips. The centre has a cluster of golden stamens.
- **x marliacea 'Rosea'** (medium)
Similar to 'Carnea', but with mature blooms of a more even pale pink.
- **'Masaniello'** (medium/large)
Attractive golden-centred blooms with broad, pointed, rosy pink petals, fading from deep crimson pink at the centre to pale pink at the edge. Blooms are freely produced and occasionally stand slightly above the profuse olive-tinted green foliage.
- **'Mrs Richmond'** (medium/large)
Produces plentiful good-sized blooms with broad, oval, satin-pink petals. The base and centre of the blooms are a darker rose colour, fading towards the tips. The dense golden stamens are orangy red on the reverse side and the blooms slightly fragrant. The intensity of colour varies quite noticeably from plant to plant.

*Below: 'Mrs Richmond'*

■ **'Norma Gedye'** (medium/vigorous)
Once established, this plant produces large blooms of an even rose pink and profuse dark green leaves.

■ *odorata* **'William B. Shaw'** (small/medium)
There are many pink cultivars of *odorata*, which usually have mildly fragrant blooms held just above the water surface. They tend to be smaller lilies, although in warm climates they may grow larger, more vigorous and have more fragrance. The blooms often close by mid to late afternoon and the leaves are round, mid to olive green, and tinged purple when young. 'W. B. Shaw' has slightly pointed, soft-pink petals with a ring of golden stamens in the centre.

■ **'Pearl of the Pool'** (medium)
A clear-pink, semi-double lily with pointed petals and a golden centre.

■ **'Perry's Pink'** (medium)
One of the many new introductions from Perry D. Slocum of North America, this one has a beautiful, almost double, deep-pink bloom with a hint of orangy carmine. The oval, slightly pointed petals surround the golden centre, which is flecked fiery orange with a red dot in the centre. Other new varieties from this source include **'Peter Slocum'** (medium/large), a dark-pink double blossom; **'Perry's Fire Opal'**, another double lily, with broad pointed petals in a vivid deep pink; and **'Ray Davies'** (medium), double mid-pink flowers with pointed petals and a golden yellow centre.

■ **'Pink Sensation'** (medium)
The pointed petals fade from deep satin pink at the bases to silvery pink at the tips. The slightly crinkled blooms have golden yellow centres

*Below: 'Pink Sensation'*

and are very freely produced. They float between the bronzed, dark-green leaves with slightly hairy stems.

■ *x pygmaea* **'Rubra'** (miniature/small)
A miniature lily with small, wine-pink flowers, deepening to a dark mauve pink, streaked white. The true variety is rare; plants sold under this name are often small *laydekeri*-type hybrids.

■ **'Rembrandt'** (medium/large)
Large, golden-centred blooms of crimson vermilion, fading to red-streaked pink in the outer petals.

■ **'Rene Gerard'** (medium)
Large blooms with pointed, rich rosy red petals, deeper in the centre and fading to pale pink flecked with deeper pink in the outer petals. A popular and free-flowering variety.

*Above: 'Rene Gerard'*

■ **'Rose Arey'** (small/medium)
The true variety has pointed petals with incurving sides, and is a vivid pink tinged rosy carmine. The stamens are tipped golden orange and the flower has a mild fragrance. Slow to establish.

■ **'Rosennymphe'** (medium)
A free-flowering variety with very open blooms, pointed petals and a golden centre. At first a beautiful shell pink, fading on successive days to a creamy magnolia. The heart-shaped leaves are purple when young, fading from dark green to olive green.

■ **'Sirius'** (medium/large)
The large blooms are purple-crimson with pointed petals and pale sepals that lie flat on the water surface. The centres are orange, tinted red, and the mid-green leaves have a few distinctive chocolate splashes.

■ **'Sultan'** (medium)
Large, bright-red blooms fade towards the tips of the slightly pointed petals.

*Above: 'Rosennymphe'*

■ *tuberosa* **'Rosea'** (medium)
A vigorous lily with medium-sized pale pink flowers. Mildly scented.

■ **'Turicensis'** (medium/small)
An *odorata*-type lily with elongated soft pink petals and a mild fragrance.

■ **'Vesuve'** (medium)
Fiery vermilion-scarlet blooms with red-streaked orange stamens.

■ **'William Falconer'** (medium/small)
Deep, blood-red, cup-shaped blooms with fiery orange stamens around a yellow centre. The leaves are reddish, maturing to a dark green with purple-brown edges.

*Above: 'William Falconer'*

*Below: 'Sultan'*

## COPPER-ORANGE CHANGEABLE LILIES

These lilies fall in the category between yellow and red. The blooms tend to darken in colour on each successive day, a number have attractive mottling on their leaves, especially on the younger leaves, and most of the varieties are of fairly refined growth – ideal for smaller ponds. The constantly changing colours of the blooms and foliage often make it difficult to distinguish between varieties.

■ **'Aurora'** (small/miniature)
The flowers open a rosy tinted yellow and deepen, through pinky orange, to an orange-red colour. Young leaves are olive green, heavily splashed, and streaked with chocolate brown, maroon brown and pale brown.

■ **'Comanche'** (medium/small)
The flowers are freely produced on established plants, standing slightly out of the water. The petals open a peachy colour, and on successive days flecks of orangy pink build up on the

*Above: 'Comanche'*

petals, especially on the inner petals, giving an overall fiery orange coloration. The stamens are a bright-orange-gold colour.

■ **'Graziella'** (small)
A free-flowering lily with blunt-petalled apricot-orange flowers, flushed deep pink and held just out of the water, with golden orange centres. The round foliage is mid green, tinted olive with heavy mottlings of pale chocolate.

■ **'Indiana'** (small)
Blunt-petalled flowers darken from pinky peach to red-stained copper-orange.

■ **'Paul Hariot'** (small/medium)
The good-sized blooms are held slightly above the water, and deepen from a rosy yellow to copper-orange, flushed red. A free-flowering lily, staying open into the late afternoon.

## TROPICAL WATER LILIES

Those who live in warmer climates, or who have the advantage of a conservatory pond, can grow a wide range of tender plants. These exotic varieties of *Nymphaea* produce numerous, often stellate, blooms in dazzling colours, held up above the water surface. The floating leaves are frequently wrinkled and occasionally mottled. Some varieties flower in the evening to the following noon.

Plant them in much the same manner as the hardy varieties, starting in early to midsummer. Position them in shallow water with no more than 10cm (4in) cover, and only lower as the lily starts to grow more vigorously. Once established, it should tolerate 30-40cm (12-16in) cover, less in cooler situations. For good growth, temperatures of 21°C (70°F) or over, and as much light as possible are essential.

Once tropical lilies have settled, they grow rapidly, and will need boosting with aquatic fertilizer. In warm climates they will bloom until early winter. In more temperate climates, remove the lilies from the pond as they cease flowering, and overwinter them in a shallow tub or pond indoors. Some of the better varieties include:

■ **'Afterglow'** Pink-tipped peach blooms with yellow centres.
■ **'Blue Beauty'** Large blue flowers with purple-tipped stamens.
■ **'Daubeniana'** A reliable small lily with tiny pale-blue flowers.
■ **'Director George T. Moore'** Golden-centred blooms of deep lilac-purple, and a ring of purple stamens.
■ **'Emily Grant Hutchings'** A night-blooming variety with large, red-tinged pink flowers with red stamens.
■ **'Evelyn Randig'** Large pink flowers with a ring of pink stamens around the golden centre.
■ **'General Pershing'** A strong growing and fragrant pink lily.

*Below: 'Afterglow'*

*Above: 'Director George T. Moore'*

■ **'Marian Strawn'** A yellow-centred white of medium size.
■ **'Missouri'** A night-blooming white lily for a roomy warm position.
■ **'Mrs. George C. Hitchcock'** A night bloomer with big rose-pink petals and darker stamens.
■ **'Pamela'** Pale lilac-blue flowers with golden sunflower centres.
■ **'Panama Pacific'** Magenta-purple blooms with purple-tipped stamens.
■ **'Red Flare'** A night bloomer with vivid red flowers.
■ **'Sir Galahad'** A night bloomer of strong growth with golden-centred blooms of clear white.

*Above: 'Paul Hariot'*

- **'Sioux'** (medium/small)
The pointed blooms are raised just out of the water, have large golden stamens and reach a fair size on mature plants. The petals deepen from a pale peach to a rich orange-pink, darker at the bases. The young leaves are dark green with chocolate flecks, but older leaves are plain olive green.

## LILY-LIKE AQUATICS

*Nymphaea* are not the only plants available for the deeper areas of the pond. There are a few similar plants that can also provide floating leaves and blooms.

- **Aponogeton distachyus** (Water hawthorn, Cape pondweed)
A splendid plant for any pool, with long strap-like leaves of dark green, flecked with chocolate brown. It produces unusual forked white blooms, which are occasionally tinged pink, float on the water surface and have black-tipped stamens and a strong vanilla scent. The plant blooms virtually all year round, stopping only in the heat of midsummer – it may not survive very hot summers – or when ice covers the pool.
   Plant the tubers just below the soil. This adaptable plant will tolerate anything from 8-60cm (3-24in) water cover but is happiest with 15-30cm (6-12in). It is quite hardy as long as the tuber is well below ice level, and will seed freely.
- **Nuphar lutea** (Spatterdock or Brandy Bottle lily)
This vigorous plant is well suited to areas that are less amenable to water lilies. It has large heart-shaped leaves and small yellow cup-shaped flowers

## THE LOTUS

The lotus (*Nelumbo spp.*) has strange leaves held out of the water on long stalks and followed by taller (50-150cm/20-60in) flower stalks with giant fragrant blooms. After flowering, the seedpods remain like enormous poppy heads.
   The lotus tuber must be planted into a very large container of good heavy topsoil. Place the tuber horizontally on top of the soil and firm the soil over the main body of the tuber. Add a thin layer of small rounded gravel over the top, at all times taking care to leave the

*Below: Nelumbo nucifera*

delicate growing tip undamaged and virtually uncovered. Start the lotus tubers off with 8-10cm (3-4in) water cover, increasing cover to 15-30cm (6-12in) once they are established. It is possible to grow them out of the pool in a large plastic planter, filling with soil to 15cm (6in) below the top and adding water as required. Give the lotus a very sunny wind-free site and use aquatic fertilizers regularly. They need warm summers (over 80°F/27°C) to grow well and can then spread vigorously in mud-bottomed ponds. They will survive winters providing the tuber is well below ice level.
   Good lotus varieties include:

- *alba grandiflora* A large single white.
- 'Chwan Basu' A small grower with pink-edged white blooms.
- *lutea* A yellow-flowering native of North America.
- 'Momo Botan' A double deep pink with a golden centre.
- 'Mrs Perry D. Slocum' Large double orange-pink flowers, fading to yellow.
- *nucifera* The Hindu lotus with rosy tinted cream flowers.
- *pekinensis rubra* Smaller growing with deep red flowers.

in the summer. It also produces fine, crinkled underwater leaves. It takes a year or two to establish, but will then tolerate deeper, colder water than water lilies (up to 150cm/60in), and even shady areas and ponds with

*Below: Aponogeton distachyus*

gently moving water. Plant it in no more than 40cm (16in) of water, lowering it gradually to its final position. Mature plants have enormous root systems so do not plant in a small pond. Similar species include the North American *N. advena*, and, ideal for smaller ponds, *N. pumila* or its variegated form.

- **Nymphoides peltata/Villarsia bennettii** (Fringed Water Lily)
A pretty little plant with long runners sending up numerous small, pale-olive-green leaves, often slightly mottled with wavy edges. During mid to late summer a succession of five-pointed yellow flowers are produced, each lasting only a day. Tolerant of a wide range of water depths, it tends to grow up and along the surface. It is best containerized and trimmed back when necessary; it can grow out of control in mud-bottomed pools.

# MARGINAL PLANTS

These decorative, mostly perennial plants are normally grown in the shallows around the pool edge, but they will grow in other areas of shallow water, around islands and in slow-moving streams, and sometimes in moist soil above the water.

Plant them in containers, taking extra care if you mix different varieties of plants in the same container, as one will often crowd the others out. Avoid putting a vigorous variety with anything more refined, and try to mix plants with different growing habits; for example *Typha minima* has a fairly deep root system and upright growth and can be mixed successfully with a plant such as *Myosotis*, which has a shallow root system and a rambling type of growth.

Some marginals can tolerate a wide range of water depths; others will rot if placed too deeply; many require water cover in the winter to protect the roots from frost. A satisfactory compromise is to position the marginals with approximately 5cm (2in) water cover, but check the ideal level of water cover in the individual plant descriptions. Note that the depth given in individual descriptions indicates the depth of water cover over the soil in the container. If you have positioned the marginal shelf at depth of 20cm (8in), you should have no problems. If necessary, you can raise or cut down the containers.

*Below:* Butomus umbellatus

If the plants are growing in peat compost, remove most of this before planting them out, or they may rot. Marginal plants must be gradually acclimatized to their final level of water cover; raise the planting containers for the first few months so that initially the plants have only 2-3cm (1in) of water cover. This is particularly important for low-growing plants of a lush leafy nature, which cannot tolerate sudden changes in water depth.

■ *Acorus calamus* (Sweet Flag)
Green, iris-like, aromatic foliage rising from a slowly creeping rhizome, with unusual poker-like flower heads pushing out from the sides of the leaves. The more ornamental *A. calamus variegatus,* with its attractive, cream-striped, green foliage, keeps its colour throughout the season, and looks best in a large clump.
Depth: 2-15cm (1-6in)
Height: 60-75cm (24-30in)
Sunshine: Full sun to half shade
■ *Acorus gramineus variegatus*
A dwarf grass-like rush with yellow striped green foliage.
Depth: Bog to 8cm (3in)
Height: 25-30cm (10-12in)
Sunshine: Full sun to slight shade
■ *Butomus umbellatus* (Flowering rush)
The tough rush-like leaves have a triangular cross section and are dark green. Umbels of pink flowers are held above the leaves on tall stems. Needs plenty of room and a large container if it is to flower well. Intolerant of hot climates.
Depth: 5-25cm (2-10in)
Height: 100-120cm (40-48in)
Sunshine: Full sun to slight shade
Flowering time: Mid to late summer
■ *Calla palustris* (Bog Arum)
Creeping rhizomes trail out across the water surface and bear attractive green, waxy, heart-shaped leaves. The small white arum flowers are not produced very freely, but mature to produce red berries.

Depth: Bog to 10cm (4in)
Height: 10-20cm (4-8in)
Sunshine: Full sun to slight shade
Flowering time: Mid to late summer
■ *Caltha spp.* (Marsh Marigold, Kingcup)
These adaptable plants have many buttercup-type flowers during the spring, and sometimes a few more in late summer. Their rounded leaves, with serrated edges, form attractive mounds of foliage. All *Caltha* species are intolerant of hot climates.
■ *Caltha palustris*
Bright yellow buttercup flowers.
Depth: Moist soil to 15cm (6in)
Height: 25-35cm (10-14in)
Sunshine: Full sun to half shade
Flowering time: Mid to late spring

*Above:* Caltha palustris

■ *Caltha palustris alba*
Golden centred white flowers, which are produced earlier than most other water garden plants. It seeds freely.
Depth: Moist soil to 5cm (2in)
Height: 20-25cm (8-10in)
Sunshine: Full sun to slight shade
Flowering time: Early to mid spring
■ *Caltha palustris plena*
Double, golden yellow flowers and

*Below:* Caltha palustris alba

deep green leaves. It does not set seed. Both *alba* and *plena* are compact in growth, and well suited to the smaller garden pond.
Depth: Moist soil to 5cm (2in)
Height: 15-20cm (6-8in)
Sunshine: Full sun or slight shade
Flowering time: Mid to late spring

■ *Caltha polypetala*

The giant of the family, and excellent for large ponds. Its big yellow butter-cup flowers are produced later than those of the other varieties.
Depth: Bog to 10cm (4in)
Height: to 60cm (24in)
Sunshine: Full sun or slight shade
Flowering time: Mid to late spring

■ *Carex stricta* 'Bowles Golden' (Golden Sedge)

An excellent waterside grass with golden leaves, tinted lime, which keep their colour until the autumn. It pro-duces taller seed heads in the early summer. The slightly smaller, rather invasive *Carex riparia variegata* has narrower, creamy white leaves striped green, and long stalks topped by black seed heads.
Depth: Moist soil to 5cm (2in)
Height: 40cm (16in)
Sunshine: Full sun or slight shade

*Above:* Carex stricta 'Bowles Golden'

■ *Cotula coronopifolia* (Golden buttons)

A dainty plant with narrow bright-green leaves, topped throughout the summer with small yellow button-like flowers. These plants will form a ram-bling clump and are ideal for filling the gaps between rocks at the waters edge. They will survive mild winters if below the water and often re-grow from seed set the previous summer.
Depth: Moist soil to 10cm (4in)
Height: 20cm (8in)

*Above:* Cotula coronopifolia

Sunshine: Full sun or slight shade
Flowering time: Late spring to mid autumn

■ *Cyperus alternifolius* (Umbrella Grass)

An attractive foliage plant, with para-sol-like umbels. It is sometimes grown as a house plant, but is quite happy in the water and, although not very hardy, will survive most winters, pro-viding the growing point is lowered well below the ice level in winter. *Cyperus longus* (Sweet Galingale) is similar to, but hardier than, its rela-tive, with stout foliage, grassy tops and brown seed spikelets. It has a sharp pointed invasive root system and is best restricted to a large plant-ing container.
Depth: 8-20cm (3-8in)
Height: 100cm (40in)
Sunshine: Full sun or slight shade
Flowering time: Mid summer to autumn

*Above:* Cyperus alternifolius

■ *Glyceria maxima* 'Variegata' (*G. spectabilis variegatus*) (Sweet Manna Grass)

The broad grassy foliage is striped

*Above:* Glyceria maxima

green and cream and is tinged pink in the spring. Once established it can become quite vigorous and is best containerized.
Depth: 5-20cm (2-8in)
Height: 60cm (24in)
Sunshine: Full sun to half shade

■ *Houttuynia cordata plena*

A good marginal plant with red-tinted stems, heart-shaped, dark-green leaves and small semi-double white flowers with strange cone-like centres. A single form has less highly coloured leaves and another form ('Tricolour', 'Chameleon', or *variegata*) has multi-coloured leaves that range from cream and green to glowing red, mottled with olive. *Houttuynia* is very adapt-able and will grow in moist soil as well as in the water, but it is best kept in containers because of its invasive root system. The roots should be below ice level to survive the winter, and new spring growth can be temporarily scorched by late frosts.
Depth: Moist soil to 10cm (4in)
Height: 15-30cm (6-12in)
Sunshine: Full sun or slight shade
Flowering time: Early to mid summer

*Below:* Houttuynia cordata plena

■ *Iris laevigata* (Japanese Water Iris) Irises look very fitting in the water garden and this is one of the best. It is neither too vigorous nor too tall, and suits most ponds. The short-lived flowers are produced in succession, and although the flowering period is rarely more than three to four weeks, it comes just before the lilies are in full bloom, making a good start to the summer flowering season. The upright plain foliage provides a pleasant backdrop for the rest of the year. Irises look most impressive in a large clump at the water's edge and, although they will grow in moist soil, they do best when grown in the water. They commonly have three petalled blooms in shades of blue or white, but selected cultivars exist with improved blooms. These include:

'Colchesteri' Large, six-petalled white blooms that are heavily mottled purply blue.

'Midnight' Fabulous six-petalled blooms in a deep velvety blue with a yellow streak through each petal.

'Rose Queen' A cross with *Iris ensata* which should be treated like that iris and grown in moist soil rather than in the water. It has delicate soft pink flowers.

'Snowdrift' Six white petals are streaked down the centre with a fine line of golden yellow and lilac blue.

*Above:* Iris laevigata 'Snowdrift'

*I. laevigata variegata* Lilac-tinted blue flowers and attractive milky white and green foliage, which keeps its variegation throughout the summer. It grows a little less tall than other forms.
Depth: 5-10cm (2-4in)
Height: 50-70cm (20-28in)
Sunshine: Full sun
Flowering time: Early or mid summer

*Above:* Iris laevigata variegata

■ *Iris pseudacorus* (Flag Iris) A vigorous European native with tall green foliage and bright yellow flowers. A very attractive addition for the wildlife pond but generally too coarse for smaller pools.
Depth: Moist soil to 25cm (10in)
Height: 100-120cm (40-48in)
Sunshine: Full sun to half shade
Flowering time: Early or mid summer

There are a number of cultivars of *Iris pseudacorus* and all will flower best if given full sun and shallow (5-10cm/2-4in) water. Some of the more widely available include:

'Bastardii' ('Sulphur Queen') Narrow leaves and pale yellow blooms, which are freely produced. Maximum depth 20cm (8in).

'Golden Queen' Deep golden flowers. Maximum depth 15cm (6in).

'Holden Clough' Strange purple-brown-stained yellow petals. Maximum depth 5cm (2in).

*I. pseudacorus variegatus* Smaller than other cultivars at 60-90cm (24-36in). Yellow flowers and striking yellow and green striped leaves, which fade to pale green in late summer. Maximum depth 13cm (5in).

■ *Iris versicolor* (American Blue Flag) Narrow leaves and purple-blue flowers, flecked with silver and gold at the base. The flowers have narrower petals than those of *laevigata* and tend to appear just a little later. There are a number of cultivars, the most widely available of which is 'Kermesina', with rich reddish purple blooms.
Depth: 5-10cm (2-4in)
Height: 60-75cm (24-30in)
Sunshine: Full sun to slight shade
Flowering time: Mid summer

Other American water irises include Louisiana hybrids and *I. fulva*, which is slightly shorter, has orange-red flowers and requires more cover in the winter to protect it from frost.

■ *Juncus effusus spiralis* Unusual corkscrew foliage.
Depth: 5-10cm (2-4in)
Height: 30cm (12in)
Sunshine: Full sun or half shade
Flowering time: Mid to late summer

■ *Lobelia fulgens* An eye-catching plant with dark maroon foliage and vivid scarlet flowers. Although often grown as a border plant, it is happy in the pond. *L. cardinalis* is similar with dark green leaves, tinted red underneath.
Depth: 2-12cm (1-5in)
Height: 75cm (30in)
Sunshine: Full sun
Flowering time: Late summer

*Above:* Lobelia fulgens

■ *Mentha aquatica* (Water mint) A sturdy plant with aromatic, purple-tinged green leaves and lilac flowers. It can become invasive; grow it in containers, trimming back runners annually.
Depth: Moist soil to 8cm (3in)
Height: 35-45cm (14-18in)

Sunshine: Full sun to half shade
Flowering time: Mid and late summer

■ *Menyanthes trifoliata* (Bog bean)
An attractive rambling aquatic with a slowly creeping rootstock, which supports three-leafed foliage and spikes of delicate, pale-pink, star-shaped flowers, which have an unusual fringe.
Depth: Bog to 15cm (6in)
Height: 15-20cm (6-8in)
Sunshine: Full sun to slight shade
Flowering time: Early to mid summer

■ *Mimulus Sp.* (Monkey Musks, Monkey Flowers)
Lush leafy stems, which eventually become clothed in bright snapdragon-type flowers. Few of its hybrids can tolerate deep water; they grow best at the water's edge, in boggy soil, at stream sides or in waterfall pools. Not all forms are hardy, but some will readily set seed. Dislikes hot climates.
Sunshine: Full sun or half shade
Flowering time: Mid and late summer

*Mimulus luteus* and *guttatus*
Frequently confused, these moderately hardy varieties have tall stems with a profusion of bright yellow flowers. *M. guttatus* has small red dots on the throat of the flowers and seeds rather too freely. *M. luteus* has larger red spots over the petals.
Depth: Moist soil to 5cm (2in)
Height: 45cm (18in)

*Mimulus ringens* (Lavender musk)
Slightly taller than other species, with thick stems and small lavender-blue flowers in late summer. It also prefers deeper water.
Depth: 8-15cm (3-6in)
Height: 50cm (20in)

Other *Mimulus* cultivars and hybrids include:
'A. T. Johnson' Yellow with more heavy red blotching than *luteus*.

*Below:* Mimulus 'Lothian Fire'

'Queen's Prize' Lower growing with bright yellow flowers blotched velvety dark mauve. Not very hardy.
'Lothian Fire' Flowering copper scarlet with bushy dark-green foliage. All prefer wet soil or shallow water.

■ *Myosotis scorpioides (M. palustris),* (Water Forget-me-not)
Although some consider this plant to be rather weedy, it is easy to control, and produces dainty sky-blue flowers over a long period. The stems ramble out across the water surface with their lush green leaves and will creep up into the bog garden or camouflage the edge of a planting container. The plants are not reliably perennial, but will set seed, and if you spread a number of cuttings around the pool, a good few will survive.
Depth: Moist soil to 8cm (3in)
Height: 15cm (6in)
Sunshine: Full sun to half shade
Flowering time: Early to late summer

*Above:* Myosotis scorpioides

■ *Myriophyllum aquaticum (M. proserpinacoides, M. braziliense)* (Parrot's Feather)
A very attractive and adaptable plant with pink stems clothed in bright

*Below:* Myriophyllum aquaticum

*Above:* Orontium aquaticum

green feathery foliage, which pops up out of the water. It will grow in a range of depths, but must be well below the ice to survive the winter.
Depth: 8-30cm (3-12in)
Height: 10cm (4in)
Sunshine: Full sun or half shade

■ *Orontium aquaticum* (Golden Club)
An interesting plant with sea green leaves with a silvery sheen. The unusual yellow and white, poker-like flowers emerge from the water and later produce pea-sized seeds. The plant is slow growing, but looks impressive when established and has a large root system, which prefers a good-sized container.
Depth: 8-25cm (3-10in)
Height: 22cm (9in)
Sunshine: Full sun or slight shade
Flowering time: Early summer

■ *Peltandra virginica* (*P. undulata*) (Arrow Arum)
A slow grower from North America, which eventually produces attractive clumps of lush, shiny, arrow-shaped leaves. The pale green arum-type flowers are followed by lime-green berries. There is a white flowering form, *P. alba (P. sagittifolia)*, which is shorter growing and less robust. It has red berries.
Depth: 8-12cm (3-5in)
Height: 50cm (20in)
Sunshine: Full sun or slight shade
Flowering time: Midsummer

■ *Pontederia cordata* (Pickerel)
Bold clumps of spear-shaped leaves on spongy stems, producing spiked clusters of blue flowers over many weeks in late summer, after most other marginals have finished flowering. There is a white form, and a deeper mauvey-blue form. *P. lanceo-*

*Above:* Pontederia cordata

**lata** is taller with narrow leaves and blue flowers, but is less hardy in winter. All these plants need sufficient water cover in winter to prevent the roots becoming frozen, and all do better in large deep containers.
Depth: 8-15cm (3-6in)
Height: 45-60cm (18-24in)
Sunshine: Full sun
Flowering time: Mid to late summer

■ *Preslia cervina*
An aromatic plant with narrow-toothed leaves on tall stems and clusters of lilac-mauve flowers. It is a relative of the mint family and, though less invasive than most mints, is still best containerized.
Depth: 8-12cm (3-5in)
Height: 30-45cm (12-18in)
Sunshine: Full sun or slight shade
Flowering time: Late summer

*Above:* Preslia cervina

■ *Ranunculus lingua grandiflora* (Giant spearwort)
The spear-shaped, pink-tinged leaves push up out of the water in early spring and develop into narrow green leaves on tall stems, topped with

giant, glistening buttercup flowers. You should definitely containerize this vigorous grower to keep the runners in check.
Depth: 5-12cm (2-5in)
Height: 60-75cm (24-30in)
Sunshine: Full sun or half shade
Flowering time: Mid or late summer

■ *Sagittaria japonica* (*S. sagittifolia var. leucopetala*) (Japanese Arrowhead)
The arrowheads produce arrow-shaped leaves in early summer and flowers in late summer. The roots run out from the main plant, forming bulb-like growths at their tips that will form new plants the following year. *Sagittaria* needs a large container to grow well. *S. japonica* has white flowers with a yellow centre; *S. j. plena* has exceptional, double, clear white flowers, which are sadly short lived; *S. sagittifolia* is the common arrowhead, slightly shorter and with dark centres to the white flowers.
Depth: 8-12cm (3-5in)
Height: 45cm (18in)
Sunshine: Full sun
Flowering time: Mid or late summer

■ *Saururus cernuus* (Lizard's Tail)
The heart-shaped leaves are pale green and the white blooms, in a long snake-like cluster, are slightly fragrant. It is best containerized to restrict its invasive roots.
Depth: 5-12cm (2-5in)
Height: 45cm (18in)
Sunshine: Full sun to slight shade
Flowering time: Mid to late summer

■ *Scirpus albescens* (Striped Bulrush)
A very useful foliage plant for the larger water garden, with tall rush-like stems, striped horizontally with white and pale green. It needs a large basket to contain the strong root

*Below:* Scirpus albescens

system and give the plant stability in winds. The tops of the stems have brown flowering tufts in the summer.
Depth: 5-15cm (2-6in)
Height: 100-130cm (40-52in)
Sunshine: Full sun or half shade

■ *S. zebrinus* (*S. tabernaemontae zebrinus*) (Zebra Rush)
Less vigorous than *S. albescens* and has banded green and white foliage.
Depth: 5-12cm (2-5in)
Height: 80-100cm (30-42in)

*Above:* Scirpus zebrinus

■ *Typha spp.* (Reedmace, Cat's tail, Cattail)
These plants, with their characteristic brown poker-like heads, are some of the best-known waterside aquatics. Choose a variety that will not outgrow your pond. Use a large container for a decent-sized clump and to restrict the penetrating root system. The pokers start to appear in early summer.
*T. angustifolia* A medium-sized form suited to most ponds. *T. stenophylla* (*T. laxmanii*) is similar but slightly smaller with narrower leaves.
Depth: 5-20cm (2-8in)
Height: 120cm (48in)

*Below:* Typha angustifolia

*Above:* Typha minima

**T. latifolia** A giant variety for large ponds and lakes, with broader leaves and thick 'cattails'. There is also a variegated form.
Depth: 8-30cm (3-12in)
Height: 200-250cm (80-100in)
**T. minima** The only variety suited to the small pond, with narrow rush-like foliage and drumstick heads.
Depth: Bog to 10cm (4in)
Height: 60-75cm (24-30in)
■ **Veronica beccabunga** (Brooklime) Waxy, oval, dark-green leaves are clothed in tiny blue flowers. Best containerized, and not recommended for bog gardens, where it can seed rather too prolifically.
Depth: Moist soil to 10cm (4in) cover
Height: 15cm (6in)
Sunshine: Full sun or half shade
Flowering time: Mid and late summer

*Above:* Zantedeschia aethiopica

■ **Zantedeschia aethiopica**
Striking arum flowers with golden centres between the large, waxy, dark-green arrow-shaped leaves. The flowers last three to four weeks, and are followed by yellow berries.

Usually thought of as a border plant, it is quite at home in the water, but lower it well below the ice level in winter. There are various cultivars: '**Crowborough**' is slightly smaller and reputedly hardier than the common form; '**Green Goddess**' is much taller with green-tipped flowers.
Depth: Moist soil – 20cm (8in)
Height: 40-75cm (16-30in)
Sunshine: Full sun
Flowering time: Midsummer

## TENDER AQUATICS AND MARGINALS

The following plants are particularly suitable for warmer climates:

■ **Aponogeton desertorum** (*A. kraussianum*)
Similar to the water hawthorn, *A. distachyus* (see page 95) with creamy yellow blooms held out of the water.
■ **Canna spp.**
Yellow, orange and pink flowers borne on tall stems, with blue-green, broad, pointed leaves. These marginals need a rich, regularly fertilized soil.
Depth: 5-20cm (2-8in)
Height: 150cm (60in)
Sunshine: Full sun
Flowering time: Mid and late summer
■ **Colocasia spp.** (Taro)
Enormous leaves droop from the tall stems, giving the plant its common name of 'Elephant Ear'. Some varieties have purplish rather than dark green leaves.
Depth: 5-10cm (2-4in)
Height: to 120cm (48in)
Sunshine: Full sun or slight shade
■ **Cyperus haspan viviparus**
Similar to *C. alternifolius* (see page 97), this plant has tall stems ending in dense clusters of brown spikelets, which may lean over into the water. Where heads touch

*Below:* Canna spp.

*Above:* Hydrocleys nymphoides

the water, a new plant arises.
Depth: 5-10cm (2-4in)
Height: 60cm (24in)
Sunshine: Full sun or slight shade
■ **Hydrocleys nymphoides** (Water poppy)
Similar to *Nymphoides peltata* (see page 95) but with thick, shiny oval leaves and three-petalled yellow flowers, which open flat.
■ **Marsilia mutica**
The hardy four-leaf water clover is a very popular aquatic in the USA.
■ **Nymphoides indica** (Water Snowflake)
Similar to the hardy *N. peltata*, *N. indica* has star-shaped flowers, and purple-tinged green leaves.
■ **Thalia dealbata** (Hardy Water Canna)
This attractive plant needs some winter protection, despite its name. The tall stems support glaucous green leaves, which are elongated and often held horizontally. The unusual purplish flowers are held between bract-like axils on top of tall stems.
Depth: 5-10cm (2-4in)
Height: 120-180cm (48-72in)
■ **Zantedeschia spp.** Brightly coloured tender hybrids in yellows, oranges and reds. *Z. elliotana* has yellow arums and smooth green leaves flecked white.

# OXYGENATORS
## (Submerged Plants)

These plants are essential for a well-balanced pond, but the various species grow most vigorously at different times of year and originate from waters of very different conditions. Not all will thrive in your particular pool, so grow a variety of oxygenators, and top up, if necessary, with those species that grow well.

Oxygenators are generally sold in bunches of cuttings and, with few exceptions, need to be planted into shallow containers (7-10cm/3-4in deep) of heavy soil. Push in the bases of the oxygenators and top off with gravel – a 20cm (8in)- square container should hold around six bunches – the cuttings will soon root. The lead weights sometimes sold with them usually cause no harm. Do not mix varieties in the same container. You can grow oxygenators on the pool shelf, and in deeper water (up to 100cm/40in), but do not put newly planted baskets into deep water if it is too cloudy for light to penetrate.

■ *Callitriche spp.* (Starwort)
Attractive plants with delicate bright green leaves, which form star-shaped rosettes when they reach the surface. Most species only grow well in harder water.
■ *Ceratophyllum demersum* (Hornwort)
An excellent underwater plant with slightly brittle, bristly, mid to dark green foliage. It does not root like other oxygenators and need only be anchored to the base with a stone or small lead weight.
■ *Crassula helmsii/Tilloea recurva* (Pygmyweed, Swamp Stonecrop)
Often offered for sale, but really too vigorous and capable of smothering other plants.
■ *Egeria densa* (Elodea densa)
Similar to the Canadian pondweed but with longer mid-green leaves. A strong grower but not hardy in areas with icy winters.
■ *Eleocharis acicularis* (Hairgrass)
A decorative, bright-green, grasslike plant that grows sideways in its container, rarely attaining a height of more than 20cm (8in).
■ *Elodea canadensis/Anacharis* (Canadian pondweed)
Small dark green leaves clothe the brittle stems. A vigorous grower and a good oxygenator.
■ *Fontinalis antipyretica* (Willow Moss)
A dark green plant with narrow stems clothed in leaflets. Slow growing and preferring slightly moving, clear water.
■ *Hottonia palustris* (Water Violet)
Delicate and finely cut bright green foliage, which thrusts clusters of pale pink flowers up into the air in early summer. A beautiful plant for shallower water. It prefers soft water and slight shade and can prove difficult to establish.
■ *Lagarosiphon major* (Elodea crispa)
Very easy to establish, with long stems clothed in dark green leaves, which curl back on themselves.

*Above:* Lagarosiphon major

■ *Myriophyllum spp.* (Milfoil)
A variety of species with very fine feathery foliage in shades of green, olive and brown. Some push tiny flower spikes a few centimetres (an inch) out of the water in early summer. They can tolerate deep water once established, but can become entangled with thread algae.
■ *Potamogeton crispus* (Curled pondweed)
One of a family of vigorous pondweeds, this plant is less rampant with long, crinkled, translucent green leaves. Small pink-tinged flower spikes are produced in early summer. It must be very fresh if it is to transplant and root well, and does best in slow-moving water.
■ *Ranunculus spp.* (Water crowsfoot)
An excellent family of oxygenators with finely cut green foliage and small white flowers held above the water in early summer. It becomes dormant after flowering, and may partially die back. Of its many species, those with small floating leaves tend to suit still pond water better.

*Above:* Ranunculus fluitans

*Above:* Ranunculus peltatus

## OXYGENATORS FOR WARMER CLIMATES

Although most underwater aquatics will tolerate warmer water, some may become rather drawn and straggly. Where the temperature regularly exceeds 18°C (65°F), you could try *Cabomba spp.; Egeria densa; Hygrophila difformis* (Water Wisteria) with emergent leaves, or the decorative *Ludwigia spp.; Sagittaria natans;* and the useful *Vallisneria spp.*

# FLOATING PLANTS

Floating plants are simply placed onto the water surface, their roots hanging down into the water. Larger floating plants may take a few days to gain their balance, but the smaller carpeting types normally settle quickly. Remove excessive growth if the plants become too rampant.

There are a limited number of ornamental floating plants native to temperate regions, but many exotic subtropical species are imported to supplement the variety. In frost-free climates, floating plants can become pests and in some countries or states their sale is restricted or prohibited. Elsewhere treat such plants as annuals, replacing them with new stock each year, after the last spring frosts, or keep them in a sunny, heated conservatory pond, or float them indoors in a bowl of water with a handful of soil to provide nutrients.

■ *Azolla spp.* (Fairy Moss, Water Fern)
An attractive carpeting floater. The fronds, which are only 1-3cm (0.5-1in) in size, are rich green in colour, turning a pinkish red in cool weather. The plants can spread very rapidly, so do not introduce them to large ponds or lakes. Winter frosts knock back its growth.

■ *Eichhornia spp.* (Water Hyacinths)
These unusual plants have swollen leaf bases that give them buoyancy.

*Below:* Azolla spp.

*Above:* Eichhornia crassipes

Their long trailing roots hang down into the water and are often used as spawning sites by fish. The waxy green leaves grow quite tall in hot weather, when the plant produces eye-catching lilac flowers, but, like many floating plants, the water hyacinth is frost sensitive.

■ *Hydrocharis morsus-ranae* (Frogbit)
A dainty plant with small, round, floating leaves no more than 7cm (2.5in) across, producing tiny, short-lived white flowers in succession in late summer. The plants send out side runners and have long, trailing roots. A fairly hardy aquatic, which drops overwintering buds (turions) to the pond base.

■ *Lemna spp.* (Duckweed)
A hardy plant with tiny, bright-green leaves, which can run riot in nutrient-rich water. Most varieties are best avoided, but **L. trisulca** (Ivy leaved duckweed), is much less invasive and has small angular leaves in translucent green that hang just below the water's surface. It is often eaten by larger fish. US federal law prohibits interstate commercial transport of duckweed and possession is prohibited in some southern states.

■ *Pistia stratiotes* (Water lettuce)
The spongy green leaves have a slightly hairy surface and form floating rosettes on the water's surface, with dangling roots. This is another frost-sensitive species. Possession is prohibited in parts of southern USA.

■ *Stratiotes aloides* (Water Soldier)
This unusual plant looks like a pineapple top, with its translucent spiny leaves. It may sink to the pond base, especially during the winter; in summer it floats half submerged, the leaves changing from translucent mauve-green to a brighter apple green. A small white flower rises just out of the water. A hardy plant with side shoots which can be snipped off and moved elsewhere.

■ *Trapa natans* (Water chestnut)
The reddish stems are buoyant and swollen, resting just below the water and radiating out to rosettes of dark-green, serrated leaves. In hot weather a small white flower is produced. Roots trail down into the water. An attractive, but not a hardy plant. It is prohibited in the USA.

*Above:* Trapa natans

■ *Utricularia spp.* (Bladderwort)
These very unusual plants – some of them hardy – have finely divided foliage that floats just below the water's surface. The foliage contains tiny bladders, which can catch small aquatic insects. Small yellow flowers are produced above the water in late summer. Bladderwort prefers softer water.

*Below:* Pistia stratiotes

# MOISTURE-LOVING PLANTS

Many varieties of plant will grow in moist soil and bog areas and look particularly fitting at the pool edge. If the soil by your pool is not naturally damp, then you will either have to create a bog area (see page 55), or use plants more tolerant of the dry conditions.

Moisture plants, like most hardy garden perennials, are best moved during the spring or autumn, but you can transfer container-grown plants during the summer, providing you protect their roots from drying out. Remember that while some moisture-loving plants will tolerate wet conditions – even temporary residence on a marginal shelf, others will die if their soil becomes waterlogged.

■ *Astilbe*
There are numerous hybrids and cultivars of this adaptable and attractive plant with its dense ferny foliage and bright plumes of feathery flowers. Excellent all-rounders.
Moisture: 1-2
Height: 40-100cm (16-40in)
Sunshine: Full sun to slight shade
Flowering time: Late summer to early autumn
■ *Athyrium filix-foemina minutissima* (Dwarf Lady Fern)
There are a great many ferns suited to the poolside, all of which must have either moisture or shade, and do not like windy positions. *Athyrium* has bright green spring foliage.
Moisture: 1-2
Height: 30cm (1ft)

*Above:* Astilbe

■ *Darmera peltata (Peltiphyllum peltatum*, Umbrella Plant)
An ideal foliage plant for the side of larger ponds. The numerous large leaves are over 30cm (12in) across and borne on tall stems, preceded by umbels of pinky flowers. Dwarf forms are available for more limited spaces.
Moisture: 2-3
Height: 100-120cm (40-48in)
Sunshine: Full sun or half shade
Flowering time: Spring
■ *Gunnera manicata*
This immense rhubarb-like plant with prickly leaves is best planted at a lake or riverside. The seedhead is pinecone shaped, with a bundle of finger-like projections up to 60cm (24in) high. *G. scabra* is slightly smaller and hardier. Cover crowns with the dead leaves in winter to protect from frost. May not survive very hot summers.
Moisture: 2-3
Height: 200cm (78in)
Sunshine: Full sun or half shade
■ *Hemerocallis* (Day Lily)
Grassy rush-like foliage is complemented by a long succession of short-lived, trumpet-like flowers, which are often fragrant. There are a great many cultivars and a floriferous yellow-flowered species, *H. flava*.
Moisture: 0-3
Height: 60-120cm (24-48in)
Sunshine: Full sun or slight shade
Flowering time: Late summer to autumn

*Above:* Hemerocallis 'Stafford'

■ *Hosta spp.* (Plantain Lily)
Bold foliage and tall stems of drooping, usually lilac, flowers. Generally very adaptable. The variegated forms keep their colours better in part shade. New varieties appear every year, and named cultivars can vary depending upon whom you buy from, so try to see the plants first.

*Below:* Hosta spp.

*Below:* Gunnera manicata

## RECOMMENDED MOISTURE LEVELS

0 Tolerates temporarily dry conditions.
1 Prefers soil that does not dry out.
2 Prefers more moist, rich soils, but not waterlogged.
3 Tolerates boggy, saturated conditions.

Moisture: 0-3
Height: 20-100cm (8-40in)
Sunshine: Full sun or half shade
Flowering time: Mid and late summer
■ *Iris spp.*
There are two main species of iris used in the bog garden. The Japanese Clematis Iris, *I. ensata (I. kaempferi)*, which has enormous flattened blooms in blues, mauves and whites, also has a variegated form with rich velvety purple blooms. The Siberian Iris, *I. sibirica,* has smaller, usually dark blue flowers above narrower leaves-.They all prefer moist, peat-enriched soil, and are intolerant of waterlogging, particularly in the winter.
Moisture: 1-2
Height: 75-90cm (30-36in)
Sunshine: Full sun or slight shade
Flowering time: Midsummer

*Above:* Iris ensata

■ *Lysichitum spp.*
The immense arum-like flowers appear in early spring and are followed by large leaves. The plants are slow growing with a greedy root system and it may be three or four years before they flower. *L. americanum* has shiny yellow spathes; those of the smaller *L. camtschatcense* are white.
Moisture: 2-3
Height: 50-120cm (18-48in)
Sunshine: Full sun or half shade
Flowering time: Mid to late spring
■ *Matteuccia struthiopteris* (Ostrich Feather Fern)
Unfurling shuttlecock-like foliage.
Moisture: 2-3
Height: Up to 90cm (36in)
■ *Osmunda regalis* (Royal Fern)
Tall green fronds with autumn colours and tall brown spore-bearing fronds.
Moisture: 2-3.
Height: Up to 120cm (48in)

■ *Primula spp.*
A superb range of plants with brightly coloured flowers. Few will tolerate wet conditions, preferring a moist, yet free-draining soil – for example, a good loam mixed with peat and grit. Split plants every two to three years in spring, and mulch occasionally with a nutrient-rich compost.

There are many species, including the midsummer flowering 'candelabra' types, *beesiana* and *bulleyana* (mauve pinks and pale oranges); *helodoxa* (bright yellow); *inverewe* (tall and bright red); *japonica* cultivars; *pulverulenta* (wine-crimson). There are also the tall, later-flowering forms with drooping bell-shaped blooms, some of which are very fragrant. These include *alpicola* (cream or violet); *cantab* (red, flushed orange); *florindae* and *sikkimensis* (yellow). Spring colour is provided by the variously coloured drumstick primula, *denticulata,* and the low-growing pink-flowered *rosea*.
Moisture: 2
Height: 15-90cm (6-36in)
Sunshine: Full sun to half shade

*Above:* Primula spp.

■ *Rheum palmatum rubrum*
A giant ornamental rhubarb, with red suffused young leaves and tall red flower plumes.
Moisture: 2
Height: 200cm (78in)
Sunshine: Slight to half shade
Flowering time: Midsummer
■ *Rodgersia spp.*
Good foliage plants for roomy yet sheltered situations. Slow but reliable growers with tall flower clusters in cream or pink. Best forms include the chestnut-leaved *aesculifolia* and bronze-leaved *pinnata* cultivars.

*Above:* Rodgersia spp.

Moisture: 2-3
Height: 120cm (48in)
Sunshine: Slight shade
Flowering time: Mid to late summer
■ *Schizostylis* (Kaffir lily)
Various cultivars with freesia-like flowers in reds, pinks and white. Useful late flowering. Cover with protective mulch in winter.
Moisture: 1-3
Height: 40cm (16in)
Sunshine: Full sun
Flowering time: Late autumn
■ *Scrophularia aquatica variegata* (Variegated Figwort)
Tall green foliage heavily splashed white. Unspectacular red flowers.
Moisture: 1-3
Height: 1m (40in)
Sunshine: Full sun to half shade
Flowering time: Late summer
■ *Trollius spp.* (Globe flower)
Attractive yellow or orange flowers on tall stems above non-invasive buttercup-like foliage.
Moisture: 1-3
Height: 60cm (24in)
Sunshine: Full sun or slight shade
Flowering time: Midsummer

*Below:* Trollius spp.

# CHAPTER SIX

# POND FISH

When you have installed your pond, why not add some livestock? Ornamental fish add extra year-round colour, and their graceful movements below the surface complement the ripples from fountains and waterfalls. They also help to keep down the levels of unwanted midge larvae and mosquitoes. Many gardeners, who start by adding a few fish to a pond, become engrossed in a whole new hobby.

A variety of ornamental fish are available for ponds; a popular first choice is the common goldfish, which is adaptable, hardy, and breeds readily. A shoal of graceful orfe suits a large pond, and for the enthusiast there are other, more exotic fish, such as the imposing koi, with its myriad of pattern and colour combinations.

Fish have a few simple requirements, which you should consider while planning your pond. Most self-contained fountain ornaments and small, shallow water features are not suitable for fish, which need sufficient volume and depth of water and reasonable water quality to thrive. A minimum of upkeep, and basic commonsense, will usually be enough to maintain the water quality and keep the fish in good condition. If the pond is sparsely stocked with fish, there may be enough plant and animal life to sustain them. However, most pondkeepers enjoy feeding their fish, encouraging them to become tame. Some fish varieties, most notably koi, have a few extra requirements and these are described in the following section.

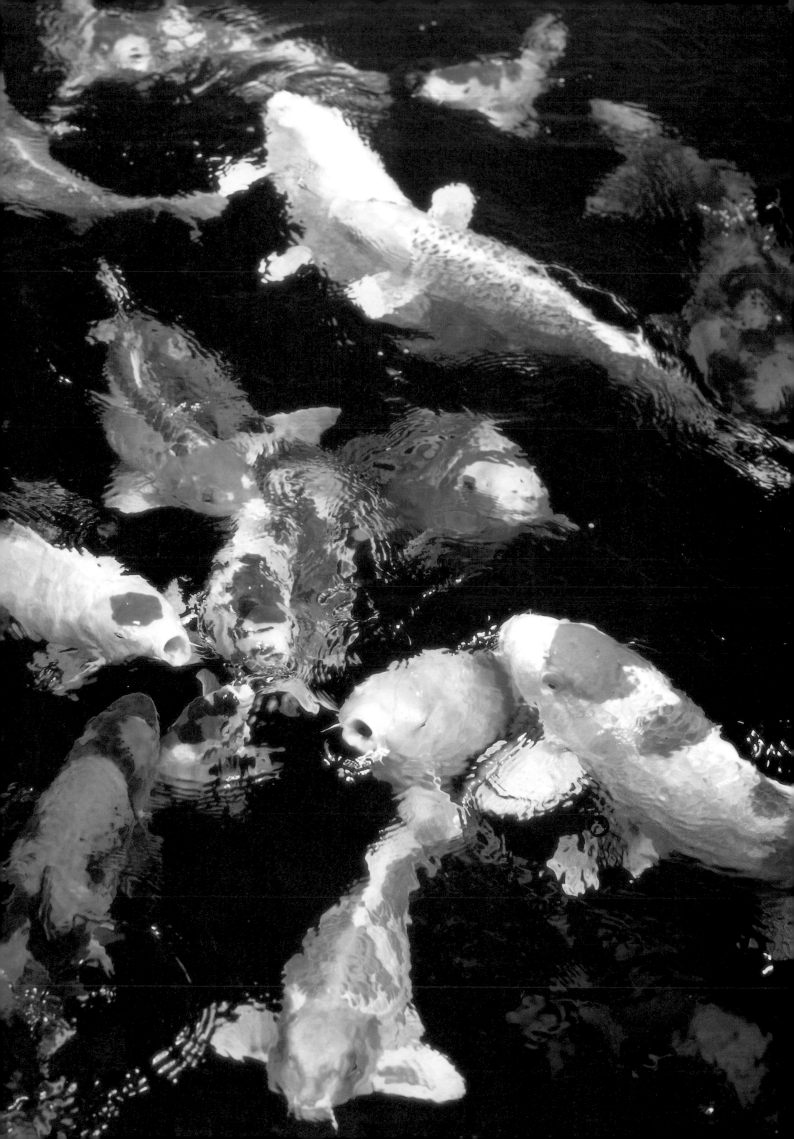

# INTRODUCING FISH TO THE POND

Although you can introduce fish to the pond almost as soon as it is completed, it is much more sensible to wait a while. The plants, in particular the oxygenators (submerged plants), need at least three to four weeks to root and establish. After this, you may safely add fish, but a longer wait may help the pond to achieve clear, balanced conditions more quickly.

Take care not to add too many fish too soon. Add a few fish in two stages during the pond's first season, leaving enough room for more to be added in future years. A limiting factor on the number of fish that you can keep is the level of oxygen in the water; this relates to the surface area of the pond exposed to the air, so calculate the surface area to find out how many fish you should introduce.

The best time of year to introduce fish is late spring through to late summer. In early spring, fish are often weak after their winter rest, and prone to stress from chills; and in the autumn, fish have less time to settle into their new surrounds before the winter arrives. Always avoid moving fish when the temperature falls below 10°C (50°F); at lower temperatures they are more sluggish and their natural immune system is less able to cope with stress and disease. (Very high temperatures – over 32°C/90°F – are also stressful to fish.)

## CHOOSING FISH

Always buy healthy stock, avoiding bargains of dubious quality. Go to a reputable supplier, and spend some time looking at the fish, to ensure that they are fit and well, before you buy. Healthy fish are lively, with erect rather than clamped fins, and their skin and fins appear unragged and free from cloudiness, wounds or bumps. In summer weather, the fish should not be sitting motionless on the base of their tank, hanging torpidly near the surface, or constantly flicking on their sides as if scratching themselves. The occasional slight nick in a fin is not a major problem, providing there is no sign of infection.

If some fish in a tank are unwell, it is better not to buy any fish from that tank. Check also to see that the fish are being kept in good conditions.

Very small fish may be frail and prone to problems, and very large fish can be much more expensive and sometimes take a little longer to settle into a new environment. Choose a few medium-sized fish (7-15cm/2.5-6in) in each type, rather than single specimens, as a group will be less nervous, will settle more quickly, and will probably include males and females.

## RECOMMENDED NUMBERS OF FISH FOR THE POND

In a new pond, introduce no more than 25cm length of fish (including tail) for every square metre of surface area (1in per square foot); for example, a pond of five square metres could have up to 125cm of fish initially, i.e. around a dozen 10cm fish, (12×4in fish in a pond of around 50ft²).

This allows plenty of space for the fish to settle, grow and reproduce. In future years, when the pond has fully established, you could add more fish.

The maximum recommended stock for established ponds is 50-75cm length of fish for every square metre of surface area (2-3in per square foot). Higher stocking levels are possible if the water is well filtered and the water quality monitored, but consider such stocking rates with great caution.

**The anatomy of a koi**

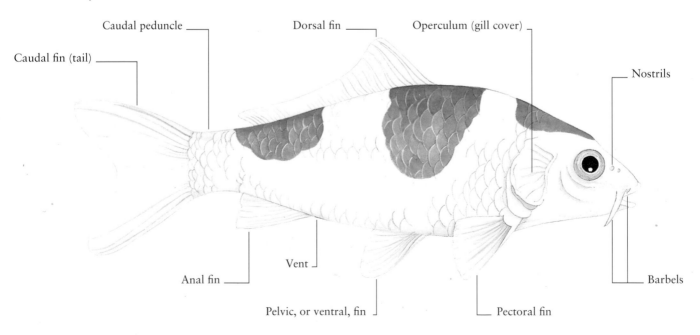

Caudal peduncle — Dorsal fin — Operculum (gill cover)

Caudal fin (tail) —

Nostrils

Anal fin —

Vent

Barbels

Pelvic, or ventral, fin

Pectoral fin

them to the water surface and into a floating bag or bowl of water, which you can then lift out. If your hands are wet, you may temporarily touch or handle the fish gently, but dry hands or nets can remove the protective mucus from the fish.

*Left: Take care to choose healthy fish from a reputable dealer. These small koi are active and looking for food; an indication that they are in good health. They should be packed carefully – using oxygen for long journeys, or if the weather is very hot.*

*Below: Large fish will struggle and can damage their fins if lifted out of the water in a net. Instead, as here, use a pan net to guide a koi along the surface and into a floating basket or bowl. It can then be examined, or transferred into a bag if it needs to be moved.*

## TRANSPORTING FISH

Carry your fish home as quickly as possible; let the supplier know if you have a long journey, so that the fish can be packaged accordingly. Fish are normally packed in polythene bags with a small amount of water and plenty of air. For long journeys the air in the fish bag can be enriched with oxygen and the bag insulated against temperature change.

Rapid changes in temperature can severely stress fish, so it is important to acclimatize them gradually to your pond temperature. Float the bag for at least 20 minutes – up to 40 minutes for bags with large volumes of water, keeping it sheltered from strong sun. When you release the fish, they will often hide and may take up to a month to settle fully; don't disturb them unnecessarily and don't expect them to feed straight away.

## NETTING FISH

You may need to net fish sometimes, for example when draining the pond for cleaning. Choose a net with a long sturdy handle, an opening at least as big as your largest fish, and a mesh that is fine enough not to damage the fish, and yet coarse enough not to impede water flow. Avoid lifting fish out of the water, especially larger fish (over 20cm/8in long), instead direct

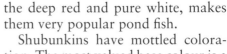

# GOLDFISH

Goldfish are popular throughout the world and make excellent pond fish. They originated in Southern China as coloured varieties of a native, dull-brown fish, and were being kept as pets before 1000AD. Since then they have spread around the world, and intensive selective breeding has resulted in the wide diversity of forms available today. The popularity of goldfish is partly due to their great adaptability. Although they are stressed by sudden changes, they can tolerate temperatures from 0°-32°C (32°-90°F), and can withstand mild pollution and low oxygen levels for short periods. They become quite tame and will rise to the surface to be fed. Comets, shubunkins, and red and white varieties are almost as hardy as the common goldfish, and ideal for the garden pond.

Common goldfish (*Carassius auratus*) have colours ranging from intense reds, through golden oranges to pale yellowy orange. Creamy white forms also occur, with a matt appearance, as they lack the shiny layer of guanine material in their scales.

Comet-tailed goldfish have long flowing tails, occasionally as long again as the body. They move surprisingly quickly and look very graceful. Comet tails are often found on other varieties, notably red and white and shubunkin goldfish.

Red and white comets are often known as sarasa comets (a Japanese description) and vary from white fish marked with red, to red fish with white undersides. The great range of patterns, and strong contrast between the deep red and pure white, makes them very popular pond fish.

Shubunkins have mottled coloration. The most valued base colour is a rich blue, speckled with black and interspersed with regions of red, white and yellow. Paler and darker blue forms are frequently produced, along with more orangy red varieties, and they complement the bright reds of common goldfish. Shubunkins have a matt surface dotted with infrequent shiny scales, and can have short or long tails. The blue colour is due to black pigment deep in the skin, and may fade when the fish is stressed. The colours of all the varieties of goldfish may change as they grow older and can become very pale on elderly fish.

The wakin, or tri-tail, is a Japanese form of the common goldfish, often with a short double tail, slightly jointed at the top. This short 'fantail' gives it the more exotic look of fancy goldfish, but it is much hardier.

## FANCY GOLDFISH

A number of more delicate forms of goldfish have shortened bodies, in some cases almost egg shaped, and are collectively known as fancy goldfish.

The most popular is the fantail with its double tail, usually divided, but sometimes jointed at the top. It comes in red, red and white, and 'calico' (the term used to describe shubunkin-type colorations on fancy goldfish). The Japanese form of fantail has a high back and is known as a ryukin; the nymph is a single-tailed fantail produced in North America.

Moors are jet-black fantails with 'telescope' eyes, which protrude eerily from their heads. Red and calico forms of telescope-eyed fish are also available, but are not as popular.

Orandas have short dumpy bodies, like fantails, but their heads are covered with an interesting growth, similar in appearance to a raspberry. There is a variety of colours, one of the most striking being a white fish with a red hood, the red-cap. All the above fancy goldfish can be found in veiltail forms, with long flowing tails, which are much more delicate.

The lionhead is similar to the oranda, but without a dorsal fin. It is a slow grower, and its lack of dorsal fin accounts for its rather quaint wiggling motion through the water. Bubble

*Below: Their bright colours, active nature, and great adaptability make goldfish one of the most popular and widely available species of pond fish.*

eyes and celestials, like lionheads, have no dorsal fin, but are without the oranda-type hood. The bubble eye has a strange jelly-like sac under each eye, and the celestial has protruding eyes, which point upwards; both are rather delicate fish, best appreciated when viewed from above.

These are some of the many fancy varieties available – intriguing or grotesque, according to your point of view. All can interbreed, although it is wiser to keep the more delicate varieties separate. Do not keep them with larger varieties of pond fish, such as koi, orfe and large common goldfish. Fancy goldfish are less hardy than the more common forms; their exotic finnage is more prone to damage and infection and can become entangled in thread algae. Their intestines are very compressed in their shortened bodies, and this can increase the risks of indigestion. If you feed them excessively with dried food, it will swell up inside the fish, putting pressure on the small internal air sacs (the swim bladder),

*Below: Chocolate orandas, bubble-eyes, red orandas and red-cap lionheads are a few of the many fancy forms. All benefit from over-wintering indoors.*

*Above: Shubunkins are goldfish with matt blue-tinted skins speckled with other colours. They will crossbreed with other goldfish.*

causing fish to lose their balance, and float to the surface or sink to the base. In severe cases, permanent damage can result. To avoid this, feed fancy goldfish on moistened foods, and intersperse their diet with commercial frozen foods containing bloodworm or daphnia. Micro-pellet dry foods are preferable to flake foods, but you should pre-soak both to drive out air and allow them to swell.

You can keep fancy goldfish in outdoor ponds and they can even tolerate low temperatures, but they may succumb in winter and are generally better suited to conservatory ponds and aquariums, where the temperature rarely falls below 13°C (55°F).

## FACT BOX

- Maximum size: 35-40cm (14-16in); fancy forms 25-35cm (10-14in); goldfish tend to grow in proportion to their surrounds.
- Maximum age: 15-25 years (fancy forms 8-12 years).
- Maturity: 18-30 months.
- Sexing: females are plumper, and males have spawning tubercles on their gill plates and pectoral fins during the spawning season.

# KOI

Koi are coloured ornamental carp. *Cyprinus carpio*, the common carp, originated in Asia, and became widespread due to its value as a food fish. Common carp are too drab to be recommended as ornamental pond fish, although the mirror-scaled form is sometimes kept in aquariums, where the large, shiny side scales can be best appreciated.

Koi originate from the Niigata prefecture of Japan, where the local villagers started to grow carp for food in the early seventeenth century, using the flooded rice paddies as ponds. They picked out the unusually coloured fish that occasionally occurred and bred them selectively. During the nineteenth century distinctive colour varieties were stabilized, including red and white forms and yellowish blue forms. New colour patterns continued to appear and many new varieties emerged during the first half of this century. The Japanese used the term nishikigoi (brocaded carp) to describe these beautifully patterned fish.

The koi trade expanded rapidly in the 1950s and 1960s, due to the much-improved methods of transporting fish. Today koi are produced in many areas of Japan and exported worldwide. They are also bred in other parts of the world – Israel, Southeast Asia and the USA are the other major sources of supply – but Japan is still the home of koi.

Koi, with their exceptional range of colour patterns, imposing size and tameness, have become very popular pond fish. They grow much larger than goldfish and have a distinctive head shape with barbels by their mouth. They are always on the lookout for food, and will come to the surface readily if they think they might be fed. Sharing many of the characteristics of the wild carp, they are tolerant of a wide range of water qualities and temperatures. Although tough and resilient, they are not quite as robust as the wild carp or common goldfish, because they are inbred.

*Above: The Kohaku is one of the most popular varieties of koi with contrasting red markings on a white ground. The edges to the red areas should be clearly defined.*

## KOI CARE

Unlike goldfish, which tend to grow in proportion to the size of their surrounds, koi keep on growing; if kept in enclosed quarters, they will become slightly stunted, but will continue to grow at a slower rate. This makes them unsuitable as longterm inhabitants of small ponds. You should give them plenty of room and deeper water, ideally 120cm (48in) or more at the centre of the pool, which should have a bottom drain. You will need to plan carefully before beginning construction on such a large pond.

Koi are not suited to typical garden ponds, as their strong lips can churn up detritus on the pool base, and they will chomp at soft-leaved plants. Unless you have only very few koi and use plants of sturdy growth, you will need to greatly reduce planting and introduce a filtration system to keep the pond water clear and healthy. An effective filter may be expensive, but is almost essential if you keep many koi (see pages 125-127). Koi will mix happily with most other pond fish, although many koi-keepers prefer to keep them on their own.

Feed koi on high-quality foods to encourage good growth and colouring, but don't feed them in low temperatures; in Japan, koi are used to severe, short winters, but they find long winters very stressful. Minimize the effects of the cold by providing shelter from winds, or insulating covers, and protect precious koi from marauders, such as herons.

*Below: Koi were first produced in the mountainous regions of Niigata in Japan, and many high-quality fish are still farmed there in the flooded terrace ponds.*

## CHOOSING KOI

When choosing koi, look for healthy fish and pick out bold colours that will be a feature in your pond. The prices of fish are related to the quality of the patterns and colours and the origins of the fish, as well as their overall size. Japanese fish are considered to have the best 'pedigree' and are generally more expensive. Koi do not breed true, and the most reputable breeders will have sorted through the fry (by hand) four times and rejected over

95% of the young koi by the time they reach 10cm (4in). Some are sold at this small size; those with the most potential are usually grown to larger sizes. A few of these selected fish, with the potential to improve their pattern, are sold at high prices. (These fish are known as 'tategoi' and have their own class at koi shows.)

Koi of 10-20cm (4-8in) are ideal for beginners to start with; 20-45cm (8-18in) fish are a good range to choose from when stocking larger ponds. Remember the great growth potential of

koi and leave plenty of room for them. Check that the dealer has given the fish sufficient time to settle and acclimatize after receiving them. Some koi-keepers quarantine their fish, but this is only worthwhile if you have suitable filtered facilities of a decent size. Cramped facilities are worse than useless. If you are in doubt about a koi's health, you would do best to avoid it, though you could ask the dealer to reserve it for a few weeks, and take it home once you are satisfied it is well. Before koi have settled in their new pond, they may try to jump out, especially if the pond is small, so put a tight-fitting net over the pond for the first few days.

*Right: A stunning variety of koi are produced. Here a tancho showa complements a shiny gold ogon – a variety particularly popular in the West.*

*Below: Specialist dealers often give valuable advice and may have a better selection of different varieties and sizes of koi from which you can choose.*

### FACT BOX

- Maximum size: some koi can grow to over 90cm (36in) in ideal conditions, but maximum size is usually 55-70cm (22-28in).
- Maximum age: generally 20 to 50 years old, but there are reports of fish over 100 years old.
- Maturity: 3-4 years.
- Sexing: males tend to be less plump than females and their gill plates have a sandpapery feel to them during the spawning season.

## VARIETIES OF KOI

The Japanese have set standards for the classification of the various colour patterns of koi, drawing up 14 major groups, 13 of which are shown on the right. Quality is judged not only on pattern, but also on colour, size, overall shape, appearance and skin condition. Kohaku, sanke and showa are very popular varieties in Japan – and in most other countries – and it is often difficult to obtain well-patterned youngsters at a reasonable price. Ogon are koi with a gold coloration and a metallic lustre, which are very popular in the West. Other varieties of ogon vary from silver and lemon yellow to deep orange, and metallic varieties of most of the other pattern groups have been created by crossing them with ogons.

Doitsu koi have smooth skins with or without large scales along the back and sides. These characteristics were originally transferred from German leather carp. Kinginrin is the group not shown in the illustrations and refers to koi that have glittery, sequin-like scales caused by irregularities in the scale surface. These 'gin-rin' koi (as they are commonly known) can be very attractive and come in the patterns of most of the other 13 classifications.

Most koi can be classified within one or other of the major groups, but there is such a diversity of patterns that you may not be able to give a detailed variety name to every koi, especially if the pattern or colour is of poor quality.

The patterns of koi can change, some varieties being more variable than others; reds can fade in some fish, whereas blues and greys tend to deepen with age, particularly in cool climates. The seemingly complex names of koi are often made from a combination of descriptive Japanese words, such as 'hi', meaning red, and 'shiro', meaning white.

Ghost koi are a cross between ogons and wild carp, with an overall grey or brown appearance and distinctive metallic edges to each scale. They are considered poor quality by the Japanese but can look impressive when large. Long-finned koi are a relatively new introduction – less hardy than ordinary koi – and it is uncertain whether they will continue to be produced in great numbers.

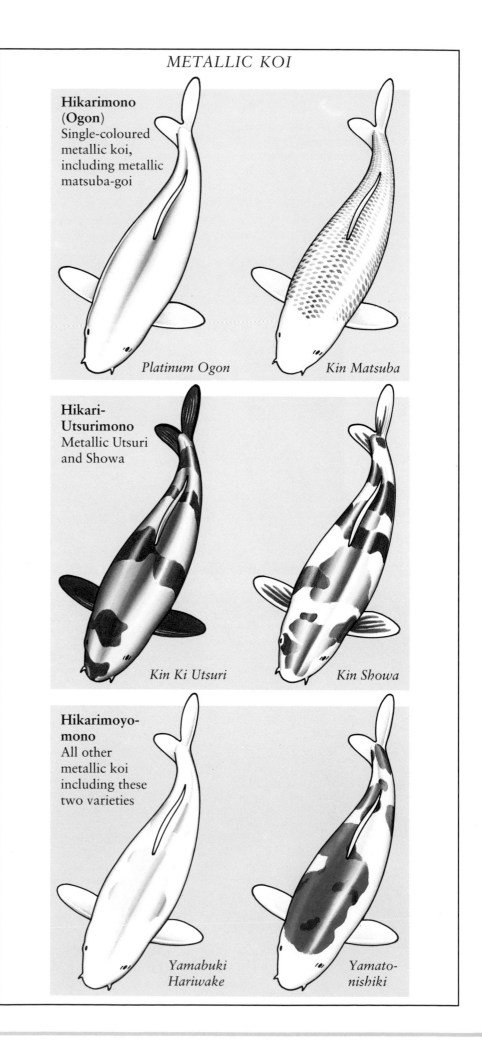

METALLIC KOI

**Hikarimono (Ogon)** Single-coloured metallic koi, including metallic matsuba-goi

Platinum Ogon

Kin Matsuba

**Hikari-Utsurimono** Metallic Utsuri and Showa

Kin Ki Utsuri

Kin Showa

**Hikarimoyo-mono** All other metallic koi including these two varieties

Yamabuki Hariwake

Yamato-nishiki

## NON-METALLIC KOI

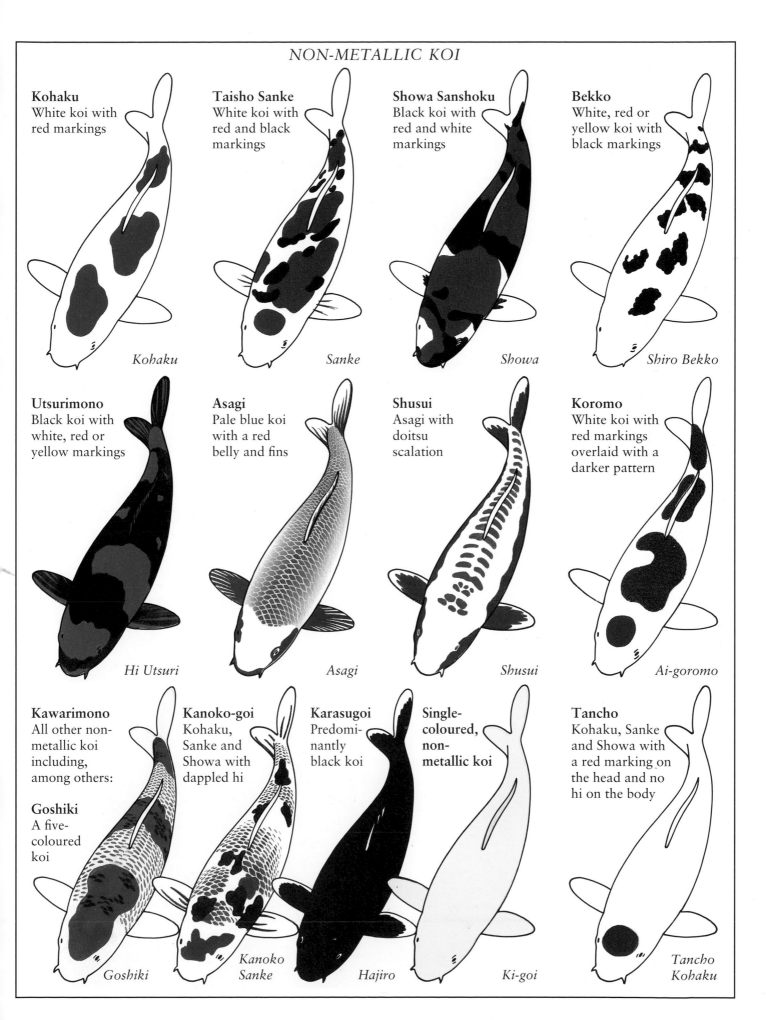

**Kohaku**
White koi with red markings

*Kohaku*

**Taisho Sanke**
White koi with red and black markings

*Sanke*

**Showa Sanshoku**
Black koi with red and white markings

*Showa*

**Bekko**
White, red or yellow koi with black markings

*Shiro Bekko*

**Utsurimono**
Black koi with white, red or yellow markings

*Hi Utsuri*

**Asagi**
Pale blue koi with a red belly and fins

*Asagi*

**Shusui**
Asagi with doitsu scalation

*Shusui*

**Koromo**
White koi with red markings overlaid with a darker pattern

*Ai-goromo*

**Kawarimono**
All other non-metallic koi including, among others:

**Goshiki**
A five-coloured koi

*Goshiki*

**Kanoko-goi**
Kohaku, Sanke and Showa with dappled hi

*Kanoko Sanke*

**Karasugoi**
Predominantly black koi

*Hajiro*

**Single-coloured, non-metallic koi**

*Ki-goi*

**Tancho**
Kohaku, Sanke and Showa with a red marking on the head and no hi on the body

*Tancho Kohaku*

# OTHER POND FISH

## GOLDEN ORFE
### (Leuciscus idus)

- Maximum size: 45-60cm (18-24in) in large ponds.
- Maximum age: over 15 years.
- Maturity: 4-6 years.
- Sexing: males have tiny tubercles on their body during the spawning season.

A hardy golden form of the European Ide, which lives in lakes and slow-moving rivers, Golden Orfe are an excellent choice for the larger pond. When viewed from above they have a narrow, torpedo-shaped body, and vary in colour from pale salmon-orange to a carrot hue, often with speckles of dark brown or black pigment on the head and along the back. They grow remarkably quickly and can put on a lot of weight.

In recent years a blue form of orfe has been developed. The colour is not particularly stable, being anaemic grey-blue on some fish, but on good specimens the intensity of pale blue is very attractive. They do not grow quite so fast as the golden form.

Orfe are quite active fish and will dart about the pond rapidly. They are most at ease when in a small shoal of half a dozen or more and once they have settled they will readily come to the surface for food. They also eat small underwater insect larvae, but do not stir up the base to the same extent as koi or goldfish. Like their wild form, they prefer well-oxygenated water, and benefit from water movement from a fountain or waterfall, especially in hot weather. They are not suited to small ponds as they will eventually outgrow them and may even jump out.

## GOLDEN RUDD
### (Scardinius erythropthalmus)

- Maximum size: 30cm (12in).
- Maturity: 2-3 years old. Rudd will spawn readily in large pools.

Quite similar in shape to orfe when viewed from above, the rudd's dorsal fin is set further back. Common rudd are a dull brown with red fins. The improved forms have burnished gold sides with a hint of orange to their brown backs, and bright red fins.

*Below: A mixed group of pond fish, including an orfe, shubunkin, rudd, goldfish, tench and koi. All will live quite happily together.*

Rudd will bask under the lily pads, shoaling actively in a similar manner to orfe. They do not grow as large as orfe, and will tolerate slightly smaller pools, but are still at their best in more expansive ponds, with some water movement in hot weather.

## TENCH
*(Tinca tinca)*

- Maximum size: typically 20-40cm (8-16in), larger in lakes.
- Maximum age: over 10 years.
- Maturity: 3-4 years old.
- Sexing: the males have enlarged and thickened pelvic fins.

This active fish lives at the bottom of the pool. It has small eyes, numerous tiny scales, a smooth mucusy skin, and tiny barbels by its mouth. The colours of the wild green form look best from the side and are difficult to see in most ponds. The slower-growing golden form is much more ornamental, a pale orange in colour with variable amounts of brown pigment along its back.

Tench are often sold as scavenging fish, but although they will eat food that sinks to the base of the pond, they will not tidy up any other waste, and goldfish are just as effective at browsing on the base. You may not see very much of these timid fish, although once settled they will come to the surface to take floating foods.

These are the main groups of fish for the garden pond. Other types include:

- **Rosy Minnow** *(Pimephales promelas)*, a North American species, is salmon-orange, and does not grow very large. It prefers well oxygenated water and may not survive the coldest winters out of doors.

- **Three-Spined Stickleback** *(Gasterosteus aculeatus)* is a small (6-9cm/2.5-3.5in) fish with an aggressive manner. The males take on a distinctive metallic blue hue and red belly during the spawning season and their intricate courtship is probably most visible in a large aquarium. It is better suited to a wildlife pond without larger varieties of fish.

- **Coldwater catfish** have distinctive 'whiskers' and tend to stay low in the water, although they will come to the surface to feed. By nature they are quite aggressive and larger specimens will nip the fins of other fish, and even eat smaller fish whole. The varieties available are the North American Brown Bullhead *(Ictalurus nebulosus)*, which grows to about 30cm (12in), and the Albino Channel Catfish *(I. punctatus)*, which is more visible, growing to around 60cm (24in) in favourable conditions. They are not ideal fish to mix with more delicate varieties and are easily stressed at temperatures lower than 10°C (50°F).

- **Grass Carp** *(Ctenopharyngodon idella)*, originally from East Asia, are sometimes sold as a cure to thread algae problems. They will indeed eat certain forms of algae, but much prefer floating fish food and, unfortunately, also like to eat many forms of oxygenating (submerged) plant. The golden (albino) form is most unusual, and large specimens, with their long cylindrical bodies, are quite spectacular. However, grass carp grow very large, in excess of 100cm (40in), and will jump out of small or poorly aerated ponds. This makes them unsuitable for most garden ponds, and their availability is restricted in some countries to prevent unmonitored release into the wild.

For climates without severe winters, there are a number of smaller fish that will survive well in outdoor ponds. These varieties are also ideal for keeping in aquariums and conservatory ponds.

The Japanese Ricefish or Golden Medaka *(Oryzias latipes)* grows to 5cm (2in), stays near the pool surface, and will breed prolifically, given adequate space.

Mosquito Fish *(Gambusia affinis)* and White Cloud Mountain Minnows *(Tanichthys albonubes)* are probably better appreciated in an aquarium, as is the golden form of the eel-like Weather Loach *(Misgurnis anguillicaudatus)* (see below), although this fish shows up well on the pond base, reaching up to 20cm (8in).

## COLDWATER FISH BETTER SUITED TO THE AQUARIUM

- European Bitterling *(Rhodeus sericeus amarus)* and the more colourful, deeper-bodied Japanese Rosy Bitterling *(Tanakia tanago)* (8cm/3in). The males have a beautiful purply blue sheen, overlaid with pink and bright blue. The females lay their eggs in freshwater mussels using an ovipositor tube.
- Weather Loach *(Misgurnis anguillicaudatus and M. fossilis)* (25cm/10in) and Spined loach *(Cobitis taenia)* (10cm/4in).
- Rainbow Dace or Red Shiners *(Notropis lutrensis)* (8cm/3in). The males of this North American species take on attractive pink and blue hues. They may nip the fins of goldfish.
- Pumpkinseeds or Sunfish *(Lepomis spp.)* (to 20cm/8in). These aggressive North American natives are best kept on their own. They have very colourful blue or green sides.
- Mud Minnows *(Umbra pygmaea)* (10cm/4in).
- American Darters *(Etheostoma spp.)* (to 15cm/6in).

*Left: Bitterling are small active fish, well suited to an aerated aquarium. Once they have settled and overcome their initial nervousness, the males take on a most attractive coloration.*

# CHAPTER SEVEN

# WATER GARDEN CARE

Like any part of the home or garden, your pond will require some maintenance. In a well-designed pond this should never become a chore, and any work you put in will reap its rewards.

Fish ask for little more than good water quality and some sparing feeding. They will very often breed in the pond, indicating that conditions are acceptable. Aquatic plants, which may require the occasional trim and splitting, fortunately do not need to be watered like other garden plants. It is neither necessary nor desirable to completely clear out and drain the pond each year; indeed, if a large pond is well looked after, this task can be delayed for a number of years.

Obtaining the natural balanced conditions and clear water so desired by pondkeepers involves no mystery or chance. There are some very commonsense steps that you can take to keep your pond in top form. It helps if you have an understanding of what makes water good or bad, as clear water is not necessarily healthy, nor green water harmful. Any steps you take to improve the water quality will benefit all the forms of life in the pond and the availability of pond filters has made this much more easy.

With some appropriate seasonal care you should be able to keep the incidence of plant pests and fish diseases to an absolute minimum. Prevention is preferable to cure, and a small amount of regular maintenance will prove to be less effort in the long run, but if problems do occur, prompt remedial action should suffice.

# WATER AND WATER QUALITY

Water (H$_2$O; a combination of hydrogen and oxygen) is a very special liquid with a number of unique properties that make it vital in supporting life on earth. For the pond-keeper, two in particular are worth noting. Unlike many other liquids, water floats when cooled to freezing point. If it were to sink, then in icy weather ponds would freeze from the base up, and wildlife would die. Secondly, water is a good solvent, which is why we use it to dissolve anything from dirt on our clothes to sugar in our tea. For this reason it is very rarely pure – even rainfall can contain a number of airborne pollutants and water running down hillsides into rivers picks up minerals from the rocks it crosses. When the water has absorbed large quantities of mineral salts, such as those of calcium and magnesium, it is classified as 'hard', and will coat your kettle with a characteristic layer of scale.

Water picks up other chemicals as it percolates through the landscape – nutrients such as nitrates and phosphates, salts of metals such as aluminium and iron, and brown tinted humic acids from peat – and eventually finds its way to our taps. Although the water works remove most solids, many dissolved materials remain in the water, and other chemicals are added, for example chlorine, to prevent bacteria from growing in the water, and lime, to make the water slightly alkaline, thus reducing the amounts of unwanted copper and lead dissolving into the water from domestic piping.

Tap water is usually ideal for use in ponds. The only precaution necessary is the removal of chlorine, which might injure water life. Plants are relatively unaffected by the small amounts of chlorine in tap water, but fish can be severely upset. In a new pond, leave the water to stand for a couple of days to allow the chlorine to dissipate naturally, then you can add plants and fish without any problem – although it is normally wiser to allow plants to establish before adding fish. If you wish to introduce water life to the pond immediately, or if you are topping up a pond with more than a small amount of tap water, use a tap-water conditioner, which will neutralize chlorine and similar chemicals (such as fluorine and bromine) and will often contain other beneficial compounds to help mature the water.

Some water supplies are disinfected with chloramine, which is more persistent than ordinary chlorine, and using standard chlorine removers (de-chlorinators) will not remove the harmful levels of the chemical ammonia, which are left in the water after the chloramine has been broken down. In these cases you will need to use a water conditioner specifically intended for use against chloramine, or feed the water through a filter containing activated carbon, or carbon and zeolites. Check with your local water supply company to find out if your water is treated with any chemicals harmful to fish, such as chloramine or pyrethrins.

## POLLUTION

There are many forms of pollution that can upset the balance of life in the pond, and, if left unchecked, can cause grave damage. Provided you have sited the pond carefully, and take reasonable precautions, however, you can forestall such problems.

From within the pond itself a slow build-up of decaying leaves, blossoms, fish waste and dead organisms may eventually cause problems and you may need to make partial water changes or even clean the pond out completely. Dust, soil and mud can also cause problems, but the most immediate danger is from poisonous chemicals washing into the water. Common pollutants include:

■ Oils and oily fumes can be toxic to water life and form a film on the water's surface, preventing oxygen from entering the water.
■ Garden pesticide sprays can kill fish within a few hours.
■ Garden weedkillers often interrupt the natural process of plant photosynthesis, stopping water plants and algae from producing oxygen. The pond is then affected by falling levels of oxygen and decaying plant material.
■ Solvents in pond paints, pipework glues and wood stains can kill fish. Allow them to dry, and rinse them if this is recommended by the manufacturer, before contact with pond water.
■ Metal poisoning can be caused by new copper-piping, metal fittings and galvanized meshes.

Other pollutants include cement dust from building work, bonfire fumes, car exhaust fumes, seepage from compost heaps, wood preservatives, garden fungicides, cigarette ends, incorrect media in pond filters, and poisonous leaves from certain plants.

If you suspect a pollution problem, there are a number of steps you can take. First and foremost, stem the source of the pollution. Carry out full, or partial, water changes to dilute the pollutant; pump the pool water

*Below: Unsightly scums of algae are to be expected from time to time and are best netted out. Excessive scum is a sign of too many nutrients in the water.*

*Above: Water lily leaves and tall poolside plants can provide beneficial shade for a pond in a very sunny position.*

through an activated carbon filter, which will absorb many chemicals; remember that if the water is kept moving by a pump, more oxygen can enter at the surface, and waste gases can escape as well. A biological pond filter will help to break down a number of chemicals that might otherwise cause problems.

## BALANCED POND CONDITIONS

Clear and healthy pond water is obtained when plant and animal life achieve a natural balance. Within two to three weeks of planting, most new ponds will go through a stage of green water caused by the high level of nutrients in the water coupled with sunlight. The nutrients originate from the tap water used to fill the pond and from the soil used for planting. The algae that cause pea-soup conditions are single-celled plants that can grow and multiply much faster than larger pond plants and take advantage of the high levels of light and nutrients found in new ponds.

Given time, other plants will start to grow, using up the nutrients in the water and giving shade to the pool. This will start to starve the green algae of the food they need. At the same time, various other organisms, including water fleas, that feed on the green algae, will start to colonize the pool. Eventually the green water will fade and, as the pond matures, balanced conditions will be obtained.

There are, however, a number of steps that you can take to aid this natural balance:

■ Plant sufficient oxygenating plants, usually about five bunches for every square metre of surface area (one bunch per two square feet).
■ Use sufficient plants to shade the pond surface. The leaves of water lilies are ideal, but floating plants will grow more rapidly, and are therefore especially useful in new ponds.
■ In sunny sites, some marginal or poolside plants on the sunny side of the pool will give beneficial shade.
■ Line basket-weave planting containers with hessian, and top them with a layer of gravel, to reduce the level of soil seepage into the water.
■ Don't add too many fish too soon; wait at least three to four weeks after adding plants, longer if possible.
■ Try to avoid using algicide chemicals in a new pond; they will check the growth of the plants, which in the long run help to control the algae.

Providing the pond is well sited — away from trees and hollows (where dirt can wash in) — and the water is a reasonable depth (45cm/18in or more), then in most cases the pond will stay clear for around nine or ten months each year once a balance has been achieved. The pond will benefit from a certain amount of seasonal maintenance to preserve good conditions. In many cases the water may become slightly cloudy each spring, but will clear as the water plants start to grow. Some ponds may stay clear all year round, having reached the so desired ideal balance.

Unfortunately, in some ponds this balance may prove difficult or impossible to achieve; the water feature may not be in an ideal site, or it may contain rather too many fish. At one time this would have led to frustration on the part of the pondkeeper, and discouraged the installation of any further water features, but the emergence of the biological pond filter has revolutionized the popularity of water in the garden.

It is important to distinguish between the simple mechanical strainers fitted to pumps and true biological filters. Mechanical filters tend to be quite small, often consisting of a small block or canister of foam or floss, which traps fine particles. These filters can very soon become blocked and need frequent cleaning. Although they improve water quality slightly, they rarely give crystal clear water. Biological filters are larger, do not require such frequent cleaning, and give crystal clear water all year round, without the use of chemicals, so they are ideal for ponds where it has proved difficult to obtain a natural balance. They are also the answer for the impatient pondkeeper who is not prepared to wait for the natural balance to arrive.

## WATER TESTS

You can test your water, both from the tap and in the pond, to find out more about the water quality. Water testing kits are widely available; the most simple involve the use of a coloured indicator, which changes colour when mixed with the water sample. An accompanying colour chart allows you to gauge the quality of the water. Check that the kit you choose will cover the range of typical conditions, and that the colour changes are distinct enough to note easily. The two most useful tests for the pondkeeper are pH and Nitrite ($NO_2$) (see page 127).

## TESTING pH

pH is a measure of acidity or alkalinity. It is stated as a number between 0 and 14, and technically refers to the amount of hydrogen ions in the solution; 0 is the most acid and 14 the most alkaline; pH 7 is neutral and is the value for pure water.

Most ponds have a slightly alkaline pH value between 7 and 8, but the range 6.5 to 8.5 is acceptable to most pond life. Problems can occur outside of this range, so it is worthwhile testing the pond pH, especially if troubles arise.

## PONDS THAT ARE TOO ALKALINE

Alkaline conditions are a common problem in ponds, especially newer ponds, and if the pH of your water is regularly over 8.5, conditions will become stressful to fish and other pond life. pH values above 9 signal a serious problem, especially if excessive growths of algae are not the cause, and you will need to take rapid steps to remedy the situation.

### Symptoms of high pH
- Fish become prone to fungal infections and other diseases as their protective mucus coating is damaged.
- Waste products in the water (ammonia) become more toxic to pond life.
- Fish gills can become damaged, and fish may die without external symptoms.
- Plant growth will be less lush and oxygenating plants may have a powdery coating of off-white calcium salts on their leaves.
- Biological pond filters will fail to work as effectively.

### Causes
*Water may be in contact with materials containing lime.*
- Fresh cementwork is a prime source of lime. Even a handful of mortar can cause problems.
- Cement products, such as blocks, paving slabs and certain reconstituted materials, can leach out lime over a long period. In hot weather, the surfaces dry out and cement dust can then be blown or washed into the pond.
- Decorative limestone, or stonework containing chalk will result in high pH, especially if rocks are crumbly, but these sources rarely prove as dangerous as cementwork.

*There may be excessive growth of green algae.*
- Most pond life gives out carbon dioxide ($CO_2$) through the natural process of respiration. During daylight hours $CO_2$ is removed from the water by underwater plant life. $CO_2$ normally forms weak acids in water, and as it is removed by the plants, the pH rises, as on balance more alkalis are left in the water. At night the levels of $CO_2$ build up again, the balance is restored and the pH falls. This is a natural cycle in all planted pools, but it is greatly exacerbated by excessive growths of 'pea-soup' and thread algae (blanketweed). If algae is the only problem, then the pH value will be low first thing in the morning, but high later in the day.

### Remedies
- Remove all sources of high lime (i.e. concrete blocks), or seal the surfaces with a commercial lime neutralizer or a pool paint.
- Net or siphon out any loose pieces of cement mortar.
- Carry out partial water changes (see page 141), which will dilute the alkalis in the water and temporarily reduce pea-soup algae.
- Take action to reduce levels of algae (see page 124), and remove excessive growths of thread algae.

If after taking these steps the pH is still high, use acidifying compounds, such as granular pond peat in mesh bags, and pond pH buffers intended to cope with alkaline conditions. Follow the supplier's instructions carefully. These compounds are rarely strong enough to neutralize lime from cement, however.

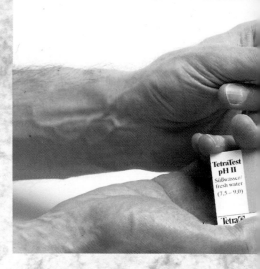

## PONDS THAT ARE TOO ACID

Acid conditions are less common in garden ponds, but when they do occur, fish and other water life can become stressed.

### Symptoms of low pH
- Fish become more prone to disease, they may have reddened fins, and they may die for no apparent reason.
- Some plants, particularly oxygenating plants, will not grow as well.
- Biological pond filters will fail to work as effectively.

### Causes
*The pond water may be very soft.*
- Some water, such as rainwater, or that which has drained off hard granite rocks or peat moors, will have a low content of calcium, magnesium and other salts. Such waters are described as soft, and have a poor buffering capacity, which means that they have a low resistance to factors causing fluctuations in the pH level. As plants remove salts from the water, they can make soft water even more soft.

*Below: Simple test kits allow you to check your pond water for pH, nitrite and other factors. This pH test kit gives a rapid measure of acidity or alkalinity.*

pH 8,0    pH 8,4    pH 8,7    pH 9,0

*The pond water may contain acids from natural sources.*

- Peat and decomposing plants release humic acids into the water.
- Organic acids from decomposing fish waste build up in the water.
- Nitrate ($NO_3$) builds up in the water, as waste products are broken down, and forms weak acids in the water.

### Remedies

- Regular partial water changes (see page 141) will dilute the organic acids building up in the water.
- The buffering capacity of soft water can be improved by adding rocks containing calcium and magnesium carbonates, that is limestone, tufa and dolomite. Add them in moderation and monitor the pH level. You may need to introduce fresh rocks after a few months, as the surface of the rocks can become sealed with a layer of biological grime.
- Use proprietary pond-buffering-salts to raise the pH level.
- In plant-free fish ponds, the addition of plants will help to reduce the build-up of nitrates.

## TESTING FOR OXYGEN

Oxygen is essential for the maintenance of healthy conditions in the pond, and for the wellbeing of fish and other pond life. Oxygen can dissolve in water wherever air and water come into contact, the main point of contact being the pool surface, which is why the surface area of a pond is used as a measure for safe stocking levels of fish. Moving water – from a fountain, waterfall, or water pump – increases the area of water in contact with the air, and also helps to circulate water from the depths of the pond to the surface. This is especially valuable in ponds heavily stocked with fish, and also during hot weather, when less oxygen can dissolve in the water. Oxygen is produced by submerged oxygenating plants and algae in the water, but only during daylight.

### Symptoms of lack of oxygen

- Fish gasp at the water's surface, often leaving bubbles floating on the water. This is especially noticeable in the early morning, when fish would not normally be at the surface.
- There may be unexplained fish deaths, especially overnight. Larger fish, and varieties such as orfe and rudd, are the first affected as they are more sensitive to a lack of oxygen.

- The water might appear inky black and have an unpleasant odour.

### Causes

- Too much of the surface is covered with lily leaves and floating plants.
- Large amounts of excess food and waste are decomposing in the pond and using up the oxygen.
- Warm, muggy weather and thundery conditions have lowered the levels of oxygen dissolved in the water.
- A pump that is normally in use has been turned off.
- Excessive growths of pea soup and thread algae are using up oxygen at night.
- The pond is overstocked with fish.

### Remedies

- Remove excessive growths of floating aquatics and lily leaves.
- Remove waste from the pond by siphoning off the base and topping up with fresh water.
- Run fountains and waterfalls continuously, or at least overnight, especially in hot weather.
- Take steps to control excessive algae growth.
- Have you too many fish? Give some away!

## TESTING FOR WATER HARDNESS

It is possible to test for hard water with simple kits. The scales used will vary according to the test, but should be converted to their equivalent in milligrams per litre (mg/l) of calcium carbonate ($CaCO_3$).

- Less than 50 mg/l = soft water
- 150-300 mg/l = moderately hard water
- More than 500 mg/l = very hard water

The majority of pond plants and coldwater fish prefer water of a moderate hardness, although some plants and fish will not thrive in very soft or very hard water. In general, unless you know that your water supply is especially hard or soft, it is not worth worrying about this.

## COPING WITH ALGAE

Green water is caused by the growth of thousands of single-celled plants in the water. Algae are quite natural – their spores are present in the air and will colonize any new body of water. There are numerous different types and they all thrive in sunny warm conditions and in nutrient-rich water. They are rarely harmful to water life, but are of course unsightly.

You can control green water by trying to achieve a natural balance, by using a pond filter, an ultra-violet unit, or (as a last resort) algicides. The natural balance depends upon starving the algae of light and nutrients, and creating conditions suited to the growth of algae consumers, such as water fleas.

Algicide chemicals are useful for controlling green water in unplanted pools, fountain displays and self-contained ornaments. Depending upon the strength of the chemicals used, you may need to re-dose at one to four month intervals. In planted pools you should use chemicals only when other means have failed. There are two main types: the brown-coloured tannin flocculants are less damaging to plants, and cause free-floating algae and other particles to sink to the base. Always siphon off the resulting sediment before it starts to decompose.

Other chemicals come in various forms – liquids, tablets and slow release blocks – most of which have been designed to be safe to use with fish. In theory they kill algae without damaging other plants, as they can enter through the thin cell walls of algae more easily than larger plant cells. In practice they check the growth of most aquatic plants, especially oxygenators, and in higher doses can kill plants. It is very unwise to use them in newly planted pools, as plants are particularly prone to damage at this stage. The main danger lies in de-oxygenation, as the chemicals often stop the process of photosynthesis by which plants produce oxygen. The dying and decaying algae also use up large quantities of oxygen, depriving fish and other pond life, so they must be removed to prevent this type of pollution. It is a good idea to remove the algae by carrying out a water change, then add the algicide to prevent the re-growth of algae. This

method uses much lower levels of the chemical, and you will often obtain satisfactory results using only half the recommended dose rates. Chemicals usually help to clear the algae, but they will not always give crystal clear water, and they work much less effectively at low temperatures (i.e. under 10°C/50°F).

Thread algae, blanketweed and silkweed are basically different names for the same problem – the numerous forms of filamentous algae whose masses of threads can be found tangled around plants, in cloudy masses on the pool base, forming dense mats on the pool side and causing frothy scums on the pool surface. They are unsightly rather than harmful, and although most ponds have a few forms present, in balanced conditions they rarely become a problem. They can arrive in a number of ways: on birds' feet, their spores can blow into the pond, and small pieces can be transferred in with water plants.

Thread algae can become a problem in well-lit ponds that are rich in nutrients. Unfortunately, most tap water supplies are becoming increasingly rich in nitrate, and this exacerbates the problem every time the pool is topped up. Fitting a biological filter will control pea-soup algae but cannot control thread algae. Indeed, in filtered ponds the clear water and lack of competition from green-water algae can actually enhance growth of thread algae.

*Above: Persistent murky water and scums of algae are more likely in ponds with too few plants and too many nutrients, such as those leaching from soil above this pool.*

The best method of control is to pull out as much of the algae as possible using a fine mesh net to scoop out the cloudy types, and a stick to pull out the more entangling types. You can also reduce the nutrients and sunlight available to the algae by growing plenty of floating and underwater plants. Try to avoid topping the pond up with lots of tap water, and make sure as little soil as possible washes into the pond.

If you fail to achieve the desired results, careful use of algicides can be very effective. Remove as much algae as possible before treating. Blanketweed algicides may have similar side effects to green water algicides, but often low doses will be sufficient to keep blanketweed at bay; ask your supplier for an effective brand.

There are a number of alternative methods of control. Plant filters and magnetic devices prove useful in some cases, (see page 129) or you could place mesh bags of special granular pond peat in the pond. The humic acids released by the peat reduce algal growth slightly and are less damaging to plants than algicide chemicals. You could also try filling mesh bags with barley straw, which helps to reduce algae growth. The silicates in the straw bind nutrients, such as phosphate, robbing the algae of food, and it seems that the straw may encourage the growth of certain organisms that feed on pea-soup algae. Both peat and straw can eventually pollute the pond, so remove them as soon as they start to decompose.

Snails are often suggested as controls for thread algae, but, although they can eat large amounts of algae, they are not sufficient to cope with its sometimes phenomenal growth rate, and they also have the unpleasant habit of eating expensive plants!

Grass carp have been used in some countries to control blanketweed, but they are not a miracle solution, and will not eat all forms of thread algae.

## HOW BIOLOGICAL POND FILTERS WORK

Biological filters must be used in conjunction with a pond pump. Water is continuously passed through a bed of filter media, where some settlement and mechanical straining of particles will take place. More importantly, the filter media act as a haven for natural organisms to flourish. The bacteria, single-cell creatures and tiny animals that are found naturally in pools – and which help to break down waste – are concentrated in the filter, where they grow protected from fish and supplied by the pump with a constant stream of food and oxygenated water.

The organisms in the pond filter play an important role in what is known as the Nitrogen Cycle. Nitrogen is a gas that makes up 80% of the air that we breath, and, when it forms compounds with other chemicals, plays a vital role in the environment. Proteins, which form an important part of many living tissues, are nitrogen-containing compounds; nitrate ($NO_3$) is an important fertilizer, which plants convert into protein.

Ammonia ($NH_3$) is a waste product excreted by fish and also resulting from the breakdown of decaying material. Ammonia is toxic to many life forms and injurious to fish, but certain bacteria in the filter feed on the ammonia and turn it into nitrite ($NO_2$). Nitrites, too, form toxic compounds that are very irritating to fish, but specialized bacteria can feed on it and convert it into relatively unharmful nitrates ($NO_3$), which are then used by pond plants as food.

Apart from bacteria in the filter, there are many varieties of single-cell organisms and fungi, and various larger creatures, such as water fleas and worms, that all feed on the different forms of waste entering the filter, and on each other too. They help to remove fine particles from the water, and some of them feed upon the algae that cause green water. They cannot eliminate waste entirely, but they convert it into less polluting material. A brownish fluffy sediment (floc) will build up in the filter and will require periodic removal.

## TYPES OF FILTER

There are a number of different biological filters on the market. The simplest are large blocks of foam fitted to the pump inlet. Although these make good mechanical strainers, they tend to clog up rather quickly, and as biological filters they are only suited to ponds of around 150-300 litres (33-66 UK/40-80 US gallons). They can sometimes be linked together into multiple units, but are then rather cumbersome to handle. Larger, in-pool submersible filters are often less visible, but they are difficult to move and very difficult to maintain.

The most popular form of biological filter is the external type. The simplest consist of a single-chamber tank, filled with various filter media. Water is pumped into the tank from the pond, flows through the media, and then out of the tank and back into the pond, either through a pipe or down a waterfall. If necessary you can hide the filter some distance from the

**A single chamber pond filter**

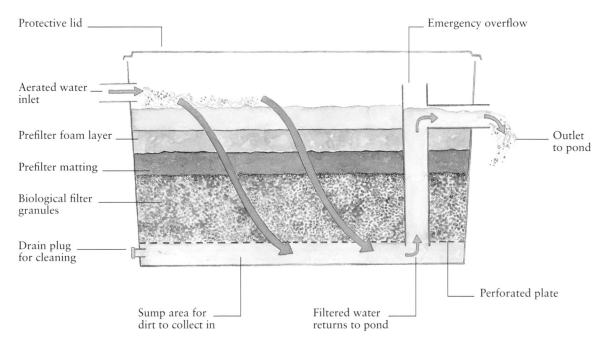

Protective lid

Emergency overflow

Aerated water inlet

Prefilter foam layer

Prefilter matting

Biological filter granules

Drain plug for cleaning

Outlet to pond

Perforated plate

Sump area for dirt to collect in

Filtered water returns to pond

*Above: This basic multi-chamber filter has three compartments for different filter media, and a sloping base and drainage valve to facilitate waste removal.*

*Left: Water is pumped into this simple filter; layers of foam remove the heaviest dirt before the water reaches the submerged main bed of biological media.*

pond, or sink it into a rockery. The size of the filter depends upon the pond size and the number of fish being kept; the smallest filters generally available – based upon a tank of around 20-litre (four-gallon) volume – are intended for pools of up to 1000-litre (200 UK/265 US gallon) capacity. For ponds that are heavily stocked with fish, or that contain very few plants, choose a filter with extra capacity. This is also advisable if you keep koi, which tend to stir the pond up more than goldfish.

## CHOOSING A FILTER

Pond filters are a relatively new development, and their quality varies considerably. Make sure you choose a filter of sufficient size, as too small a filter will not cope, and will require very frequent cleaning. Unfortunately, some manufacturers have made unrealistic claims for the capacity of their filters, so buy your filter from a reputable independent dealer and ask for advice on the best filter for your situation.

Pick a filter containing a high-quality, long-life filter medium and find out how easy the filter is to clean; better models have drainage plugs to facilitate cleaning. Make sure that the water will be sufficiently aerated, using spray bars, jet nozzles or venturi apparatus. A lid will keep leaves out of the filter and provide shade, although a loose-fitting mesh cover is often adequate. An overflow facility will prevent disasters should the media clog.

More advanced filters have a multi-chamber design. The initial chamber enables settlement and removal of large particles (pre-filtration). It often contains a non-clogging medium, such as filter brushes, and can be easily drained and cleaned without disturbing other parts of the filter. The pre-filtered water then flows through the remaining filter chamber(s), which can be filled with other types of biological filter media, and as they require only infrequent cleaning, biological organisms can grow in them relatively undisturbed.

The best multi-chamber filters are made from tough glassfibre and have sloping bases to facilitate waste removal. They are generally quite large; extra care will need to be taken in hiding them. Some can be adapted and sunk into the ground beside the pool, where water flows into the filter by gravity and is pumped back into the pond from the other end of the unit. Some specialist pond constructors will custom-build a filter on site to suit particularly large ponds.

Disguising your pond filter can take some ingenuity. Close to the pond you can hide the filter in a rockery or a raised walled area, topped with seating or plants. Remember to provide access to the filter and to make provision for draining waste from the filter. Alternatively, you could situate it further from the pond, behind bushes or in a shed, remembering that if the filter is protected from frost it will be easier to run during the winter.

At one time, undergravel pond filters were popular. These are constructed by placing an array of perforated pipes in a section of the pond (usually not the base) and covering with a gravel medium, through which water is drawn, and returned to the pool. These are not too unsightly, and work very effectively initially, but they are difficult to clean and maintain. After two or three years you will need to strip them down, and if they clog unnoticed, the organisms will die and pollute the water. External filters are much more reliable.

## POND FILTER REQUIREMENTS

Biological pond filters have a few simple requirements if they are to function properly.

The filter must be run 24 hours a day – the organisms in the filter need a constant supply of oxygenated water to survive. Choose a reliable pump to

**A multi-chamber pond filter**

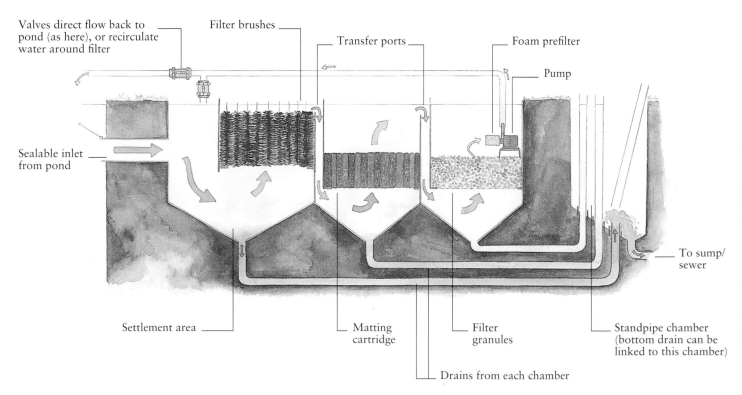

Valves direct flow back to pond (as here), or recirculate water around filter

Filter brushes

Transfer ports

Foam prefilter

Pump

Sealable inlet from pond

To sump/sewer

Settlement area

Matting cartridge

Filter granules

Standpipe chamber (bottom drain can be linked to this chamber)

Drains from each chamber

feed the unit, preferably with moderate running costs. If you turn off the filter for any length of time, the organisms will die, so you should drain the filter before restarting it. Filter organisms can survive pump stoppages of up to a day in cold winter weather, but in summer they may start to suffer after only half an hour.

Give the filter time to mature. It can take three to eight weeks for filter organisms to establish themselves in the media. You can accelerate the maturing process by using proprietary bacterial cultures, or some mature media from another filter. A handful of mud from an established pond will also seed the filter with organisms, but may introduce unwanted parasites.

If you put a few fish in your pond at this time, they will provide some waste for the filter organisms to feed on, but during the maturing process, levels of waste compounds, such as ammonia and nitrite, which can severely stress fish, will build up in the water. To avoid problems, try not to introduce large numbers of fish into the pond at this time, and only feed fish very sparingly until the filter settles. The levels of ammonia and nitrite ($NH_3$ and $NO_2$) can be monitored using simple test kits and will give an indication of whether the filter has matured or not. High levels can irritate fish causing them to flick on

their sides (flash). If you have large numbers of fish, you can reduce nitrite toxicity with a salt treatment (see page 136). If high ammonia levels are a problem, don't use salt, but consider using zeolite compounds, which can absorb some of this chemical.

Follow the manufacturer's recommendations regarding flow rate. Too high or low a flow rate will reduce the efficiency of the filter. If your pump is too powerful, restrict the flow with a valve, or fit a bypass to direct some of the flow directly back into the pond. Remember that the outlet of most pump-fed filters is intended to empty unrestricted back into the pond, and therefore cannot be used to power fountain ornaments or jets, although it can be directed into a waterfall.

Maintenance of the filter involves cleaning of the pre-filter or settlement area whenever waste begins to build up. This should not take long, and you should do it fairly frequently; simply rinse it with pond water if it starts to clog. Very vigorous cleaning, or use of chlorinated tapwater, will damage the beneficial biological organisms.

Avoid using pond medications while the filter is maturing and never allow undiluted chemicals to enter the filter; medications containing more than trace amounts of methylene blue dye are particularly damaging to filters. It is useful to be able to isolate

## SOLVING FILTRATION PROBLEMS

Sometimes the water may not clear even after the filter has been running for a considerable time. There is usually a reason for this that you can remedy. Ask yourself the following questions:

- Is the flow rate through the filter correct?
- Have any medications been used in the pond that might have upset the filter?
- Has the filter been turned off at any time?
- Is the filter the correct size for the pond?
- Does the pond need a few partial water changes? Or is it so dirty that it really requires a total clean-out?

You can also do the following:
- Check the chemical balance in the pond (see pages 122-123) – very acid or alkaline water can reduce activity of filter organisms.
- Raise the pump inlet at least 15cm (6in) off the pool base.
- Use some of the filter-maturing agents available.
- If the filter is coping well with the biological waste from the pond, but green water is a persistent problem, consider using an ultraviolet (UV) unit to boost the filter's effectiveness.

*Left: Water flows from the pond via a large pipe into a settlement area and then through various media before being pumped back. Dirt can be drained to waste and valves allow the filter to be isolated from the pond.*

*Right: Lifted decking reveals this final chamber of a filter system. Water flows horizontally through rows of filter brushes and a cartridge of filter matting.*

your filter from the pond, because if water can be pumped around the filter only, bypassing the pond, this will keep the filter active while the pond is being medicated or drained.

In warm climates leave the filter running year round. In more temperate climates the filter can be insulated in winter and left running at a low flow rate. Raise the pump closer to the pond surface to prevent excessive cooling of the water at the base of the pond. It is sometimes possible to place a small heater in the filter to keep ice at bay, alternatively, drain the filter at the first frosts, and rinse it through, leaving it dry over the winter, and rinse and restart it in the spring. This avoids the problems of icing up, but does mean that the filter must go through the maturing process again.

## FILTER MEDIA

There are many types of filter media available. Some are excellent at catching dirt, others have a high surface area, ideal for the attachment of filter organisms. Others are very open and allow high flow rates of water without clogging. No one medium can be good at everything; compromise, or choose a combination of different media.

Flow rates for different media vary; in general higher flow rates can be used with more open media, and in multi-chamber filters, where most of the heavy solids have been removed by pre-filtration. The filter should be able to deal with a volume equivalent to that of the pool once every four hours. For koi pools this should be increased to once every two hours, or even once every hour.

■ **Angular gravel** is cheap and has a reasonable surface area, but it is heavy and tends to compact and clog. Spar gravel is more expensive but has a greater surface area.

■ **Lightweight granules** are not too expensive, are lighter than gravel, and have a good surface area for biological activity. They are generally rounded, so they are easy to handle and less likely to compact. The two main types are sintered pulverized fuel ash, an excellent medium, which is fairly cheap but still rather heavy, and volcanic pumice, which is more expensive and tends to float. Granules of 7-15mm (0.3-0.6in) are best.

■ **Plastic media,** such as ring media and hair-roller types, are very light, open and non-clogging, have moderate surface areas and can be expensive. They are more useful as a settlement and pre-filtering media, and large quantities are needed for effective biological action.

■ **Filter brushes** are light, non-clogging and easy to clean. Their price varies greatly. Although they have some biological activity, they are most useful as a pre-filtering medium in multi-chamber filters.

■ **Filter foam** is widely used, but note that only non-toxic open-cell foam intended for use with fish is suitable. This is very lightweight but expensive, and comes in various grades. You can use sheets as a pre-filter on top of granular media, but you may need to clean them frequently. You can also use foam as a biological medium if you situate it after pre-filter media. Fine grades have the highest surface area but clog more rapidly than medium or coarse foam; profiled types clog up more slowly. Foam's major limitation is its short lifespan; two to four years maximum; 10-18 months if it requires frequent cleaning. It is best used with other media.

■ **Filter matting** is a coarse material made from plastic or nylon fibres. It is tougher than foam and you can either

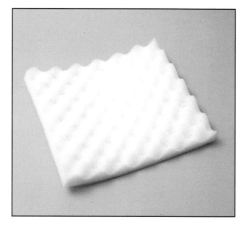

*Above: Angular gravel, such as Canterbury spar, is a traditional filter media, but it is very heavy and difficult to clean.*

*Below: These granules of sintered pulverized fuel ash are a good general-purpose biological medium.*

*Above: The various brands of lightweight ring media are non-clogging, but generally have less surface area than fine media.*

*Below: A chamber filled with filter brushes is ideal for removing dirt from water before it passes through other, finer media.*

*Above: Foam has a massive surface area for biological activity to take place, but it clogs rapidly in dirty conditions and is expensive.*

*Below: Filter matting is a lightweight matrix of resin-bonded plastic fibres with a large surface area. It is easy to clean.*

use it as a pre-filter material, or in cartridge arrays in multi-chamber filters following pre-filtration. It is expensive, but has a high surface area and can be used with high flow rates. It is very popular with koi-keepers, particularly in Japan.

■ **Zeolites** are special alumino-silicate rocks, which absorb ammonia and other toxic chemicals from the water. They are most useful with new maturing filters, positioned after the other media. Place them in a mesh bag, as they need to be recharged every six weeks by soaking in a strong salt solution. Never use them in ponds when the pond is being treated with a salt medication.

■ **Activated carbons** can be used intermittently to remove staining chemicals and pollutants from the water. Place the carbon in a mesh bag in the water flow. Discard the carbon after six to ten weeks, when it will be saturated with waste products.

*Above: Zeolites are special minerals, which can be used in new filters to remove impurities, such as ammonia, from the water.*

*Below: Activated carbon granules adsorb chemicals from the water and help to remove pollutants and excess medications.*

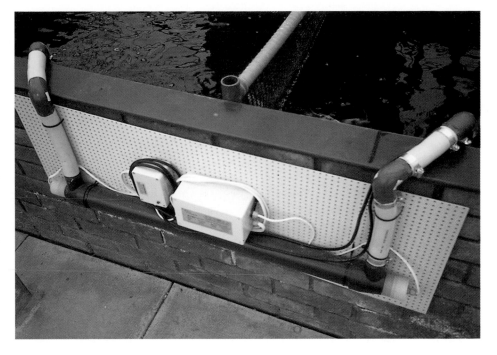

## EXTRA FILTER AIDS

■ **Ultra-violet units** are useful for the control of green water in ponds. They are best used in conjunction with a biological filter and are not a substitute for an efficient filter. In many cases it may be wiser to spend money on uprating the biological filter.

They work by passing water close to a source of UV light, which damages the algal cells. The UV light also encourages fine protein particles to clump together, making them more easily removed by the biological filter and so improving water clarity. UV light also destroys some bacteria and fish parasites, but at the low doses used in pond units, this is insignificant. The units are normally fitted after the main pond filter, where the cleaner filtered water is less likely to deposit solids in the unit, and allows the UV light to penetrate further into the pond water.

Use the units with care, protecting the electrical connections from damp, and don't look at the burning lamp. Switch the lamp on whenever the water is hazy. The lamp's output fades with time, so you should replace it annually in the spring, at the beginning of the season.

■ **Centripetal tanks** are specially designed settlement tanks fitted in front of pond filters. They remove a large proportion of suspended solids from the water and are useful for very big ponds and those containing large numbers of koi.

*Above: In this Ultra-violet unit, water is passed close to a UV light tube,*

*damaging green water algae and enhancing the effectiveness of the main filter.*

■ **Plant filters** are useful for ponds that contain very few plants. They consist of a bed of strong-growing plants, situated in the outflow from the filter, which remove chemicals, such as nitrate, from the water and can therefore reduce growths of thread algae in the pond. They are most effective in warm countries where the plants can grow all year round. The best plants to choose are watercress (*Rorippa sp.*) in temperate regions and water hyacinth and water lettuce (*Eichhornia* and *Pistia*) in warmer countries.

■ **Sand and cartridge filters** are sometimes suggested for garden ponds, but they tend to clog rapidly and require frequent maintenance and powerful pumps. You should therefore use them only in a swimming pool, where the dosing of strong algicide and anti-bacterial chemicals makes them more practicable.

■ **Magnetic filters** were originally developed to reduce scale in domestic water supplies and have been fitted to recycling systems to reduce the levels of algae. In theory they limit the availability of nutrients to pea-soup and thread algae, but it is hard to prove what effect they have, and it may be months before you notice any significant improvement.

# PLANT CARE

Plants in the pond require no more maintenance than those in any other part of the garden. You may need to pull out the occasional weed seedling, but if you use planting containers, the dangers of weeds running out of control are minimal. Plants benefit from trimming back to remove dead tissue in the autumn and some tender plants may require extra protection in the winter.

There will come a time when you will need to trim the plants in the pool severely to restrict growth, or replant them completely. If a plant is beginning to spread too far out of its container, trim back the new growth in the spring to keep it in shape.

Where plants are in basket-type containers, their roots can run out into the pond mulm and draw nutrients from the waste on the base, but they will eventually run out of essential nutrients and their vigour will start to wane. You can boost their growth with a slow-release aquatic fertilizer, most of which are available as tablets, pellets or sachets. Push them into the soil, near the plant roots, in order to reduce the risk of fertilizing the water and so encouraging algae growth. Liquid fertilizers are available but tend to be less effective.

## PLANT PROPAGATION

Even with regular fertilizing there will come a time when each plant requires lifting, splitting and replanting in fresh soil. If you have used small containers, you may need to do this after only one or two years, otherwise every three to five years should be sufficient. Dividing the plants gives you the opportunity to increase the number of containers of a plant, or to replant in a larger container to give a more impressive clump. Remove any seedlings, and pot them separately.

Divide waterplants during the growing season, picking a cool day to prevent plants from drying out. Remove the plant containers from the pond and place them on a suitable work area; a polythene groundsheet will help to keep the area tidy. Remove the plants from their containers, cutting these open if the plants have become very overgrown. Make sure that you have sufficient tools and spare planting baskets, hessian liners, soil and gravel.

### ■ Marginal plants

Tease the growing points of the plant apart, trimming excess roots as you go, and dividing the plant at natural breaking points. Rinse off excess soil into a bucket of water. Choose the youngest, freshest sections of growth for replanting, and trim off any older or damaged pieces. Replant in fresh soil as for new plants (see page 84). Top the container with the old gravel, and add some new gravel if necessary. Return the container to the pond after rinsing off loose soil, and make sure that the plants have the correct amount of water cover.

### ■ Oxygenators

Simply trim off 15-25cm (6-10in) of the fresh growth at the top of the existing strands of oxygenator. Cut

**Trimming plants**

*Above: When replanting marginals, such as this Iris, cut off any old and* *dying leaves, old rootstock, and spent flowers, retaining only the freshest growth.*

out all the middle section of straggly growth and replant bunches of the fresh growth in with the existing roots. If necessary, remove the layer of gravel from the containers and add in a fresh layer of soil 2-5cm thick (1-2in). Oxygenators do not require a great depth of soil and the cuttings will normally root after a few weeks. Ideally, protect the containers from fish by placing them in a fish-free pond, or covering with coarse plastic mesh, for three to four weeks.

### ■ Water lilies

The plants must not dry out while you are at work, so douse them with a watering-can at intervals. Before you remove any growth, note the style of growth of the lily rootstock. Some types have a rhizome or tuber-like growth across the surface of the soil, others have a more gnarled, upright growth. It is important that the rootstock is replanted at a similar angle.

Retain the newest sections of growth, at the ends of the rootstock and on sideshoots, for replanting. Even a small 'eye' off the lily crown could be replanted separately, but for most success, remove a larger section of the growing point (or crown) – pieces 7-20cm (3-8in) in length are ideal. Cut the piece of crown so that it is at least as long as it is broad – longer (two or three times the width) would be better. Cut the rootstock cleanly to avoid bruising (some lily roots may stain your hands).

Trim off the majority of thick anchoring roots, which tend to die back anyway; if many are left, they can rot and infect the crown. Leave a few of the large roots to help anchor the crown, and leave some of the finer, nutrient-collecting roots. Cut off any damaged tissue and remove all older leaves and buds. (If you leave too many leaves, the plant will be difficult to anchor, as its buoyancy will tend to pull it out of the container.) Replant using the same method as for new water lilies (see page 88).

### ■ Bog plants

Treat moisture-loving plants in the same way as herbaceous border plants and divide them in the spring or autumn; some will tolerate being divided during the growing season provided they are kept sufficiently moist after replanting.

## PLANT PESTS

Water plants are no more prone to disease than other garden plants. Indeed, if you keep the pond full they will never suffer from the stress of lack of water and will consequently be stronger to cope with attack.

### ■ Insect pests

Blackfly are easy to spot but other insects can cut disfiguring chunks from leaves. Control pests by rubbing them off the plants, or dislodging them with a jet of water. Once they are in the water, pond fish will eat many of them. If there are no fish in the pond spray a systemic garden insecticide onto the leaves. As long as you direct it at leaves only, the level in the water will normally be safe for pond life. If you have fish either remove the plants for treatment elsewhere, or use a fish-safe insecticide. A number of fish parasite treatments contain organophosphate insecticides (see page 136). Prepare these at the dose rate recommended for the pool and spray onto the plants to avoid upsetting fish and do not use with sensitive fish, such as orfe and rudd.

*Above: Bog garden plants are best divided in the spring – a little earlier than the truely aquatic plants – or in the autumn.*

*Below: This lily leaf shows typical signs of insect damage. Remove badly affected leaves and consider treatment.*

### ■ Distorted leaves

Leaves of all plants can become distorted if damaged while young by insect pests, chills or snails. Occasionally lilies suffer from an infection that causes leaf distortion, but the rootstock may not be affected throughout. Cut out and discard any parts of the crown that appear to be affected.

### ■ Snails

Large numbers of snails (*Limnaea* species in particular) can cause great damage to all water plants. There is no effective chemical control for snails that is also safe with fish, which will eat some snail eggs but will not eradicate them. Population explosions of snails are generally self-limiting, and the numbers usually decrease after a while, but you can remove some snails by dangling a cabbage stump in the water, on which they will usually congregate.

### ■ Fungal infections

Some marginal plants (notably *Caltha spp.*) are prone to mildew infections in late summer. Pick off badly infected leaves and destroy them, then either remove the plant for spraying, or paint on a solution of systemic fungicide. Do not allow large amounts of fungicide to drain into the water as these chemicals can kill fish.

Some water lily leaves may suffer from black blotches, or turn dry and blackened at the edges. Cut off any affected leaves at the base and discard them. In severe cases, paint a systemic fungicide onto the remaining unaffected leaves.

### ■ Lily crown rot

This term is used to describe a number of fungal and bacterial diseases of water lilies. The leaves, including younger ones, turn yellow, and black patches spread from the centre of the leaf. Affected leaves are often easily pulled off because the crown at the base may be affected; if so, examination will reveal it as black and rotten. Remove affected lilies from the pond.

In less severe cases, new growth may be seen from side shoots. Remove the rootstock, cut off all affected tissue and replant undamaged sections in fresh soil. Spray the crown with a systemic fungicide and leave the plant in a separate pool or trough to recover. Newly planted or recently moved lilies are most at risk, especially if they have been chilled. Mottled-leaved varieties seem to be the most susceptible, but other varieties may also become affected.

Severe types of lily crown rot can sweep through established stocks causing great damage. The incidence of this is very rare, but obtain professional help if you suspect this.

# FISH CARE

If you keep the water in good condition and do not overstock the pond, the fish will require minimal care. In most cases some seasonal maintenance in and around the pond will be adequate; but if you are keeping koi, or larger numbers of other fish, filtration is a definite advantage.

## FEEDING FISH

If your pond is well planted, and sparsely stocked with fish, they will very often survive without extra food. However, if you feed your fish, they will become larger, stronger, and tamer. There is an enormous range of foods – pellets, sticks and flakes in various sizes and recipes, the majority of which float, bringing the fish to the surface and allowing you to net any uneaten food.

Modern fish foods are a big improvement on the old biscuitmeal types, providing a balanced diet and containing anything from 25–40% protein, and all the necessary trace elements for pond fish.

There are different blends to provide variety; some are rich in wheatgerm, which is easily digested and therefore ideal for feeding in cooler weather; others contain algae-meal and carotenes to enhance the colour pigments of the fish, and others are designed to encourage rapid growth.

Choose a fish food recommended by your supplier and buy small quantities, as the foods start to deteriorate once opened, especially if they become damp. Fresh food is much appreciated by pond fish, and stale food can harm fish by damaging their livers. Choose a pellet small enough to be taken by all the fish; you can mix this with larger pellets if necessary. Flake foods can be powdered to provide food for fish fry, but even tiny fish will nibble at larger pellets as they soften. In general flake foods tend to be rather messy in outdoor ponds, and are best kept for indoor aquarium use; they can also cause indigestion in some short-bodied fancy goldfish.

Pellet foods may seem rather dull to us, but fish love them. Most include flavour attractants to help the fish locate them quickly. Fish tend to be quite conservative in their tastes, so that, once accustomed to one particular brand, they may take a little time to adapt to other foods. They will occasionally eat small pieces of bread, and boiled kernels from maize and peas; or tubifex worms, daphnia, and shrimps – but always use safe frozen or dried forms, as live ones carry a risk of disease.

Feed your fish during the day rather than in late evening, as it takes them longer to digest food in the cooler overnight temperatures. (Fish are cold-blooded animals whose body temperature, and rate of activity, drops with the external temperature.) Fish should therefore be fed less in cooler weather and more in warmer weather, except at very hot temperatues (over 30°C/86°F), when you should reduce the amount. One small meal each day is quite adequate for pond fish, although you could feed them three or four times a day in warm weather.

In cool spring and autumn seasons feed only on warmer days, and in the winter stop feeding once daytime temperatures regularly fall below 10°C (50°F). Most pond fish will actually carry on eating small amounts of food down to 5-6°C (41-43°F), but it can take them up to two or three days to digest the food. If you do want to feed some food at low temperatures, choose easily digested wheatgerm-rich types. If there is a short mild spell in the middle of the winter, refrain from feeding fish, beginning again only once the warmer weather arrives in the spring.

Do not be fooled by the hungry attitude of fish; their small digestive systems are not suited to large meals and if they are given too much food, most will simply pass through them virtually undigested. This is wasteful of food and will pollute the pond.

When you are feeding the fish, give them only as much as they will consume in two to five minutes. Remember that in cooler weather their appetites will be reduced. Most fish foods

*Below: These food sticks contain more colour enhancers and higher levels of protein than standard pond fish recipes, making them ideal for koi.*

*Below: Standard food sticks can be fed to all pond fish. They are lightweight and float for a long time, encouraging fish to come to the surface to feed.*

*Below: Pellet foods containing high levels of wheatgerm are more rapidly digested than other types and are therefore useful for feeding in cool weather.*

are very concentrated and a small amount is all that is required. If you are away for a few days the fish will come to no harm. Most pond fish are browsers and prefer to nibble throughout the day at plants and insect life in the pond. In established ponds there is usually sufficient natural food to tide the fish over and they can survive without food for quite a long time. Do not be tempted to give them a large meal before you go and another after you get back – this is not only unnecessary, but may, in fact, harm the fish.

Most pond fish will become tame in time. Some varieties, such as koi, are easier to tame, basically because they are greedier! Accustom the fish to being fed at the same spot in the pond, once a day. Don't scatter the food too widely, and stand motionless beside the pool so that the fish get used to seeing you while they are feeding. Then stop feeding them for three to seven days, but continue to spend some time each day beside the pool. Recommence feeding, but give only a few pellets, and sit close to the pond. If you wish to encourage hand feeding, hold the food just under the surface of the water. At first you may need to hold your hand under for some time, but eventually some of the bolder fish will come up to the surface to take food from your hand. Continue to feed sparingly until those fish come readily to you – others will normally follow. Once you have successfully tamed a few fish, you can gradually increase the level of feeding. Remember to scatter some food for the more nervous fish.

If tame fish become skittish and unfriendly, it usually means that they have been frightened by a bird or cat. They will normally become tame again once the danger is removed.

*Above: Koi will often become tame enough to eat from your hands. Don't be fooled by their greedy appetites; overfeeding will quickly pollute the pond.*

*Below: Pellet foods are often enriched with colour enhancers. These contain carotenes, which boost red coloration; other blends use algae meals.*

*Below: A staple diet pellet is ideal for general feeding and will float for a long while; allowing excess food to be removed. Choose a pellet size to suit your fish.*

*Below: Flake foods are mainly used to feed aquarium fish but can also be fed to smaller pond fish. They are ideal for fish fry if crumbled between your fingers.*

## FISH HEALTH

Like humans, fish can become ill, especially when they are stressed, but if you keep your pond water in good condition, do not overcrowd the fish, and you make a point of buying only healthy fish, disease should be a very rare occurrence.

Unhealthy fish become lethargic, may stop feeding, and their fins are often folded in, rather than held out. Other outward signs of disease are described below. Stress, often due to poor water quality, is the main cause of disease; if this is the case, any amount of medication will prove ineffective. It is most important to remove the source of stress before attempting to treat the fish.

If problems occur, check the water quality first, however clean and healthy it may appear (see page 127). If necessary, carry out partial water changes and stop feeding the fish until the problem is dealt with, which will cut down on one of the main sources of waste, and thus of pollution.

Sudden losses of fish usually indicate pollution in the water, or a lack of oxygen. Losses over a longer period of time can be caused by stress and disease. Diseases tend to be most prevalent at times of year when the fish are stressed; in the spring the fish are weak after the winter and, as temperatures rise, waste in the pond starts to decompose. In midsummer fish are spawning and can damage each other; their hormone levels are also raised at this time of year, making them less able to fight disease.

■ **Anchorworm and fish louse** are larger crustacean parasites, which, though they rarely cause fish deaths, can weaken fish if present in large numbers. The wounds they cause can become infected and affected fish will often jump, scratch and flash.

Anchorworm (Lernea) are visible as small (3-12mm/0.12-0.5in) whitish tags hanging from virtually any part of the fish, the head of the parasite being embedded in the fish. As the anchorworm has a long and complex life cycle, it is often necessary to carry out a prolonged course of treatment with specific anti-parasite medications. In severe cases, remove the parasites with tweezers and use a topical treatment to clean the wound.

Fish lice (Argulus) should be treated with a specific anti-parasite medication, usually containing organophosphate, but some fish, such as orfe and rudd, are sensitive to these and will require alternative treatment.

■ **Carp pox** describes the waxy off-white blobs found on some carp and koi – often on the fins, though it can affect any part of the body. Although

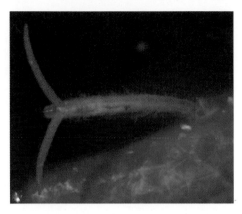

*Above: Anchorworm are unsightly parasites causing wounds on fish.*

*Adults need to be removed with tweezers; pond treatments will control juveniles.*

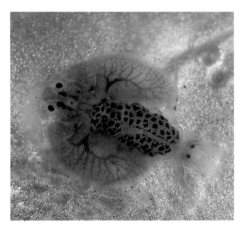

*Above: Fish lice can grow up to 12mm (0.5in) across. Their disc-like bodies lie flat on the fish's skin, piercing it to feed.*

*Right: Ragged fins are a result of bacterial infection, often following stress. Improving conditions is often sufficient in mild cases.*

sometimes mistaken for fungi or white spot, carp pox rarely causes much harm, and affected fish are usually lively and continue to eat. It is caused by a virus similar to the human herpes virus. Pox may occur if the fish has been moved or chilled. In many cases the fish's immune system will fight off the infection after three or four weeks, but if there is no improvement, flick the growths off with your thumb nail and dab the area with tincture of iodine. Pox may reoccur.

■ **Dropsy** is a symptom of internal problems in the fish, characterized by a bloated appearance and scales protruding like a pinecone. It is often accompanied by protruding eyes (pop-eye). The cause can be any number of internal complaints – only a few of which are contagious. Treatment with salt and anti-bacterial medications can sometimes help and antibiotic therapy is more effective, but in many cases dropsy will prove fatal.

■ **Finrot** is generally caused by poor water conditions and stress, resulting in a bacterial infection. To treat, improve the conditions and treat the pond with an anti-bacterial medication. Topical treatments are also very effective. Severe cases are rare, but may require antibiotics. The fin regrows with transparent tissue, pigment taking some months to recover.

■ **Fungus** is a common disease, visible as fluffy off-white tufts on the fish's body, which can become stained green or brown by algae. Fungus is a secondary infection; the spores are always present in the water and will

*Right: Fungus is a secondary infection, which can kill fish if left untreated. It is important to discover the underlying cause of the infection to prevent any re-occurrence.*

invade the skin where the protective mucus coat has been removed, for example by raised pH levels or physical damage following spawning or attack by birds or cats. Fungus will also attack fish severely affected by other diseases.

Treatment involves removal of the original source of stress, and medication, either topically or in the pond water, with a proprietary preparation. Small areas of fungus can be treated very effectively.

■ **Gill problems** should be suspected when fish become very lethargic and glide around near the pond surface or by moving water. The gill plates beat faster than normal, or very erratically. Fish may die with no outward sign of illness, but examination of the gills will reveal patchy or ragged filaments, often blotched white or grey rather than the usual even pink-red. The problem is caused by bacterial or fungal infections of the gills. This is normally a secondary problem following damage from stress, often caused by ammonia, nitrite and chlorine, or gill parasites.

Remove all sources of stress and treat the pond with salt, which clears excess mucus from the gills, or with anti-bacterial medications. Ensure that the pond is well oxygenated, and treat also for parasites if these are suspected. In severe cases, antibiotic therapy will be required. Prompt treatment is essential, as advanced cases are normally fatal.

■ **Leeches** are present in most ponds, but only one or two of the many varieties attack fish. To remove a leech, net the fish, dab the leech with a strong salt solution and remove it with tweezers. Alternatively, organophosphate treatments will often control the adult leeches, though not the leech eggs.

■ **Mouth fungus** is, in fact, a bacterial infection, resulting in reddened lips and loose white tissue around the mouth. It can be caused by a number of bacteria, including *Flexibacter columnaris,* and can pass from fish to fish, or through infected nets. Treatment is similar to that for ulcers.

■ **Slimy skin** is a description of the bluish white hue on the surface of fish that are affected by skin parasites, which live in the mucus coating of the fish. Occasionally the skin and fins may be reddened as well. Most fish carry a few parasites and may flash now and again because of irritation; this is not worth worrying about. However, if fish are regularly flashing, scratching, or jumping at the water's surface, take action. In severe cases the fish may become very lethargic, as their gills are also affected.

Treatment involves minimizing any forms of stress, and use of general anti-parasite medications intended for single-cell/protozoan parasites. Skin flukes are a little less common but give similar symptoms; their eradication may require more potent medications.

■ **Twisted spines** in adult fish are sometimes caused by an electric shock following a thunderstorm, or as a result of faulty electric equipment. Overdoses of medications containing organophosphate insecticides will also damage the nervous system and twist the fish spine.

*Right: Bent spines in young fish can be caused by internal parasites or genetic defects. Damage to the nervous system is the main cause in older fish.*

■ **Ulcers** are a bacterial infection on the body surface. They cause an unsightly wound which is often reddened with white patches around the edge. Bacteria can also attack the fins and mouth in the same way. Although not very common, this can become a major problem if it occurs. There are a number of causes:

■ Damage from birds, cats or large parasites, such as anchorworm, can become infected. Usually only one or two fish are affected.
■ Scratches in the mucus of the fish become infected by bacteria. Ulcers on the affected fish release more bacteria into the water, increasing the risk of disease spread. A number of fish may become affected.
■ Raised areas on the fish break into open sores. The bacteria are present in the fish bloodstream and cause the ulcers from within. This type can be quite infectious.

Ulcers are often caused by various forms of *Aeromonas* bacteria, but other bacteria may be involved. The severity depends upon the particular strain of bacteria; stress and poor conditions play a major role in spreading the disease and all steps should be

*Below: Ulcers are particularly unpleasant bacterial infections that can prove difficult to treat. Improving conditions is beneficial.*

taken to minimize stress and improve hygiene — by disinfecting nets after every use, for example. You can usually treat infections resulting from simple damage effectively with a pond anti-bacterial medication. Topical treatment of the wound is also very helpful. In cases of more severe infection, combine treatment with salt therapy (see table). If suitable facilities are available, isolate all affected fish, remembering that poor isolation facilities will stress the fish, and are worse than useless. In persistent cases, consult a veterinary professional specialising in fish diseases.

■ **Wasting disease** can be caused by various internal problems including liver damage, internal parasites and fish tuberculosis. In a few cases, specialized anti-parasite treatments or vitamin supplements might help.

■ **White spot** describes the numerous pin-head-sized white pimples that are caused by the encysted stage of this protozoan parasite. The spots are scattered all over the body, and may be difficult to see from a distance. Larger white blobs are not white spot, neither are the pimples (spawning tubercles) found on the gill plates and pectoral fins of male goldfish.

Treatment involves the use of anti-parasite medications in the pond. As the life cycle of white spot (or 'ich') can be quite long at lower temperatures, and only certain stages are susceptible, retreat the pond after four days if the temperature is above 15°C (60°F), or after seven days if it is below this temperature.

*Below: White spot or 'ich', is a parasitic disease often triggered by chills or sudden stress. Early treatment with a pond medication should prevent fish losses.*

## FISH TREATMENTS AND MEDICATIONS

| | |
|---|---|
| ■ Fungal treatments | Proprietary treatments containing Malachite green. Topical treatments are also effective (see below). |
| ■ Controls for parasites with free-swimming stage | Proprietary broad-spectrum parasite treatments containing one or more of the following: Malachite green; Acriflavine/Ethacridine; Dimetridazole; Methylene blue; Formalin; Metronidazole; Quinine. |
| ■ Controls for fluke-type parasites | Proprietary parasite treatments containing: Malachite green with formalin; Organophosphate chemicals*. |
| ■ Controls for anchorworm and fish louse | Proprietary specific treatments containing: Organophosphate chemicals* (Trichlorphon; Naled). These may need to be repeated to control anchorworm. Anchorworm can also be controlled with Diflubenzuron. |
| ■ Antibacterial treatments for minor infections | Proprietary broad spectrum treatments containing one or more of the following: Malachite green; Acriflavine/Ethacridine; Methylene blue; Formaldehyde (Formalin); Sodium Chloride. Topical treatments are also effective. |
| ■ Antibacterial and antibiotic treatments for severe infections | In food: Oxolinic acid (and other quinoline antibacterials); Oxytetracycline. In water: Nifurpirinol; Sodium Nifurstyrenate; Oxytetracycline; Ampicillin. By injection: obtain professional advice. |
| ■ Topical treatments | Some proprietary antibacterial treatments; tincture of iodine; Povidone iodine; Mercurichrome; proprietary treatments containing Benzalkonium chloride – topically or in a short-term bath; proprietary antibacterial, antibiotic and protective pastes and ointments. |
| ■ Sodium chloride (additive-free salt) | A useful medication, which can be used in conjunction with some other treatments. Dose rates: 1g/litre (0.1%) as a general tonic; 3g/litre (0.3%) as protection against nitrite toxicity; 5g/litre (0.5%) for reduced levels of free-swimming parasites. The above levels can be used until a cure is effected. 7-9g/litre (0.7-0.9%) as a supportive treatment for one to three weeks while treating wounds and ulcers. Raise and lower high salt levels (above 0.3%) over a period of days. Goldfish and koi are more tolerant of high salt levels than some other pond fish. |

**NOTES**

*Organophosphate chemicals will kill orfe and rudd; use with great care with other fish too.

Follow directions for all proprietary treatments carefully (overdoses can kill fish) and check pond volume. Where proprietary medications are unavailable, refer to reference texts for dosage rates of chemicals. Many chemicals, in particular antibiotics and methylene blue, can destroy biological filter activity; treat fish in an isolated system if possible. Some dye treatments and higher levels of salt can affect plant growth. Indiscriminate use of antibiotics can result in treatment-resistant forms of bacteria; obtain veterinary advice. Local regulations may affect the availability of drugs.

## BREEDING FISH

Most fish will breed in ponds providing the conditions are acceptable. You will need some mature fish, male and female. The exact age at which fish mature, and the distinguishing marks between male and female, vary from species to species. Fish enter spawning condition at certain times of year, generally depending upon the temperature of the water and the length of daylight. Goldfish are prolific and may spawn any time between late spring and early autumn if the water is warm enough, but most other pond fish will spawn in early and mid-summer. Some fish only spawn in very warm summers, or in very large pools; others have specific environmental requirements to enable them to start spawning.

Males chase the egg-laden females around the pond, often swimming near the top edge of the pool and through underwater plants, then nudge the belly of the female, encouraging the release of the eggs, which they fertilize with milt. If a number of males are chasing, the female fish can get quite badly knocked, and may need to be isolated for a while to recover. Spawning often takes place during the morning, and koi may start to spawn at first light.

Many thousands of eggs are released in each spawning, but only a few will survive; some are eaten (by other fish in the pond), many fail to be fertilized by milt, and others become infected by fungi present in the water. Those that do survive are difficult to see – the tiny spheres are about a millimetre across and clear or translucent amber depending on the species. They are sticky when first released and tend to attach themselves to underwater oxygenators and the roots dangling from floating plants. If you lift them out of the water, you will see these eggs as tiny specks of jelly, clinging onto the plant.

To help the eggs survive, provide dense growths of underwater plants, or floating plants, such as water hyacinths and water lettuce (*Eichhornia* and *Pistia*), that have large root systems; or buy spawning ropes made of soft fibre materials. If there is a great danger of fish eating the eggs, remove the egg-coated plants or ropes to a fish-free hatchery.

Regular feeding will keep fish in good health; to encourage them to spawn during warm spells in mid-summer, top the pool up in the evening with some cool tap water, then follow this with a very light feed to bring all the fish together in one place. They will often spawn the following morning, as the water temperature rises.

Goldfish eggs take between three and seven days to hatch, depending upon the water temperature. The tiny fry that emerge are almost invisible and attach themselves to any nearby surfaces or plants. At first they feed on the remains of their yolk sac, but then they head off into the water to find more food. Minute crustacean water fleas and other small organisms form a large part of the fry diet, along with protozoan creatures and algae on the surfaces of nearby plants. As the fry grow, they move on to larger foods, and within a few weeks they will have reached 6-12mm (0.25-0.5in). They will be visible as tiny flecks in the water with prominent eyes, often basking in the warmth of the shallows. The fry can be fed at an early stage. Special liquid and powder fry foods are available, and larger fry will eat powdered flake and pellet foods. The best food is natural microscopic pond life, which provides a constant supply of fresh food.

The early days are dangerous for fry. They can be eaten by larger fish or captured by insect larvae, beetles and

*Above: In warm seasons, goldfish will spawn readily in most garden ponds; the males vigorously chase the egg-laden females.*

*Hydra.* If the water quality drops or they become overcrowded, they will become stressed and vulnerable to parasite and bacterial ailments. Most pond fish give no parental care to their offspring, and produce large numbers of eggs to increase the chances that some will survive.

The fry of many fish, including goldfish, are drably coloured to help disguise them, but colours will be noticeable on shubunkins and koi from quite an early age, some being brightly coloured by the time they are 20mm (0.8in) long. In warm climates, goldfish start to colour (from the underside up) after only two or three months, but in temperate climates the colour change may take from six months to two years. Some goldfish revert to the wild type coloration and remain a drab olive brown.

Fry that have not reached 20mm (0.8in) long by the autumn are unlikely to survive the winter. Goldfish are genetically a very 'plastic' species, which means that you may have fry with two or three tails, missing gill plates or even, occasionally, with only one eye. These genetic defects may not show up until the fish are larger, but these fish will often live quite happily to a great age.

# POND CARE

## CLEANING THE POND

Like any part of the garden, a pond requires some regular maintenance if it is to be kept looking at its best. If you have sited the pond away from overhanging trees, and stocked it with a good balance of plants, then frequent clean-outs will be neither necessary nor desirable, and some appropriate seasonal care (see pages 142-145) will be sufficient for several years.

There will come a time in the life of any pool when the level of detritus on the base builds up to a level that requires attention. For example, in medium-sized pools, a depth of detri-

*Below: Late summer is a good time to clean out a large pond. An autumn cover-net would be needed here to keep out falling leaves from the surrounding trees.*

tus in excess of 8-10cm (3-4in) merits attention. To obtain some temporary relief in larger, more natural ponds, use products containing champagne chalk. Scatter this fine powder in the water and it will settle on the base, aiding the breakdown of organic waste. However, these products do not work in every situation and are only really a stop-gap measure.

If you decide to clean the pond, plan in advance to minimize the disruption to pond life. This is an ideal opportunity to add a waterfall, ornament or stepping stones to your pond. Spring is not a good time for a "spring" clean; the water may be cold and conditions unpleasant to work in; fish are weak, following the winter, and prone to stress; plants are not in full growth and therefore not suited to dividing and replanting. There is also the danger of upsetting any amphibians

spawning in the pond or damaging their tiny offspring. Early and mid-summer are slightly better times for a clean-out, but young fish fry could be injured or lost, and the plants will take time to recover and may not flower as well during the rest of the summer.

Late summer is ideal; most plants will have completed flowering, but will still be in active growth, and the majority of fish fry should be large enough to be netted carefully. Pick a day that is not too hot so that plants do not dry out, and stop feeding the fish the day before.

Prepare your equipment before you start. Remove marginal plants first, splitting and replanting them while the pond is draining, and store them temporarily in a shady spot, watering them regularly to prevent them drying out. Wrap any wilting plants in damp newspaper for temporary protection. Net off floating plants and keep them in buckets or trays of water.

Place a temporary container for the fish somewhere near the pond, but shaded from the heat of the sun. A round paddling pool with a good surface area and no sharp internal projections, which might damage the fish, is ideal, though you could use a plastic

*Above: A simple temporary tank with aerated water and a cover net is ideal for keeping fish in while you are cleaning the pond or medicating or quarantining fish.*

## LEAKS AND POND REPAIRS

A dropping pond level can be very disconcerting, and will reveal an unsightly rim around the pond edge. In many cases there is a simple explanation and straightforward remedy.

Evaporation is a major cause of water loss, especially in hot or windy weather – remember that water is lost not only at the pool surface, but also through the surface of plants growing out of the pond, and from bog areas. It is quite common for the water level to drop 5cm (2in) in a summer week.

Splashing also causes water loss – the spray from fountains and waterfalls can spread a considerable distance, especially in warm or windy weather. Adjust the height of fountain

water cistern, or even a wooden frame draped with a cheap liner instead. Fill this with the cleanest water drawn from near the suface of the pool. Unless the water is particularly foul, save as much as you can at this stage, so that the balance will be quickly restored in the refilled pool. Use the rest of the water from the pond for watering flowerbeds and shrubs.

It is easier to catch the fish when the pond is nearly empty; using a reasonably sized net to move them, lift the fish swiftly over into their temporary quarters (see also page 109). Check the fish for any signs of injury or disease and if there are many fish in the temporary container, ensure that it is sufficiently aerated by installing a circulating pump or aquarium airstone. Cover the container with a tight-fitting fine mesh net to prevent the fish from leaping out (diamond-mesh stretching nets are unsuitable as small fish can get caught in them). Don't feed the fish at this stage.

Drain the pond as low as is feasible and doublecheck for any small fish that you have overlooked. Remove the layer of detritus on the pond base with a dustpan and bucket rather than the pump, and dig it into flowerbeds, or spread it thinly onto the compost heap. If you need to step into the pond, check that the base will support your weight; wear soft-soled footwear in a liner pool, and use a round-edged plank to spread your weight in a preformed pool.

Rinse the pond down and brush off any excess blanketweed from the sides. Don't use detergents; paint any stubborn growths of blanketweed with a solution of pool algicide. You can start to refill the pond straight away. Carry out any extra work on the plants while the pond is filling, and reposition them in the pool as soon as it is sufficiently full. Take the opportunity to add any new plants and make up for any losses, and add a water conditioner to the inflowing water to neutralize any chlorine. If you managed to save a lot of the old water, run some of this into the pond.

If the fish do not seem unduly stressed by their temporary quarters, leave them a while longer to allow the water in the refilled pond to warm slightly. Transfer the fish back to the pool with care (see page 109).

Top up the pool with the remains of the saved water and return any floating plants. The pool will take some time to settle and may appear rather bare at first and unfiltered ponds will be rather cloudy for a few weeks. You can start to feed the fish again, but only sparingly at first. Avoid adding any new fish until the pond has completely recovered. After its overhaul, the pond will be in good condition for the winter and plants should grow strongly the following spring.

(see also page 109) ... (see page 109)

## CHECKLIST OF EQUIPMENT USEFUL FOR CLEANING PONDS

For draining and cleaning:
- A suitable pump and sufficient hose and cable.
  Alternatively a large-bore (over 20mm/0.8in) siphon hose.
- Clean buckets.
- Dustpan and coarse brush.
- Waterproof boots.
- Water supply hose for rinsing down and refilling.

For splitting plants:
- Polythene groundsheet to keep the work area tidy.
- Containers of water to keep floating plants in.
- Damp newspaper to cover and protect plants while they are out of the water.
- New planting containers, if necessary.
- Hessian liners, fresh soil and topping gravel for replanting, plus fertilizer tablets.
- A garden knife and scissors and a trowel.

For storing fish:
- A suitable holding container and cover net.
- A water or airpump for aeration.
- A sufficiently large catching net.
- A tap water conditioner for refilling the pond.

sprays to compensate, and consider water loss at the planning stage.

Capillary action can draw vast quantities of water from the pond – folds in pond liners, pieces of protective matting on top of the liner, and growths of thread algae, can act as wicks drawing water into the surrounding soil. Double check around the pool edge for damp patches and adjust liner folds or remove matting and algae to compensate.

In streams and waterfalls, algae growing on pouring lips, or leaves collecting at falls, can raise the level sufficiently for water to escape over the sides. Biological filters can also overflow if they become clogged.

If the pool level continues to drop, then there may be a leak. Continue to top up the pond until you find time to investigate. Turn off fountains and waterfalls (but try to keep biological filters functioning) to discover if these have been the cause of the water loss. If the water still drops, let it find its level, then examine the waterline for damage. Cracks in cement, which tend to open with time, should not be too difficult to pinpoint, but small areas of damage in glassfibre or liner ponds may be harder to locate. In dry weather, look out for any telltale damp regions of soil. Tap preformed ponds around the waterlevel, as the sound will alter if there is water behind a particular area. Press gently on liner ponds to find if the soil behind is soft and wet at any point.

How you repair a leak will depend on the lining material you have used. General-purpose underwater patches are available, but you should clean and dry the damaged area before patching for a longterm repair.

Clean out concrete cracks with a wire brush and widen them slightly to give a good surface for the filling to key into. Various repair compounds are available, which are often longer lasting than a standard rendering mortar. Coat the dried surface of the repair with a flexible sealant paint or a mastic tape to seal in lime, and cover the crack. Remember that cracks tend to open up again, particularly after frost. The only permanent answer to bad cracking is to use a flexible liner.

Abrade glassfibre ponds around the damaged area to give a rough surface. Cover the hole with a glassfibre patch and layers of resin, or for small

## PART WATER CHANGES

Water changes improve the quality of the water in a pond far more than a mere topping-up ever can. Wastes tend to build up in a pond, and even a biological filter cannot remove them all. As water evaporates from the pond, waste and mineral salts become more concentrated, and topping up with water cannot dilute these fully.

Drain some water from the pond before refilling; ideally this should be pumped or siphoned from the dirtiest conditions on the base of the pond. You can siphon out waste – providing there is a point in the garden below the surface of the pond – using a large bore hose (20-30mm/0.8-1.2in), and starting the siphon by filling it with water from a tap or pump. Alternatively, submerge the hose in the pool to expel air, cover one end and lift it out of the pool and to the lower level. Fix a solid piece of pipe to the end of the hose in the pond to facilitate vacuuming the base. You may need to clear leaves from the suction end of the hose from time to time.

Drain out up to 20% of the pond volume at a time; larger water changes are more likely to upset the balance of the pool. Top the pond up from the tap, jetting the water in to aerate it, and add a tap water conditioner.

patches, epoxy glassfibre paste. Use sufficient hardener in the mix to give a tough surface, and after drying, rinse well to remove harmful chemicals.

Repair liners and preformed plastic ponds with specific patches and glues. Clean surfaces well and use a small amount of solvent cleaner to remove grease. Old plastic does not bond well and some plastics are very difficult to glue. Uncured butyl mastic tape or patches are the best means of repairing butyl; warm all surfaces to increase adhesion. This material will also stick to a number of other plastics, but will not bond surfaces together if tension is pulling them apart.

## HAZARDS

Children, especially the very young, can be at risk around water, whether it is shallow or deep, and you must take safety precautions if unsupervised children are likely to play near the water. Raised ponds, out of reach of small children, and pebble fountain features are design possibilities. Alternatively, place a strong steel mesh temporarily over small ponds (use a 15cm/6in grid painted with black enamel), or put up a fence around the feature. Remember to keep electrical controls out of reach of children.

Herons can decimate fish populations, but are less of a problem in built-up areas that are distant from other ponds and lakes. They will raid ponds very early in the morning and are not afraid to come close to houses. To dissuade herons, you can string an almost invisible nylon line around the pool edge, 30-40cm (12-16in) above ground and 20-30cm (8-10in) back from the water. They will hit the line when walking up to the pool and fly off. Unfortunately, once a heron is familiar with a pond it may swoop down from above. A net over the pond, or nylon line zig-zagged across the water will help. Provide fish with plants or covered areas where they can hide. Herons are cunning hunters, unlikely to be put off by decoys.

Other birds, such as crows, magpies and seagulls may take the occasional fish, expecially ones that are lethargic.

*Left: Incorporate extra liner at the construction stage to catch seepage and reduce water loss from a high waterfall.*

*Above: A raised wall around the pond will help to keep out small children and will dissuade cats and herons from plundering fish.*

Cats have different characters, and some may be avid fishers. Keep the fish out of reach by ringing the pond with lush growths of marginal plants, or building a raised wall around formal pools. Cat-repellent chemicals have mixed results, and some are dangerous to fish.

Dogs rarely go for fish, although they may drink from the pool. Some lively dogs may be partial to the odd swim and this can disrupt plants. Keep friends' dogs well away, and train your own not to swim at home.

Frogs and toads generally pose no threat to pond life, but occasionally they may mistakenly grab pond fish while spawning in the spring, and this can damage or kill. If you do remove amphibians, take them to a suitable wet site many miles from your pond; they have good homing instincts and can often find their way back.

Gnats and mosquitoes are much less of a problem around water containing fish, as they devour the insect larvae. If insects become a nuisance, site an electrocuting unit, with attractant violet bulb, near the pond.

Other pests and predators vary from country to country. Some rodents may attack fish or plants, others can damage exposed pond liners – PVC types in particular. Water voles and coypus can damage water plants and burrow through pond edges; mink and otters may take fish. These predators are more common in rural areas than in towns.

# SEASONAL WATER GARDEN CARE

## SPRING

In spring the pond comes to life after its winter rest. The marsh marigolds *(Calthas)* and early bog primulas *(Primula denticulata, P. rosea)* are the harbingers of spring. Fish are still lethargic in the cold temperatures and often rather weak. You can start to feed them again as the weather warms, ideally using easily digested wheatgerm-rich foods. Feed around midday so that the warmth of the afternoon can aid digestion, and stop feeding if cold weather is forecast.

If a pond cover net is in place, leave it until the marginals start to grow up, as it will help to protect lethargic fish from hungry herons at a time when natural plant cover is limited. After re-moving the net, trim back any dead foliage, but remember to provide some protection, as late frosts set some plants back. The spring is a good time to plant up, or alter, the bog garden and other areas outside the pond, but, in many regions, is too cold for dividing pond plants themselves.

Waste and leaves that have built up on the pond base since the autumn can suddenly start to decompose as water temperatures rise. This is upsetting to the pond balance and stressful to fish, so it is very beneficial to carry out a partial water change at this time to remove waste and freshen up the pond.

Following the winter, it is wise to check all electrical equipment and cables for weather damage. If you turn off pumps during the winter, clean them and ensure that parts are moving freely before restarting them.

Pond filter organisms will be increasing their activity, and if you reduced the flow rate through the filter, you can now gradually increase it to normal levels. Reinstate any filters that were turned off during the winter, giving them a good rinse first, and speed up the rate of biological activity by using commercially available starter cultures.

Amphibians will be spawning in the pond. Keep an eye on the fish and remove any toads that grab hold of fish in error. Protect spawn from hungry fish by removing it to a fish-free pool, or by segregating it behind some plastic mesh.

Spring is a good time to plan extensions to water features. The ground is usually workable, and any new pond could be ready to stock with plants and fish by late spring.

*Below: Early flowering plants are a welcome sign of increasing activity in the pond; time to tidy up after the bleak winter months.*

## SUMMER

In early summer the plants and fish will move into active growth, helping the pond to look more attractive after the drab winter months. With fountains and waterfalls running, the rate of evaporation will start to increase and you may need to top up the pond from time to time. Green algae can flourish at this time of year, and the pond may become a little cloudy until the plants reach full growth. Net out any thread algae, and try to be patient – algal problems often cure themselves. If pea-soup algae has been a persistent problem, consider fitting a biological filter.

This is the time to add new plants to the pond, and once they have settled you could also add fish. Build up stocks of oxygenating (submerged) and floating plants to encourage clear water. Do not add tender aquatics to the pond until the risk of frosts is over. Some plants may benefit from being divided and replanted, and you could use fertilizer tablets to boost the growth of existing plants.

Weed out any unwanted seedlings from bog plant areas and put down a mulch of chopped bark or peat to smother new weed growth and hold moisture into the underlying soil.

Fish will be feeding much more readily and can be moved on to fresh, high-protein foods when the water temperature rises above 15°C (60°F). In the warmer weather, fish parasites can also multiply, so you should look out for disease problems. Treat with a specific medication if you notice particular problems, or, if in doubt, use a broad-spectrum medication.

Biological filters are under a great deal of pressure at this time of year, as the biological organisms in them may not be multiplying quickly enough to cope with the increasing fish waste and algae growth. Clean pre-filters to prevent clogging, taking care not to upset filter organisms. Avoid over-cleaning media and try not to let strong medications enter the filter.

This is a good time of year to install lighting systems, which will allow you to make the most use of the area around the pond during summer and autumn evenings.

During mid and late summer the pond is at its best with plants in full bloom, fish active and the sights and

sounds of moving water particularly welcome. In hot weather the pond level may drop quite rapidly, requiring more frequent topping up. Oxygen levels can also drop, and pond life will benefit from pumps being run night and day.

It is still a good time to introduce or divide aquatic plants, making sure that plants do not dry out in the sun. Snip off any spent blooms to keep the garden looking neat.

New fish will acclimatize well during the summer. Feed them to promote rapid growth and encourage tameness, but be careful not to over-feed. Spawning can take place from early summer onwards and by late summer you may see a number of fish fry. Be ready to isolate any female fish that are being excessively harassed by spawning males and give young fry cover by providing dense underwater plant growth, or remove them to another pond, free of large fish.

Clean biological filters if they are dirty, taking care not to flush out too

*Above: Make the most of the long summer days beside the pond, with the cool reflections of lush leaf growth, giant lily blooms, and the splashing of darting fish.*

many of the biological organisms. Clean pump strainers if they become clogged and remove the pump occasionally for cleaning and check to see if the bearings need replacing.

Late summer is the time to consider a pond clean-out, but this will not be necessary every year if you have carried out regular maintenance. A small partial water change will help to remove waste from the pond. Pond vacuuming systems are available, but siphoning out dirt is often just as effective, and a fine mesh net can be used to remove larger pieces of debris on the pond base. Pump-powered vacuuming systems are more useful for koi ponds, which have few plants, but they need to be used on a regular basis to prevent the pump pre-strainer becoming clogged with dirt.

## AUTUMN

Many plants will flower until the autumn frosts, and some, such as the water hawthorn *(Aponogeton distachyus)*, can carry on until ice covers the pond. A number of poolside plants glow with autumnal hues, and pond fish colours, too, may intensify in the cooler weather.

Autumn is the time to tidy your pool. Trim back dying plant growth, but leave some material to protect plants from the frost. Remove tender aquatics to their winter quarters before frosts. Lower less hardy plants, such as *Zantedeschia aethiopica* and *Lobelia fulgens*, into deeper water if in containers, or give them a protective mulch if in the bog garden.

Oxygenating plants are often rather straggly by this time of year, and if you leave them growing at the surface, they may become frozen in ice and the uppermost growth will be killed. Trim off the top growth and replant.

Early autumn is the latest time to consider a complete pond clean-out.

Otherwise, change part of the water (around 20%) to freshen the pond and leave it in good condition for the winter. Remove as much waste as possible from the base of the pond. Leaves are a major cause of pond pollution and removal of floating leaves is not sufficient to prevent significant quantities reaching the pond base, so put a strong square mesh (1cm/0.4in) net over the pond and remove leaves that gather on top of it. If the net is held taut, many leaves will blow off rather than settling.

The fish should be strong and healthy after the summer, but take the time to check them for any signs of disease, as it is virtually impossible to treat them successfully during cold weather. The summer's spawnings of fry should be visible and growing well. Carry on feeding while the fish show interest, but give smaller amounts of more readily digested foods. Stop feeding if very cold weather is forecast. Do not move fish or introduce new ones if pond temperatures drop below 10°C (50°F).

Container-grown water plants introduced to the pond in the autumn will make a good show the following year. However, mid-autumn is too late to divide aquatics, and it would also be unwise to introduce bare-root plants. The autumn is an ideal time to plant up the bog garden or divide bog plants, which prefer to be moved outside their peak growing period.

Give filters a good clean before the winter sets in, taking care not to wash out all the active filter organisms. As the weather becomes colder, the flow rate through the filter can be reduced to prevent excessive cooling.

*Left: Autumnal colours signal the end of another flowering season and the need to net over the pond before heavy leaf falls.*

*Left: Sparkling crisp frosts highlight foliage around the pond. Despite the lack of activity below the surface, make sure that a hole is melted in persistent ice.*

Do not break the ice, as shock waves can stun or kill fish. Instead, melt the ice with a pan of hot water, or a small pond heater (60 to 150 watts), suspended at the water surface from floats. These heaters are not sufficient to warm all the water, but can maintain a hole in the ice. It is easiest to fit them before icy weather. Very large ponds may need a number of heaters.

Floating balls or planks of wood on the surface will not increase gas exchange, and cannot protect concrete pools from frost damage. Polystyrene floats with an air passage through them can help gas exchange to an extent, but will still freeze over in prolonged cold weather.

To avoid cooling the water, turn off fountains and waterfalls where possible, or at least turn them down. Raise submersible pumps well off the base to leave the lower regions undisturbed for pond life. Remove pumps if they are not being used, then clean and store them according to manufacturers' instructions. If you leave them in the pond, run them occasionally to prevent build-ups of silt and scale from seizing the bearings, making sure that they are deep enough not to be frozen in ice. Drain and insulate external pumps.

If frosts· are expected, drain and rinse through biological filters, leaving them disconnected and dry during the winter, unless you keep valuable fish, which will benefit from the running filter. Take action to prevent ice forming in the filter.

Koi do not like very prolonged, cold winters, so provide extra protection by placing covers over part of the pool, but remember to remove them in the spring to prevent too rapid a rise in pond temperature. Some koi-keepers install larger water-heating systems to keep their ponds above 10°C (50°F). Fish will then feed all year round, grow faster, and can be appreciated even in the depths of winter. However, this is expensive on fuel and not always practical. An alternative is to build a pond inside a conservatory where it will be protected from the ravages of winter.

## WINTER

As cold weather sets in, life in the pond slows down for the winter. Some plants form resting buds which sink to the base of the pond for protection, and some amphibians will settle into the detritus on the pond base. The fish enter a state of semi-hibernation at temperatures below 5°C (40°F), gliding about slowly in the depths of the pond. Refrain from feeding them until the warmer spring weather – in short mild spells they can usually find some natural food.

Leave pond cover nets in place. Although the risk of leaf pollution is reduced, birds, such as herons, are more likely to attack at a time when the fish are unable to react quickly and have very little plant cover.

In the coldest weather, the warmest part of the pond is near the base, where dense water settles. Here the temperature is only 4°C (39°F), or even lower if ice encroaches from the surface, but the cold itself rarely causes death to hardy species, such as goldfish, providing the pond has been built deep enough.

Problems may occur if the ice layer seals the surface for more than a few days, preventing fresh supplies of oxygen from entering the water and stopping waste gases from escaping. In this case, melt a hole to allow the necessary gas exchange at the water surface. Sweep snow off the ice to allow light to enter the pond and keep oxygenating plants active, but leave some snow as an insulator against further cold.

# CHAPTER FIVE

# WILDLIFE PONDS

A garden pool acts as a magnet for wildlife: aquatic insects, amphibians, microscopic water life and birds. Wildlife in the garden is of great educational merit to children, helping them to understand some of the principles of ecology; and older generations can benefit too, relaxing as they view the activities of colourful damselflies or bathing birds. We are becoming increasingly aware and concerned about our environment, and 'green' issues. We know that the draining of marshlands and pollution of water leaves its toll on the natural habitats of aquatic life, and many species are in danger of extinction. By building a pond in your garden, you are creating a haven for wildlife, and helping to improve the environment. Both wildlife ponds and ornamental garden pools can act as home to a profusion of aquatic organisms. It is quite possible to have wildlife without the untidiness, combining the best of both a decorative pond and a wild pond, by incorporating a few simple features to encourage water life, and designing the pond to make maintenance easier than in a truly wild pond. Here we look at how to do this and at the creatures such a pond may attract. To maintain your wildlife pond follow the general advice given on pages 138-141, but remember that a total pool clean-out will severely upset established pond life, so try to save as much of the water as possible and return some of the detritus to the cleaned pond. Alternatively, in large ponds, clean only one half at a time, leaving the other half to a later season or the following year.

# DESIGNING A WILDLIFE POND

A single pond is unlikely to be able to provide for the needs of all forms of water life, but it is possible to attract a wide variety of wildlife by creating a diverse range of conditions. Try to provide the following:

■ Shallows and depths; a variety of levels.

■ Plenty of plants to give cover, but with some open areas.

■ Access at the pool edge for animal life – either a shallow slope or a suitably textured edging, such as turf.

■ Margins around the pond, so that it will interrelate with its surrounds.

Site your wildlife pond away from overhanging trees, where it will receive a fair amount of sunlight. The maximum depth of the pond should be at least 45cm (18in), and preferably 60cm (24in), to prevent rapid fluctuations in water temperature. Some pond life likes to retire to cooler deep water, so if the pool is large enough, provide an area 75-90cm deep (30-36in) for these species. These recommendations are similar to those for ornamental ponds and water lily cul-

ture, and even in much larger wildlife pools, 150cm (60in) will be sufficiently deep. You can adapt the design of a standard ornamental pool to encourage wildlife by widening the planting shelves to allow for more plants and to provide shallow areas, which will warm rapidly in the sun. Incorporate some extra shelves to give a variety of depths to suit most wildlife, sloping the shallowest shelves gradually to the edge to facilitate the access of animal life. The other sides of the wildlife pond should slope fairly steeply to ensure a good volume of water for the given surface area, providing a stable environment without sudden temperature fluctuations.

Liner material is best for constructing such a pond, although concrete could also be used. You can adapt ornamental ponds, including most preformed pools, to create more levels, by placing pieces of slate on upturned planting containers, and placing a stone or slate between marginal planting containers and the edge to form a shallow sloping exit ramp.

This method of wildlife pond construction is by far the best for smaller

wildlife ponds (under 30m²/300ft²) and will give good results even in much larger ponds. Plants grown in containers are easy to maintain and trim back as necessary, and as the soil is mostly restricted to the containers, you can drain the pond without a major upheaval.

An alternative method of design imitates a natural pond, with gently sloping sides and a layer of soil on the pool base, achieved by sandwiching a pond liner between two layers of protective matting. Cover the top surface with at least 5cm (2in) of soil to allow plants to grow, and provide pockets of deeper soil for larger plants. The gently sloping sides prevent all the soil from washing into the pond base, and the upper layer of protective matting acts as an anchor for plant roots, so encouraging the binding of the soil to the pool sides. Where soil slippage is likely to be a problem, use thicker layers of matting on top of the liner before you spread the soil.

This method of construction is particularly suited to large ponds, when you can use a very thick layer of soil (15-20cm/6-8in) on top of the liner to protect it. This might allow you to use a cheaper grade of lining material (although it is wise to use the best

*Below: This design imitates a natural pond, with soil over the liner, gently sloping sides and plenty of plant cover. Such a pond needs to be on a large scale.*

### Imitating a natural pond

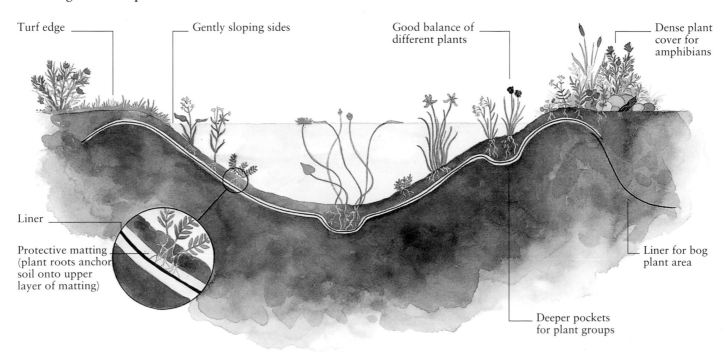

Turf edge

Gently sloping sides

Good balance of different plants

Dense plant cover for amphibians

Liner

Protective matting (plant roots anchor soil onto upper layer of matting)

Liner for bog plant area

Deeper pockets for plant groups

grade you can afford). This type of pond is also more rapidly colonized by water life, the gradual slope of soil allowing easy movement of animals across the pool base, and encouraging the rapid spread of aquatic plants.

However, there are a number of drawbacks with this type of construction for small ponds. Plants grow unrestricted, and the weedier native varieties rapidly swamp small areas; those with sharp root systems may also damage pond linings. You will find it difficult to clean out, and if you are digging out or splitting plants, be very careful not to puncture the lining. To achieve the required depth in a small pond, the sides have to slope more steeply, so the soil will slip to the base. If the sides slope in a more gradual fashion, but to a lesser depth, there will be a low water volume for the given surface area, which encourages very rapid warming of the water in summer, thus creating an unstable environment for water life. In small

ponds the high proportion of loose soil will cause the water to become excessively rich in nutrients, resulting in more frequent problems with green water and algal blooms.

*Above: The dense backdrop of foliage at the pool edge and good variety of water plants make this feature attractive to both wildlife and spectators.*

## THE GREEN GARDENER

Environmental issues are of increasing concern as we become aware of the damage that we are causing to the world around us. Building a wildlife pond in your garden is one way of helping to conserve the environment, and your choice of materials and pond-related products will also help. Try to bear in mind the following:

- Pond construction materials are intended to be long lasting and are therefore not biodegradable. Most cause some damage to the environment: concrete uses mined minerals and a great deal of energy in its manufacture; plastic materials and glassfibre resins all utilize oil resources, and a few, notably PVC, can release toxic gases if burnt.
- Electrical equipment, such as pumps, can use a fair amount of electricity. A high quality, energy-efficient pump, while more expensive to buy, should last longer – saving money and electricity.
- Woodwork around the pond should, where possible, be easily

renewed softwood. However, owing to its propensity to rot, and the dangers of using preservatives by the pond, hardwoods may be the only option. Try to use locally grown hardwoods or those from well-managed tropical woodlands.

- Chemicals should only be used when absolutely necessary. Garden pesticides based on pyrethrins, while less harmful to humans and mammals, are more deadly to fish than some other types. Biological pest controls are being developed, and may prove a viable alternative. All fish medications can upset the pond balance, and should be used with great care.
- Algicides, too, will often upset other plants and pond creatures. Those containing copper sulphate are more persistent and can cause more damage. Tannin-based flocculants are less harmful to plant life, but can still disrupt the natural pond balance.
- Peat extraction can damage wetlands, but garden peat is a very poor medium for growing plants underwater. Instead, use compost

or chipped bark in the bog garden as a soil improver and mulch.
- Stonework often comes from unsightly quarries. Use only as much as you need and make good use of any rocks you dig up in your own garden.
- Pond filter media are not all environmentally sound. Choose a longlife type, such as sintered granules made from pulverized fuel ash, which makes good use of an otherwise waste material.
- Ornamental pond fish, unlike some exotic pets, are virtually all farmed and not caught from the wild. Make sure that your pond plants come from managed resources, rather than from native sources.
- Tap water that is good for fish and plants is good to drink. If it upsets your fish, then what is it doing to you? Chlorine (to keep bacteria at bay) should be the only additive you need to remove from tap water for your pond's sake (see page 120). If you are worried about other contaminants, then let your supply company know of your concerns.

# PLANTS, FISH AND BIRDS

## PLANTS AND THE WILDLIFE POND

Plants are very important in the wildlife pond, helping to maintain a natural balance and encouraging healthy pond water that remains clear for most of the year. You should include a good variety of native plants in the pond, as they supply indigenous varieties of aquatic organisms with sources of food and shelter, but don't feel that you must restrict yourself to these plants. Although many are attractive, some are rather dull, and by intermingling a few more exotic types you will help to brighten the overall appearance, giving a more interesting and decorative effect (see opposite and also pages 96-101).

Some native plants grow very vigorously, rapidly becoming too large for the smaller pond, so use containers to limit their spread and trim back any long creeping rootstocks before they become a problem. Some of the strongest growing reeds and rushes have sharp roots, which may damage pond liners. Confine these to solid-sided pots trimming off any escaping roots, and repotting every few years to prevent the plants from losing vigour.

A good range of underwater oxygenators, marginals, floating plants and plants with floating leaves will all help to encourage wildlife, and remember to plant an area beside the pool to link it with other parts of the garden and to provide cover for amphibians. Marsh and bog plants are most suitable and you could merge these with an area of the garden filled with native plants to attract other forms of insects and animals. Turf edging is another good alternative for wildlife ponds.

*Below: This wildlife pond combines a profusion of native plants, moving water, sunny areas and cool shade, providing a range of conditions to suit a wide variety of pond life.*

## MARGINALS FOR WILDLIFE PONDS

These marginal plants are ideal for an informal wildlife pond, but the more invasive types should be containerized (C) when used in smaller settings.

- **Alisma plantago-aquatica** (Water plantain)
  Tall panicles of pale pink flowers, which seed freely. 45cm (18in).
- **Cardamine pretensis** (Cuckoo Flower)
  A rambling waterside plant with pale lilac flowers. Ideal for boggy soil. 30cm (12in).
- **Eriophorum angustifolium** *(Scirpus angustifolius)*(Cotton Grass).
  White silken tufts above wiry foliage. 30cm (12in).
- **Hippuris vulgaris** (C) (Mare's Tail). Narrow pine-tree-like foliage. 30cm (12in).
- **Juncus ensifolius** (C) (Dwarf soft rush).
  Brown spikelets on rushy foliage. 30cm (12in).
- **Phragmites communis** (C) (Norfolk Reed).
  Tall foliage with purple-tinged plumes. The variegated form is more decorative. 200cm (78in).
- **Ranunculus flammula** (Lesser Spearwort).
  Narrow-leafed foliage and small buttercup flowers. 30cm (12in).
- **Sparganium ramosum** (C) (Bur reed).
  Decorative spikelets among vigorous foliage. 100cm (40in).

*Above:* Eriophorum angustifolium

*Above:* Ranunculus flammula

*Above:* Sparganium ramosum

## FISH AND THE WILDLIFE POND

In large natural ponds and lakes there is usually a range of fish life, but at a fairly low density. Some of these fish, such as pike and perch, are predatory, some eat mainly plants, and others eat the insects and small creatures that inhabit the pond. A balance is reached where no one group of fish dominates. This balance is virtually impossible to recreate in a small wildlife pond, where predatory fish would eat all the smaller fish, but without them the other fish would multiply and consume most of the smaller animal life in the pond, including insects, insect larvae, smaller amphibians and their eggs. You can supplement the fish diet artifically, and if there is lush plant cover some wildlife will survive, but, to encourage diversity of other forms of aquatic life, you may have to exclude fish from your wildlife pond.

If you do want to keep fish, consider the smallest varieties, such as sticklebacks, which will eat some forms of aquatic life, but are less damaging to larger creatures. Alternatively, limit fish to one of each species, or two of the same sex, or, if you have a series of ponds linked by waterfalls, house fish in the lowest, and reserve the upper ponds for wildlife.

If you wish to remove ornamental fish from your pond to encourage wildlife, give them to a friend or sell them through the local papers. Do not be tempted to release them into the nearest brook or canal, where they could seriously upset the existing balance of wildlife, especially if they are exotic imported species.

## BIRDS AND THE WILDLIFE POND

Garden birds greatly appreciate a pond, which they will use as a source of water for drinking and bathing, especially in dry summers and during frosty spells in winter. They prefer gardens that are relatively undisturbed by humans and cats, and will be more likely to visit the pond if there are nearby trees or shrubs for them to take cover in. Smaller birds value areas of shallow water around 5-8cm (2-3in) deep, and you can create an ideal spot for them by situating a shallow shelf in a waterfall pool, where a gentle flow of water over the shelf will keep the area clean and reduce the risk of it freezing in cold weather. A few flat or angular stones in and around the area will provide stable standing ground for the birds, which may also clean their beaks on the stone edges.

Larger birds, such as herons and seagulls, can be pests and should be discouraged if you keep fish.

Ducks and other waterfowl are not recommended for smaller wildlife ponds, as they will eat beetles, shrimps, insect larvae and underwater plants from the pool base, and some varieties will also eat small fish. They also churn up the water, erode the pond bank and leave a trail of feathers and droppings.

If you particularly want waterfowl remember that other forms of wildlife may suffer. The pond should be as large as possible, without too many trees around, as these prevent flying access. It should also have some sloping soil banks, and some dense reed beds or long grass nearby to provide nesting cover.

# ENCOURAGING AMPHIBIANS

Amphibians spend part of their life cycle in and around water. They include frogs, toads, newts and salamanders, and they have intriguing stages in their development as they metamorphose from larvae into adults. Different amphibians have slightly different requirements in the types of ponds they prefer, but all will need a means of getting in and out of the pond. Bear in mind, however, that most amphibians will spend part of their life cycle out of the water, and it is therefore important to provide a suitable area for them outside the pond. Leave an area of long grass, or a flower bed with dense plant cover. Nooks, crannies and crevices will provide protection from drying heat and marauding birds and cats. A few pieces of flat rock or old wooden boards with hollows underneath can act as a hiding place for resting toads. Even a rockery, despite its apparent dryness, can give valuable cover.

Many varieties will find their own way into your garden, soon colonizing the pool. Once they have become established, they will keep coming back, as they have good homing instincts. If you are too impatient to wait for natural colonization, it is possible to introduce eggs or larvae to the pond. You can often find clumps of eggs in natural pools in the spring, but be sure to obtain permission from the pool owner before removing anything, and do not take too much; two to three clumps of frogs' eggs is usually sufficient for an average-sized pond. If you take too many, there will be insufficient food for them in the pond. You might also put the originating colony of amphibians at risk. Some nature conservation groups arrange swaps of spawn in the spring between pondkeepers with excessive spawn and those starting colonies.

Some amphibians are protected by law to reduce the risk of their numbers dwindling. Do not introduce exotic imported amphibians which may escape into the surrounding countryside once they have matured.

## FROGS

Frogs have a smoother, more moist skin, and tend to have more heavily webbed feet than toads. The more common varieties (*Rana spp.*) are often the first amphibians to colonize new pools, even small, less mature ponds. The great clumps of eggs they lay in the water have a coating that soon swells to provide a protective jelly-like layer. These egg masses tend to be laid in the shallow areas (around 8-12cm/3-5in deep) on pond shelves and on top of dense growths of submerged oxygenating plants, and they float just under the water surface, hatching in around a week.

The young frog tadpoles cling onto the side of the pond or plant material for a few days before becoming free swimming. They feed on algae and plant material scraped up by their rasping mouths. Oxygen is absorbed across their skin surface and through their feathery gills, which, though visible in young tadpoles, soon become covered with a protective flap of skin, and water is then passed over these internal gills and out through a small opening – the spiracle.

One to two months after hatching, hind legs develop and help the frog tadpole to swim through the water. Some are even able to remove free-floating algae from the water as a source of food. Around a month later, the front legs – which have been developing internally – pop out through the spiracle. The gills become less important as lungs take over the breathing. The frog tadpoles spend more time in the shallows where they can easily take air from the surface. By

**Exit ramps for amphibians**

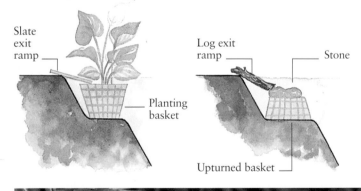

Slate exit ramp

Planting basket

Log exit ramp

Stone

Upturned basket

*Left: If it is not possible to adapt your pond material to create a gentle slope at the edge, use your ingenuity to make a suitable exit ramp that will allow amphibians to leave and enter the pond at will.*

*Left: Common frogs will often turn up in your pond without any effort on your part, and once established will keep coming back.*

*Above: Toads prefer gardens with plenty of dense plant growth to hide among when they are out of water.*

*Right: Adult smooth newts absorb oxygen across their moist skin and through their lungs.*

now their intestines have adapted to a carnivorous diet of small insect larvae and crustaceans, as well as any dead and dying tadpoles. You can supplement their diet at this stage with commercial fish flake and pellet foods. The tadpoles look considerably more frog-like and their tails start to shorten.

Normally within four months of hatching the tail has almost disappeared, and the baby frogs start to venture out from the pond. Only a few will have survived from the egg stage, as many eggs are eaten by fish and other larger pond life. Older tadpoles and adult frogs may also eat some of the eggs and young tadpoles. Some tadpoles succumb to a lack of food, especially if there is overcrowding or if the weather is particularly cold. These conditions may also prolong development. In very small ponds the water may become too warm for the tadpoles, and in steep-sided ponds the baby frogs can drown if they are unable to climb out. They are also very vulnerable to attack from predators, especially if there is not much cover around the pond edge.

Adult frogs may remain in and around the garden, feeding on insects, snails and slugs, and can be quite useful in keeping down the level of plant pests. They will normally return to the pond two to three years after hatching to mate and lay eggs.

## TOADS

Toads have drier, more warty skin than frogs and tend to prefer larger, deeper ponds that are more mature and settled. The male toads, which are noticeably smaller than the female, grasp the females' backs while mating – occasionally grabbing hold of a pond fish in error. The eggs are laid a little later in the spring than are those of frogs and they hang lower in the waters forming long rope-like strands that are tangled around submerged plants. The eggs and tadpoles have an unpleasant taste to fish and so are unlikely to be eaten.

Metamorphosis is shorter than for frogs, usually taking two to three months. Toads are more tolerant of dry conditions and can spend more time away from the pond, travelling greater distances, but they cannot leap, tending to move by crawling or hopping. They will often dig into soil for protection and sometimes over-winter in the mud on the pond base.

## NEWTS

Newts are tailed amphibians with moist skin. Respiration takes place across their skin surface as well as through lungs in adults (gills in larvae) and through the mouth lining. Spawning usually occurs in late spring or early summer, when the males take on their brightest coloration with crests along the backs of some species. Following courtship, the male releases a packet containing sperm, which is captured by the female, and the eggs are fertilized inside her body. She then lays each egg individually onto the submerged leaves of oxygenating and floating plants, sometimes carefully wrapping the leaf around the egg. It is very important to provide a range of native plants to enable this activity.

The young newt tadpoles are a pale brown colour with almost translucent tails. They have distinctive, feathery external gills that remain noticeable for much longer than those of frogs and toads. Towards the end of the summer the newt will have developed all four legs and will emerge from the water (in some cases the larvae will not emerge until the following year).

Newts are carnivorous from birth, eating insects, insect larvae, slugs and snails. The young newts, or efts, live in moist areas of tall grass and undergrowth, sometimes some distance from the pond. Out of the water their skins become tougher. Some species overwinter under rocks and wood, returning to the water the following spring. They may take two years or more to mature and usually return to the same pond to spawn.

# OTHER WILDLIFE

A few weeks after you have completed the wildlife pond, numerous smaller forms of animal life will arrive. The enormous range of arthropod creatures that will colonize the pond include the arachnid water spiders and mites, the crustaceans, such as water fleas, and the incredibly varied insects.

## INSECTS

Plants added to the pond are sure to carry other forms of life, and insects will lay their eggs into the water. You will soon see the larvae and pupae of midges and gnats, gyrating in the water and hanging at the surface and, if you look closely, minute caddis fly eggs laid in spirals inside loops of jelly strung along the water's edge.

To encourage insect life, provide a wide range of native plants – underwater varieties, emergent marginals and floating plants. Detritus provides the ideal home for many forms of pond life, and seepage from planting containers and nearby bog areas will give a sufficient layer of soil on the base of the pool within a few weeks. To speed up colonization in new wildlife ponds, introduce a bucketful of mud, netted from the base of an existing pond. However, not all forms of life will settle immediately – some creatures prefer more mature ponds.

The pond skaters (Gerris sp.) live on the surface film, with water

*Below: Diving beetles*

*Above: Lesser water boatman*

crickets and pond measurers, feeding on small insects that have fallen into the water. The surface tension keeps them buoyant, and they flit about, along with minute pink or dark purple springtails. Water boatmen also dart about in the water, often hanging below the surface until disturbed. The largest of these water bugs are the carnivorous diving beetles (Dytiscus sp.) – aggressive attackers of pond life, eating other insects and small fish.

Some of the most attractive aquatic insects are the large dragonflies and smaller damselflies (Odonata), which fly above the pond surface from early to late summer. They are various colours from luminous metallic blues through to banded greens, yellows and reds. These very visible insects are the final stage of a life cycle that may have lasted anything from one to three years. During their month of adult-

*Below: Mayfly*

*Above: Scarlet darter dragonfly*

hood they will mate, scattering their eggs onto the water surface or laying them carefully on the submerged stems of reeds. The eggs hatch into underwater larvae, which grow up to 5cm (2in) for some species, living on the pond detritus, attacking and eating small insects and larvae. For their final metamorphosis they clamber up the stems of marginal plants and break out of their old cases, gradually expanding their wings. You may sometimes find the spent larval cases hanging from plant stems.

Similar insects include the mayflies (Ephemeroptera), which emerge from the water as drab dun flies before changing into the short-lived adults. All these insects have distinct underwater larvae (or nymphs), which have feathery external gills.

Other water-loving insects have equally unusual larvae: the caddis fly larvae often hide in elaborate cases made from pieces of sand, grit and plant material; chironomid midges have bright red larvae – the familiar 'bloodworm' – which live on pond bases and are readily eaten by fish.

## CRUSTACEANS

Large crustaceans are normally only found in streams and slow-running water, but ponds are home for a host of smaller types. The water louse (Asellus sp.) and water shrimp (Gammarus and Crangonyx spp.) scurry around the base of the pond eating decaying material. They grow to around 20-30mm (0.75-1.25in) long and vary in colour from translucent white to pale brown.

Water fleas, such as *Daphnia sp.*, grow up to 4mm (0.15in) in size and feed on free-floating algae, helping to clear the water.

Copepods, such as *Cyclops sp.*, grow a little larger than water fleas and feed on algae and other minute organisms. Ostracods – oval orangey pink creatures, rarely more than 2mm (0.08in) in length – tend to crawl over the pond base, eat decaying waste, and can often be found inside biological pond filters.

## SNAILS

Snails *(Mollusca)* tend to grow best in hard water, which provides minerals, such as calcium, to make their tough shells. Their usefulness in ornamental ponds is somewhat overrated; although they eat some forms of thread algae, they rarely manage to keep it under control and can multiply at an explosive rate under favourable conditions. They also sometimes attack and damage healthy pond plants and can also act as intermediate hosts for fish parasites. (In some tropical countries, they can carry flukes that cause bilharzia in humans.)

Commonly found pond snails include the ramshorn snail *(Planorbis sp.)*, growing up to 2.5cm (1in) across, and the great pond snail *(Limnaea sp.)*, up to 5cm (2in) tall (which may damage plant life). Both lay jelly-like egg clusters on plants.

The freshwater winkle *(Viviparus sp.)* is sometimes sold for ponds. It is unusual in that it gives birth directly, to live baby snails.

*Below: Freshwater shrimp*

*Above: Pond snail*

Freshwater mussels *(Anodonta, Unio and Dreissena spp.)* can sometimes survive in well-matured ponds with a layer of silt on the base. They filter their food out of the water and release tiny mussel larvae *(glochidia)*, which can sometimes be found clinging onto fish. Some varieties grow to over 20cm (8in) long; they are unsuited to new and smaller ponds.

## WORM-LIKE WATER LIFE

You may find *Tubifex* worms, which are eaten by fish, in the mud on the pond base or flatworms *(Planarians)* – which range in colour from white to grey, green, brown and black – gliding over stones and plants in search of food. Leeches are frequent in ponds, and have extending bodies with suckers at each end; few will attack fish or humans. Numerous other worms live in ponds and filters, many of them similar to ordinary garden worms.

## OTHER MICROSCOPIC WATER LIFE

Ponds are usually teeming with microscopic aquatic creatures, all important in the natural balance of the pond and its many food chains.

*Hydra* live on the surfaces of plants and stones; their tiny tentacles catch passing small animals and stun them with stinging barbs similar to those of sea anemones. Rotifers (infusorians) are minute filter-feeding creatures, mainly free-floating in the water, and are an important source of food for larger animals, including fish fry. Some attach to surfaces and play a major role in biological filters.

Algae may be thought of as pests by many pondkeepers, but they play a vital role as a food source for small pond life. Their delicate cells, seen under the microscope, reveal an incredible diversity of forms. At certain times of year, algae may multiply at an explosive rate, triggered by changes in the weather and by increases in nutrients, but they rarely last long. The 'blue-green' types of algae cause the most noticeable 'blooms' (as excessive algal growths are known), but all types of algae will bloom in the right conditions.

*Protozoa* are single-celled creatures, but they carry many complex appendages. They are frequently coated in minute hair-like 'cilia', which direct food (such as aquatic bacteria and other tiny particles) out of the water and into the protozoa's 'mouth'. Some are free floating, others attach themselves to surfaces. Some varieties are parasitic; a few can cause major infections in stressed fish.

The range of creatures in the pond is almost limitless. As a wildlife pond matures, various other organisms, such as sponges and moss animals *(Bryozoa)*, will colonize. There is literally a whole new world beneath the water's surface. The closer you look, the more you will discover.

# GENERAL INDEX

Page numbers in *italics* indicate captions to illustrations; those in **bold** indicate primary treatment of the subject. Other text entries are shown in normal type.

# PLANT INDEX

Page numbers in *italics* indicate captions to illustrations. Other text entries are shown in normal type.